LISTENING THROUGH THE NOISE

LISTENING THROUGH THE NOISE

The Aesthetics of Experimental Electronic Music

JOANNA DEMERS

OXFORD
UNIVERSITY PRESS

2010

Oxford University Press, Inc., publishes works that further
Oxford University's objective of excellence
in research, scholarship, and education.

Oxford   New York
Auckland   Cape Town   Dar es Salaam   Hong Kong   Karachi
Kuala Lumpur   Madrid   Melbourne   Mexico City   Nairobi
New Delhi   Shanghai   Taipei   Toronto

With offices in
Argentina   Austria   Brazil   Chile   Czech Republic   France   Greece
Guatemala   Hungary   Italy   Japan   Poland   Portugal   Singapore
South Korea   Switzerland   Thailand   Turkey   Ukraine   Vietnam

Copyright © 2010 by Oxford University Press, Inc.

Published by Oxford University Press, Inc.
198 Madison Avenue, New York, New York 10016

www.oup.com

Oxford is a registered trademark of Oxford University Press.

Library of Congress Cataloging-in-Publication Data
Demers, Joanna Teresa, 1975–
Listening through the noise : the aesthetics of experimental electronic music / Joanna Demers.
p. cm.
Includes bibliographical references and index.
ISBN 978-0-19-538765-0; 978-0-19-538766-7 (pbk.)
1. Electronic music—History and criticism. 2. Avant-garde (Music) 3. Music—Philosophy
and aesthetics. 4. Music and technology. I. Title.
ML1380.D45 2010
786.7'117—dc22 2009036518

Recorded audio tracks (marked in text with ●) are available online at www.oup.com/us/listeningthroughthenoise
Access with username Music1 and password Book5983
For more information on Oxford Web Music, visit www.oxfordwebmusic.com

Printed in the United States of America
on acid-free paper

ACKNOWLEDGMENTS

First and foremost, I would like to thank the artists whose work inspired me and got me through many early mornings.

I would also like to express my gratitude to the following sources of research and publication support, without which I would not have been able to finish this project: the American Association of University Women's American Fellow Postdoctoral Grant; the University of Southern California's Advancing Scholarship in the Humanities and Social Sciences Grant; and the American Musicological Society's Joseph Kerman Publication Subvention. I also owe thanks to my colleagues at USC's Thornton School of Music, whose intellectual and professional support were exemplary. Robert Vaughn's willingness to order strange and wonderful electronic music for USC's music library made this a much richer book than it would have been without his help.

My parents, Jim and Joan, and brother, Ed, have cheered me on from my first music lessons onward, and I thank them for their love and encouragement. Norm Hirschy is as kind and nurturing an editor as one could ever hope to meet, and I thank him for seeing this project through to completion. Kim Cascone, Richard Chartier, Ezekiel Honig, Thrill Jockey Records, Steve Takasugi, Touch Records, and Miki Yui graciously licensed audio examples for this book's companion Web site. I received indispensable feedback and suggestions from many friends, including Giorgio Biancorosso, Kevin Dettmar, Luisa Greenfield, Andy Hamilton, Brian Kane, David Nicholls, Scott Paulin, Patricia Schmidt, Steve Takasugi, and Ming Tsao. I am especially grateful to Mandy Wong for her friendship and insight on philosophy, electronic music, and synth-pop; our conversations brightened what could have easily been a tough and lonely slog.

To say that I am grateful to my husband and daughter does not begin to describe what I feel. Inouk and Nola are the most wonderful treasures in my life, and I thank them for everything.

CONTENTS

ABOUT THE COMPANION WEB SITE

www.oup.com/us/listeningthroughthenoise

Oxford has created a password-protected Web site to accompany *Listening through the Noise*, and the reader is encouraged to take full advantage of it. Licensed examples from nine tracks discussed in the book are included on this resource, taken directly from the original recordings. These online audio examples are found throughout the text and signaled with Oxford's symbol ◗. Access with username Music1 and password Book5983.

LISTENING THROUGH THE NOISE

Introduction

In some quarters of academia, *aesthetics* is a dirty word. It calls to mind aspects of Western intellectual history that some feel are best left abandoned, such as ivory-tower professors who spout theories about the good and the beautiful without having had much contact with either. For skeptics, aesthetics is synonymous with ungrounded theorizing about the value of artworks. The discipline seems unforgivably suspect because so many works of aesthetics over the years have considered a small subset of artworks, inevitably residing in the Western canon, as standard bearers for the quality of art made anywhere, by anyone, and at any time. While claiming to be an objective measure of what it is that artworks do, aesthetic theory seems irreconcilably ideological, an instrument for reinforcing the values and prejudices that have kept a few artists and art consumers in comfort, while making sure that many more artworks and artistic practices lurk in obscurity and comparative poverty.

Aesthetics is, then, an unpopular pastime, although a few brave souls still write aesthetic theory (Danto 1997; Kraut 2007; Kuspit 2004; Levinson 2006). Many other scholars have critiqued aesthetics by means of cultural studies and sociology, disciplines that start not with theories about artistic merit but rather with empirical data concerning artistic practice. Cultural studies and sociology seem methodologically sound because they rely on ethnography and case studies, techniques that presume to minimize the author's prejudices about a subject and empower practitioners and spectators to speak for themselves. With multicultural, feminist, gay and lesbian, and postcolonial studies continuing to flourish and generate torrents of ethnographically based scholarship, aesthetics cannot help but appear out-dated, if not objectionable.

Still, a few recent examples of music scholarship have undertaken the daunting task of rehabilitating aesthetics to square it with sociology and cultural studies. Davies (2005), Kivy (2003), and Levinson (2008) have published studies of the philosophy of Western art music. Hamilton (2007) and Scruton (1997) have also written aesthetics of music, focusing on Western art music but also considering popular and experimental genres to a limited extent. Butler (2006) explores electronic dance music (EDM) in a text that functions simultaneously as a music-theory analysis and an aesthetics. Hesmondhalgh (2007) combines aesthetics with informant testimonies in his writings on popular music reception. Kronengold's work (2005; 2008) examines several popular-music genres of the 1970s and 1980s in terms that are explicitly taken from aesthetic theory. This short list does not include the numerous works of musicology and music analysis that address aesthetics but do so without using the word. Any critical writing that seeks to explain what art is, why we produce it, and what distinguishes art from nonart is aesthetics, and thus, in a sense, musicology by definition is a project of aesthetics.

My book presents an aesthetic theory of experimental electronic music since 1980 and does so with an awareness of both the risks and the potential gains of such a pursuit. Let me state at the outset that this book is not a history or ethnography of electronic music, although I try whenever possible to use testimonies from artists, listeners, and critics in electronic-music communities. There are several good histories of electronic music, including those by Chadabe (1997), Holmes (2002), Manning (2004), Prendergast (2000), Shapiro (2000), and Toop (1995; 2004). This book also does not purport to be a technical discussion of the processes for generating electronic music, a subject that Roads (1996; 2001) has covered thoroughly. Instead, *Listening through the Noise* offers an aesthetic theory of recent electronic music, a theory that acknowledges the interconnectedness of aesthetics with culture and society. But given all of the bad press that aesthetics has received, what insights can an aesthetics of electronic music provide that a straightforward sociology of electronic music cannot?

SCOPE

Sociologies of cultural expression tend to report and document behavior rather than interpret it. Some of the questions sociological research attempts to answer are: How do participants (i.e., musicians and listeners) derive pleasure and meaning from their music? How do participants acquire and share knowledge about their music? As such, the sociological method focuses on participants rather than observers. An aesthetics, on the other hand, involves more subjective intervention. An aesthetic theorist must interpret forms of expression to yield insights that might not necessarily be apparent to participants. The questions that this book attempts to answer include those basic to philosophy, questions that sociology would not necessarily be best equipped to tackle: What is electronic music? What about it is experimental? What distinguishes it from nonelectronic music? What is specific to electronic music that is absent in other artistic practices and media? These are not the sorts of subjects that usually drive the discourse of electronic-music communities, because participants tend to assume that the reasons for creating and enjoying their art are self-evident. Electronic musicians have little time for contemplating why their music is ontologically different from nonelectronic music; they may well be more interested in the traits that make a particular work unique in and of itself.

While ethnographic methods are intrinsic to disciplines like anthropology and cultural studies, aesthetic theory brings something to electronic music that ethnography cannot. Electronic music is not one single genre but rather a nexus of numerous genres, styles, and subgenres, divided not only geographically but also institutionally, culturally, technologically, and economically. Because of this breadth of activity, no one single participant or informant can speak about *all* of electronic music with equal facility. This is where the aesthetic interpretive subject comes in, an observer who reflects critically, albeit imperfectly, about what these disparate communities share. Aesthetic theory cannot and should not claim a truth content that comes easily to ethnography. It is intractably a product of interpretation but, for this reason, challenges and empowers the observer to see the forest where participants might see only individual trees.

So, to address the questions above: Electronic music is any type of music that makes primary, if not exclusive, use of electronic instruments or equipment. It encompasses electroacoustic music, which often enlists acoustic instruments along with electronics, as well as purely electronically produced sounds. Electronic music thus inhabits a large expanse of genres, styles, and practices. This book does not qualify as a survey, a cultural history, or anything approaching a comprehensive study of these different genres. Rather, I consider a few genres selectively, including musique concrète, post-Schaefferian electroacoustic music, techno, house, microsound, glitch, ambient, drone, dub techno, noise, chill-out, soundscape, and field recording. From these individual examples, I extract a set of principles that can answer the second question of how electronic music differs from nonelectronic music (more on this appears below). The traits that distinguish these genres from one another are indispensable for understanding electronic music as a whole. Still, throughout this book, I refer to "metagenres," larger groupings of genres. I argue that participants often claim allegiance to one of three metagenres as a means of claiming high-art credibility. These metagenres are institutional electroacoustic music, electronica, and sound art. *Institutional electroacoustic music* functions thanks to the support of governments, private industry, and educational centers like universities. *Electronica* means different things in different contexts but normally applies to commercial electronic music that is nominally popular, although little electronica sells any great volume of recordings. *Sound art* describes works that use nonnarrative sound (either in combination with or to the exclusion of visual elements), often in a site-specific context in which sounds interact with their venue. Not all sound-art works contain electronics, but the works I discuss in this book do.

At the start of the twenty-first century, a good deal of the world's music contains electronic sounds that come from instruments such as synthesizers, samplers, or laptops. Few would be so inclusive as to argue that any work featuring a synthesizer should automatically count as electronic music, but approaching an adequately descriptive definition of electronic music proves challenging nonetheless. One reason for this is that electronic music has had several definitions during the twentieth century. In academia, electronic music has referred to works composed in or near universities (e.g., the Center for Computer Research in Music and Acoustics, CCRMA, at Stanford) or governmental institutions (public radio stations in Germany and France or research centers like the Institut de Recherche et Coordination Acoustique/Musique [IRCAM] and the Groupe de Recherches Musicales [GRM]). During its infancy, this music was produced chiefly in France, Germany, Italy, and the United States, and its creators traced its lineage from European avant-garde composers like Edgard Varèse and Karlheinz Stockhausen. Institutional electronic music initially encompassed musique concrète (French tape composition using everyday or natural sounds), and *elektronische Musik* (German synthesized electronic music). Today, institutional electroacoustic music includes works featuring sampled and synthesized materials as well as those involving traditional instruments subjected to signal processing. The audiences for institutional electroacoustic music consist of small communities of academics and practitioners. Participants in these communities tend to view their music as elite and intellectual rather than popular or accessible.

Electronic music has traditionally meant something very different in the sphere of popular music, which itself is, of course, not one homogeneous entity but rather a loose conglomeration of rock, psychedelic, ambient, and EDM genres, along with film music. Many gain their first exposure to popular electronic music or electronica by listening to mainstream pop radio, which has canonized songs by acts ranging from Depeche Mode to Radio-head. Others discover electronica while watching science fiction films like *Forbidden Planet* (1956) or *A Clockwork Orange* (1971), whose soundtracks feature instruments such as oscillators and synthesizers. Still others first hear electronic music while listening to seminal pop albums such as the Beach Boys' *Pet Sounds* (1966) or underground successes such as Tangerine Dream's *Phaedra* (1974) or Kraftwerk's *Trans-Europe Express* (1977). Electronica generally spurns institutional affiliations and revolves instead around pioneering individuals such as Wendy Carlos, Robert Moog, or Brian Wilson, or else the instruments themselves, such as the theremin or the Moog or Korg synthesizers.

The qualifier *experimental* might initially promise to narrow the field of electronic music, but this adjective is itself far from clear. Beal (2006) contrasts the institutional avant-garde, bookended by Schoenberg and Stravinsky, against experimental composers who rejected both serialism and neoclassicism to develop idiosyncratic styles. For Nyman (1999), the term *experimental music* refers specifically to the mid-twentieth-century indeter-minacy movement headed by John Cage, Christian Wolff, and Fluxus artists, a movement he distinguishes from the mainstream avant-garde of com-posers like Boulez and Stockhausen. This notion of *experimental* is contin-gent on unusual notational systems enfranchising performers to interpret anything from tempi to pitch, as well as whether or not to create sounds at all. Nyman's experimental music includes mostly acoustic pieces, although some electronic works are mentioned. Nyman's vision is anticipated by Benitez (1978), who contrasts experimental music's disposition toward indeterminacy with avant-garde music's intentionality. Yet in general usage, *experimental music* is any music that rejects tradition and takes risks through running counter to musical conventions; the term pertains equally to jazz, dub, and hip-hop. As Piekut (2008) notes, experimentalism is not a meta-physical essence but a series of unusual practices whose strangeness stands out in relation to whatever the mainstream happens to be. We could con-clude from this that experimental electronic music is anything that chal-lenges the conventions of electronic music. Yet this leaves us with a moving target, since conventions in electronic-music history have usually been short-lived. I therefore define *experimental* as anything that has departed significantly from norms of the time, but with the understanding that some-thing experimental in 1985 could have inspired what was conventional by 1990.

Any notion of recent experimental music is bound to overlap with sound art, which draws from many of the same influences as mid-century experimentalism. Varèse's call (2007) for a new means of expression based on the principle of "organized sound" was an early affirmation that electronic music could lay aside traditional forms and instrumentations to work directly with sound. Several artists interpreted Varèse's statement literally, viewing their own creations not only as works of music but as sound sculptures. Meanwhile, the rise of installation art, happenings, and Fluxus all indicated methods for incorporating sound within the artwork. Yet, as Licht (2007) argues, experimental music and sound art are not the same, for the simple reason that the aims of sound art are often antithetical to longstanding traditions governing the composition, consumption, and appreciation of music. The locations in which it is disseminated make sound art especially resistant to classification; sound-art venues include art galleries, public spaces, and both physical and online installations. Some sound artists have training or background in music, but others do not. Some sound artists record their works in order to distribute them beyond their place of origin, while others reject recording, viewing their work as ephemeral and inseparable from their originating contexts. Although I agree with Licht that *sound art* and *experimental music* are not interchangeable, many participants do treat them as similar, if not synonymous. For this reason, sound art figures throughout this book, especially in discussions of site.

There remains perhaps the most contentious issue: How can this book simultaneously consider academic and popular forms of electronic music along with electronic sound art? Most people don't tend to think of experimental music as popular or commercially successful. Yet there are innumerable examples of miscegenation between supposedly "high" and "mass" culture, enough so that to keep the spheres separate is proving to be an increasingly untenable choice. Witness, for instance, the experimental forays of Vince Clarke, Radiohead, or Frank Zappa, artists who have made names for themselves as popular musicians. One of the more impressive music-industry successes of the last twenty years was to persuade listeners to buy EDM for contemplative, sedentary home listening—a genre known as intelligent dance music (IDM). And as for sound art, even those who are sympathetic to it may hesitate to include it within discussions of *music*, let alone dance music that features a steady rhythm or pulse. Yet the innovations of artists such as Björk and Aphex Twin somehow straddle these divisions comfortably, drawing attention as much from pop-music journalists as from gallery curators and academics.

The compromise I propose is to focus on experimental electronic music produced since roughly 1980. The year 1980 is pivotal for several reasons. For most of the previous decade, synthesizers were expensive and bulky, and the few artists who had access to them were either successful rock stars or academic composers at research universities. By 1980, digitalization triggered a precipitous drop in the price of synthesizers, making them affordable for less-than-superstar working musicians, amateurs, and even children (Cateforis 2000; Vail 1993). Unlike earlier analog synthesizers, the reasonably priced Korgs and Casios that flooded the market came with "patches" or preset materials, meaning that synthesizer users no longer had to know how to program their instruments (Théberge 1997). Early-1980s synthesizers were also lighter and smaller and therefore more portable. One of the biggest markets for these synthesizers was EDM, which, following the death of disco in 1979, emerged in underground dance clubs in the form of house and techno. Synthesizers also defined the sounds of New Wave and postpunk acts such as Human League, the Talking Heads, Gary Numan, and Duran Duran, which enjoyed heavy rotation on the first twenty-four-hour music video network, MTV.

Launched in 1981, MTV was critical to the expansion of electronic music, for the simple reason that music videos rendered normal the sight of synthesizers and other electronic equipment. The success of the video network gave lie to the notion that it took an electric guitar and a drum set to make a proper band. Many young viewers took this message to heart and developed home studios with little more than a synthesizer, a sampler, or a sequencer. The quality of electronic instruments and editing technology has increased exponentially ever since, while prices have continued to remain low, such that today, virtually anyone with a personal computer can afford to produce professional-quality electronic music from inside the home for less than a few hundred dollars. In short, digital synthesizers have made music making much more egalitarian than at any other time in history. Today's instruments require no expertise in reading or writing music notation, and users need no prior experience with playing instruments. Samplers and synthesizers allow musicians to cull together instrumental sounds with a mouse, and editing software makes possible the importation of sound effects, acoustic spaces, and even apparatus sounds of old playback equipment.

The year 1980 is a turning point for another reason. Although there are compelling reasons to respect the divides separating high-art from mass-culture electronic music made earlier in the century, slippage between the two spheres began to accelerate after 1980. This is not the dominant opinion; Emmerson (2000, 1) cautions that popular and academic electronic musicians "may plunder the other's materials, but an unease and distance still remain." I demonstrate, however, that the rhetoric of distinction, deeply ingrained in all forms of experimental music, is paradoxically what electronica, institutional electroacoustic, and sound art share in common. And this insistence on distinction is deceptive, because popular and high-art genres of electronic music seem to be settling on shared preoccupations even as they claim to be diverging from one another.

METHODOLOGY AND ORGANIZATION

My methodology takes its cue from Wolff's work on aesthetics and the sociology of art (1993), specifically her argument that the two are codependent. Aesthetics must attune itself to the culture, history, and social context of art and its practitioners and consumers. If not, aesthetics ends up working as a tool of ideology, emphasizing certain aspects of selected works that happen to agree with the writer's values. On the other hand, aesthetics cannot reduce artworks to their cultural, historical, or social backgrounds; otherwise, there would be nothing to distinguish art from nonartistic activities. Aesthetic theory, for Wolff and for me, must be sensitive to sociology while also being courageous enough to offer statements about why art is specific to itself and distinct from other activities.

This book relies to the greatest extent possible on statements from electronic-music artists, listeners, and theorists to ground its observations in empirical data. However, I admit freely that I draw a number of subjective conclusions about the nature of electronic music. I do so without claiming some purchase on the definitive truth about electronic music, for clearly there is no one truth about it. And although no one individual can be right about everything in music (or life in general), I want to avoid a paralyzing sort of relativism that sometimes impedes scholars from making any sort of conclusive interpretive statements about music. No one individual can ever hope to get everything right, but that is no reason to believe that an individual can get *nothing* right. By carefully studying the subject, the genres, the recordings, and the critical literature, we can get some things right.

Part of the key to getting things right in electronic music involves understanding genre, and here I rely on the invaluable work on the subject by Frow (2005), Kronengold (2008), and McLeod (2001). It's helpful to think of genre as a sort of social contract between musicians and listeners, a set of conventions that can more or less guide the listening experience. With enough experience, a listener comes to know what to expect in a techno track and why techno generally behaves differently from, say, house, even though both are fundamentally similar forms of EDM. The interesting moments in any genre occur, of course, when expectations are in some way thwarted, when a work does something it is not "supposed" to do according to the rules of its genre. My strategy throughout this book is to listen with two minds simultaneously, attending to how genre situates individual works amid larger groups of works, while also attending to what stylistic features otherwise distinct genres might share. Genre is of the utmost importance to any discussion of electronic music, because genre rules electronic music, dividing participants into camps that often perceive themselves as incommensurate with one another.

Now for the sticky subject: aesthetic value. Some readers might question the motivations behind this book, and with justification, since aesthetics used to be the discipline of choice for those wishing to push their artistic agenda in praising certain works while disparaging others. Even among aesthetic theorists today, there is no agreement on whether the very project of aesthetics can carry on without pronouncements about the quality of artworks. Hamilton (2007) and Kraut (2007) approach aesthetics from their backgrounds in analytic philosophy and therefore avoid asserting the superiority of the works they discuss. Rather, the two questions that interest these writers are: What is music, and what distinguishes it from nonmusic art forms? Kraut, in particular, insists on the distinction between aesthetic theory and art criticism, the latter belonging to art-world practice rather than metaphysics. Hamilton and Kraut seem to occupy the minority among many other aesthetic theorists who openly judge art quality. Adorno (1997), Scruton (1997), and Wolff (1993) all view value criteria as intrinsic to understanding art: we cannot understand art completely unless we take into account whether we feel an artwork has succeeded or failed and how it competes with other works. Wolff also points out that the very act of formulating aesthetic theory necessarily entails questions of artistic value, of what to discuss and what not to mention. An author who claims complete objectivity and value-free neutrality is thus being disingenuous, since every observer has a point of view.

This book takes a position much in line with Wolff's. The relative aesthetic value of one work over another is not my central concern here, and I try to avoid making statements about my personal likes and dislikes. However, I reject assertions that we can thoroughly bracket out the subject of aesthetic value or that anyone can represent electronic-music aesthetics objectively and comprehensively. Aesthetics and criticism overlap, but they are not identical.

As for the methodology of analysis itself, this book proposes that we ask of electronic music some of the same sorts of questions that Adorno and some post-1950 art critics have fruitfully posed. Adorno's *Aesthetic Theory* (1997) has exerted a powerful and positive influence on my writing through its premise that musical material engages in a dialectic with surrounding society, never completely reflective while never completely autonomous, either. I disagree with Adorno on many of his judgments about musical value, but I admire his ability to identify the tension between subjectivity and objectivity in the artwork. I point to an analogous tension in many electronic works that conceive of sound as a literal object, material supposedly lacking authorial bias or personal expression. As art critic Michael Fried (1998) controversially argues, minimalist sculpture of the 1960s conceived of a similar type of material, three-dimensional objects that were intended not as artistic creations but rather as mute, physically imposing objects. Fried's formulation of "objecthood" and its reception in writings by Hal Foster (1996), Miwon Kwon (2002), and other art critics can help us contextualize tendencies in electronic music and sound art amid larger doubts in late-twentieth-century art about the continued relevance of art as an autonomous enterprise removed from real life. We can trace the search for nonreferential materials from Dada to John Cage, from Fluxus to minimalist sculpture, and from musique concrète to drone music and microsound. Indeed, this search inherits many anxieties from nineteenth-century art music and musicology over whether music should be absolute or programmatic.

Remembering music from previous centuries is in fact a useful technique, since this book's premise is that electronic music is fundamentally different in character and in aspiration from any music that preceded it. Consider that before the advent of electronic music, the sound of almost any instrument or singing voice would alert listeners within a short amount of time that they were hearing a musical sound and not, say, a sound of nature, chance, or a nonartistic machine. The timbres, attacks, structure, and syntax of preelectronic music all work together to underscore music's status as a special type of organized sound that is separate from the sounds of everyday life. It goes without saying that not all listeners bring the same sort of experience or musical expertise to the sounds they hear, and listening experiences clearly vary according to history, culture, and the music itself. Still, we can be relatively certain that most people who have grown up in a particular culture can recognize its music *as* music even if they know nothing else about its production or meaning.

Until the electronic era, such qualities set apart music from everyday life. They functioned as framing devices in a manner analogous to how a picture frame demarcates a painting from the wall on which it is mounted and, by extension, the outside world. And frames of all sorts are important, for although we might be used to ignoring them and focusing instead on the materials they contain, frames serve the valuable function of identifying art *as* art. When the framing devices of Western art music—tools such as tonality, dance rhythms, predictable forms, standard orchestration, and concert venues—began to disappear or undergo critique, so, too, vanished many reasons for regarding music as separate from the outside world. Not coincidentally, electronics and the discourse surrounding electronic music were critical in the dismantling of the musical frame. When Pierre Schaeffer began to lug his turntable engraver around Paris to record the sounds of trains, he permanently transformed musical aesthetics, introducing the possibility that the sounds of the outside world could be considered as aesthetic objects. But here lies the dilemma. Once electronic musicians took apart the musical frame, what did they do with the Pandora's box of sounds unleashed into the concert hall? How does one listen to unmusical, every-day sounds?

The ways in which we listen to unmusical sounds hinge on whether we believe that sounds signify or possess meaning. And this very topic consti-tutes the essence of recent electronic-music aesthetics. In response to the earlier question of what distinguishes recent electronic music from other media, I argue that it is a concern with the meaningfulness of sound. To an extent unrivaled in all previous forms of music, recent electronic music is obsessed with the question of whether sound, in itself, bears meaning. And while participants are unanimous in their curiosity about sound's meaning-fulness, they are very much divided in their opinions about the matter. For some, it is impossible to hear sound separately from the contexts that lead to its creation and consumption. For others, successful electronic music purifies sound to its most basic materials, elements that possess no residual associations to the outside world. This book derives its three-part structure according to three discernible conceptions of the meaningfulness of sound: as sign, object, and situation. I divide each part into two chapters, each of which addresses one or a few genres and their strategies for eliciting (or avoiding) signification. (I should also mention that chapters 1 through 5 are case studies of specific genres, while chapter 6 presents a more general dis-cussion of the three metagenres in tandem. Readers looking for the red thread may find that the introduction, chapter 6, and the conclusion provide an adequate overview, while the five intervening chapters furnish more detailed analyses.)

Part I examines genres that operate on the assumption that sound func-tions as a sign, a relationship between some signified thought and some sig-nifier sound. Chapter 1 begins with post-Schaefferian electroacoustic music and its efforts to control the listening process. Preelectronic Western art music fueled extensive debates and polemics concerning the semiotic prop-erties of music, specifically concerning whether music can be heard or read as a language. And at many instances in that history, audiences heard, read, and understood musical utterances with exactitude. In certain styles, for instance, a descending bass line communicated lamentation, a strident 4/4 rhythm conveyed militancy or horses, and a chromatic melody described sensuality. But in electronic music, especially the post-Schaefferian electro-acoustic music that chapter 1 considers, the absence of musical parameters such as tonality or regular rhythm pitches music into a no-man's-land. With the absence of musical syntax, should we hear nonmusical sounds as abstract utterances or as representative of their origins in the outside world? Should we hear a recording of a rising tide lapping on a beach as music? As non-music? And what would be the difference between two such experiences? Post-Schaefferian electroacoustic music is especially conflicted about such questions, in part because of the ease with which it abstracts sounds from the outside world. Schaeffer's own approach in using such materials was to advocate that listeners practice "reduced listening," a bracketing out of the cognitive associations that would normally accompany recognizable materials. But many post-Schaefferians, even those who might have studied with Schaeffer himself, reject this manner of imposing a discipline on listeners. Instead, they think that it is incumbent on composers to work with, rather than ignore or repress, external associations of sounds as integral aspects of their works. Post-Schaefferian music can thus be characterized as a debate about the extent to which the semantic content of a sound can be manipulated. Running parallel with this is an anxiety over how much post-Schaefferian music should leave the discourse of music behind. With seemingly unlimited technical abilities for incorporating the sounds of the outside world, some electroacoustic composers create works that bear little, if any, affinities to music as it has been known. Yet others use the rhythms and syntax of post-tonal serialism. The choice of whether to retain or reject the trappings of music and whether to use mimetic or abstract sounds tells a great deal about whether composers see in their materials purely iconic representations of the outside world or more metaphoric, distanced referents.

Chapter 2 explores how electronica conceives of sound material as a metaphor. Compared with post-Schaefferian electroacoustic music, electronica spends less time dictating listeners' responses. Sounds of the outside world, sounds of other works, and sounds newly created all figure in electronica. What matter in electronica are not the origins of sound so much as the metaphors that portray sound as malleable material, the product of construction, reproduction, or destruction. Frequently, though not always, these metaphors go hand-in-hand with actual sound-production techniques. Construction is often synonymous with sound synthesis, reproduction with sound sampling, and destruction with the defacement of the phonographic medium. But of course, the most interesting moments in electronica occur when the metaphor describing sound does not correspond with the actual means of producing it. When digital-signal processing hides or disguises the provenance of a sound, listeners can hear in an old sound something supposedly new.

Part II assumes a position antithetical to the genres discussed in part I. Here, sound is not a sign but rather an object, an entity with no preexisting semantic content. And although the genres that part II profiles are nominally minimalist, they closely approach Schaeffer's ideal for reduced listening, because they contend that listeners can disregard whatever external associations sounds might have. As such, the genres in chapters 3 and 4 are the modern-day answers to absolute music, music that spurns narrative, explanation, or other references beyond itself. Chapter 3 looks at the minimal objects in microsound, a form of electronic music that utilizes brief, usually quiet particles of sound. Microsound artists exhibit surprising consistency in their search for sounds that are supposedly expressionless, and I connect this predilection to a similar desire among minimalist visual artists of the 1960s for "objecthood," where sculpture appropriates discrete objects for their physical rather than referential attributes. Chapter 4 explores maximal objects in drone music, dub techno, and noise music, subgenres that test the physical limitations of listeners through excessive durations and volumes. These various manifestations of excess all purport to transcend meaning, to push sound beyond semiosis to a state in which it communicates directly to listeners' bodies.

In part III, the pendulum swings back toward forms of electronic music that conceive of sound as meaningful but hear that meaning deriving not so much from the sound's innate characteristics as from the ways in which sound reflects its situation, its placement both within the physical world and within networks of cultures and other musics. Chapter 5 discusses ambient and chill-out, soundscape, field recordings, and sound art for widely differing tacks on how sound can communicate space, place, and location. Chapter 6 takes a step back to consider the three metagenres of institutional electroacoustic, electronica, and sound art. Participants in each metagenre describe their music in terms borrowing from the discourse of experimentalism, a discourse that pits a distinguished minority against a commercial mainstream and an indifferent public. Despite the fact that the three metagenres insist on their difference from one another, however, all three encourage a type of listening that resembles less what we think to be traditional musical listening (at least in Western art music) than a move toward a new type of attention, which I call aesthetic listening.

AESTHETIC LISTENING

It is not my intention to democratize electronic music by imposing a solidarity that would not otherwise come naturally. Part of the pleasure in listening to this music involves giving in to this rhetoric of distinction. First-time electronic-music listeners are rightly fascinated by what they hear and frequently conclude that some works are "edgier," "more sophisticated," or "more demanding" than whatever they might define as the mainstream. Yet I do want to expose the shared tendencies on all sides of the high/popular divide, because they point to something unmistakable and crucial: a growing sense that listening to electronic music constitutes an act that is fundamentally different from how listeners have been used to hearing Western art music for the previous five centuries. Chapter 6 and the conclusion take up this new experience, which I dub aesthetic listening as opposed to conventional music listening. Aesthetic listening resembles the way many listeners hear popular and some non-Western musics. In listening aesthetically as opposed to musically, we may choose to attend to development, or else we may pay only intermittent attention to sound while also attending to other sensory phenomena. Aesthetic listening also acknowledges that nonmusical sounds, the sounds of the outside world, can have aesthetic interest and that we can listen to them for more than simply their informational value. That aesthetic listening has arisen in electronic music is nothing short of revolutionary. Electronic music in its three metagenres pits itself as a high-art form yet, unlike previous forms of Western art music, does not demand attention to form or development. The experience that electronic music affords reflects more accurately the ways in which humans actually do hear the world and is thus less dogmatic about how we *should* hear it.

The art critic and philosopher Arthur Danto (1997) has spoken of the "end of art," the moment in twentieth-century art when ready-mades, objets trouvés, and commercial advertising so permeated high-art scenes that they destroyed any remaining justification for differentiating between "art" and "nonart." Danto naturally refers to John Cage, who similarly urged listeners to open their ears and minds enough to consider all sounds as music. Throughout the following chapters, and above all in the conclusion, I want to apply some of Danto's and Cage's conclusions to electronic music, but with some important exceptions. For all of the enthusiasm that Cage's philosophy has generated, it did not succeed in making listeners hear every sound as music, nor did it make listeners approach the other extreme in hearing all sounds, even those of the concert hall, as sounds outside the musical frame. I agree with Danto insofar as electronic music has precipitated an "end of music" or, rather, the end of practices and philosophies that took for granted the separation of Western art music from the sounds of the outside world. The subliminal pulsations in a work by microsound composer Kim Cascone or the ferry shuttling captured in a field recording by Toshiya Tsunoda may sound foreign, industrial, or simply mundane, but they do not sound conventionally musical. Yet the fact that listeners submit to certain rituals in hearing these sounds, whether by putting on headphones or going to a performance space to hear a live rendering, demonstrates that we still hear these sounds in artworks differently from how we would if we encountered them in everyday life. The customs governing how we listen to electronic music do not demand the same sort of continuous discipline as concert-hall attendance, with listeners sitting in silence and attending to a piece from start to finish. Listening to electronic music is intermittent and interrupted; listeners may leave a venue and then return (or not), press pause on their iPods but restart several hours later, or transfer their attention from the repetitive beats of the dance floor to a conversation they are overhearing at the bar of the club. All of these activities constitute listening that is aware of the aesthetic value of sounds, not strictly as conveyors of meaning but not strictly as musical utterance, either.

But I am getting ahead of myself now. Before we can consider the end of music and other grand subjects, we need to unpack my claim from above, that electronic music's primary concern is with the meaningfulness of sound. Let me explain what that means.

PART I

Sign

1

Listening to Signs in Post-Schaefferian Electroacoustic Music

Let me begin with an obvious statement: electronic music sounds and behaves differently from nonelectronic music. The earliest critical reactions to electronic music were quick to seize on the strangeness of its sounds, which seemed incommensurate with anything musical. A *New York Times* critic wrote of a 1953 Parisian electronic-music festival:

> One's first reaction when listening to France's "musique concrète" or Germany's "electronic music" today—almost twenty-five years after the initial experiments—was a feeling that the technician had now taken over and wanted to show the composer what he could do with the help of modern equipment. Hearing "musique concrète" for the first time, one could not help being bewildered. One can sympathize with listeners who make comparisons with railway terminals, steel foundries and tapes played back at a wrong speed. (Gradenwitz 1953)

In 1961, another critic described musique concrète and electronic music as random tape noise (Schonberg 1961), and a third complained that experimental electronic music denied listeners familiar sounds and syntax that even dissonant serial music provided (Helm 1961). Collages of industrial noise, synthesized drones, and sounds played in reverse seemed utterly foreign to musical language as it was then conceived.

Electronic music is strange because it is so malleable. Like conventional music, it can enlist acoustic instruments to produce the pitches, scales, and rhythms of traditional musical discourse. Yet, unlike conventional music, it can also incorporate sounds of the outside world, leading Emmerson to write that electronic music is "the first musical genre ever to place under the composer's control an acoustic palette as wide as that of the environment itself" (1986, 18). Electronic music can also fashion new sounds that have never yet been heard. Just consider the title of Paul Théberge's monograph on music and technology, *Any Sound You Can Imagine* (1997), or the strategy of many electroacoustic composers to engineer new sounds by manipulating grains, the acoustic equivalent of subatomic particles. This breadth of possible sounds makes electronic music both musical and nonmusical, representational and abstract, familiar and arcane.

Consider this simple fact and its ramifications. No matter the genre, listening situation (whether live or recorded), or audience, all forms of electronic music make manifest the strangeness of sounds that have only recently become imaginable and executable. All electronic music is a meditation on the act of listening to sounds both old and new, therefore a meditation on the cognitive processes that accompany listening. But electroacoustic music embodies perhaps the most fraught attitude toward this new reality of sound, since it is at its core ambivalent about whether it should eschew the formal and structural parameters that would readily link it with traditional, acoustic music. The sheer freedom of electroacoustic music constitutes both its strength and its burden. With the latitude to use both conventional musical figures and random, seemingly unintentional sounds, electroacoustic composers have generated an amount of theoretical literature concerning the act of listening that is unrivaled in any other genre of music. This literature argues over the extent to which composers, materials, and listeners themselves can control the listening process. At its heart, this discourse is concerned with the signifying properties of sound: whether sound can be heard separately from any social, cultural, natural, or historical associations. Electroacoustic-music discourse is also concerned with whether electronic music can and should be heard as music, as aestheticized sound, or something else as yet undefined.

To appreciate how unique electronic music is, consider the obvious: nonelectronic music, by definition, is performed by nonamplified, acoustic instruments or the human voice. Until electricity became available, music was generally produced with a relatively small choice of instruments and vocal types. Timbre, the characteristic "color" of any sound, has thus been one of the most stable elements of musical production; in other words, nonelectronic music is identifiable *as music* (and identifiable in a very short period of time, usually within a second or two) on the basis of its timbres. Western music since the Middle Ages can thus be heard as a series of refinements of the other parameters of musical production that could be varied, traits such as rhythm, melody, harmony, texture, and form. Goehr argues that throughout its history, Western art music has struggled to be taken seriously as an art form (2007, 120). Inherent in these struggles has been the urge to transcend music's grounding in the here and now of live performance and the exigencies of vocal and instrumental timbre, which make music always sound like music.

The desire to legitimize music fueled a debate over whether Western art music could leave behind its existential qualities in order to signify something beyond itself. This debate came to a head during the eighteenth and nineteenth centuries, as European concert music polarized itself into the absolute and programmatic camps. In brief, the absolutists claimed that music could comment only on itself and should not contain references to the outside world. The programmatics regarded music as essentially narrative and advocated the use of external references within musical works as signs of music's pertinence to the outside world. The tug-of-war between these two camps imprinted itself on the discipline of musicology, such that until the 1980s, most scholarship emphasized the formal or intrinsic aspects of musical works while deemphasizing music's extrinsic and referential qualities. Buoyed by developments in literary criticism, the civil rights movement, feminism, the gay rights movement, and the writings of Theodor Adorno, "new" musicologists in the 1980s and 1990s introduced critical methodologies borrowed from hermeneutics and cultural studies (McClary 1991). Other musicologists advocated semiotic approaches that distinguish between compositional intentions and listening reception (Agawu 1991; Clarke 2005; Nattiez 1990). Today, musicological scholarship is still debating the relative merits of formalist and hermeneutic approaches (Abbate 2004; Berger 2005; Puri 2006).

Electroacoustic musicians are also interested in whether music can, does, and should refer beyond itself to the outside world, which is not surprising, since so many electroacoustic musicians are trained within the Western art-music tradition. In fact, the theoretical positions that many electroacoustic musicians espouse recall the longstanding formalist/hermeneutic debate in both nonelectronic Western art music and musicology. But the translation from traditional to plugged-in instruments is not without its snags. Unlike nonelectronic music, electronic music *can* transcend timbral limitations and just about every other existential limitation of traditional musical discourse. Electronic music can incorporate sounds of the outside world with ease and can generate new timbres that defy identification as music (or anything else). As such, electronic music can be mimetic and representational or abstract and obscure. In this new terrain, old theories about music's separation from (or dependence on) culture and history may no longer be pertinent. Instead, we need to talk about sounds themselves, not only as units of musical syntax but also as sounds. Are sounds always referential? Is it possible to hear sound before it has been laden with the associations of culture, history, or society?

In short, does the act of listening to electronic music necessarily involve relating sounds to what is already familiar? If not, how do we make sense of the experience of listening to abstract, nonreferential, unrecognizable sounds?

I have until now referred to electroacoustic music as one discrete entity, which is misleading, since there is certainly not one single community of electroacoustic musicians and listeners but rather networks of producers and audiences throughout the world. There are certain general traits, however, that are consistent throughout electroacoustic music. It tends to be produced in educational or research institutions, usually universities or governmentally subsidized centers that specialize in music and computing. Some famous examples of such institutions are IRCAM (Institut de Recherche et Coordination Acoustique/Musique) and GRM (Groupe de Recherches Musicales), both in Paris and both supported by the French government; CCRMA (Center for Computer Research in Music and Acoustics) at Stanford University; CRCA (Center for Research in Computing and the Arts) at the University of California, San Diego; and Princeton University's music department. Those who compose, perform, and write about this music are often academics or scientists who regard themselves as researchers rather than, or in addition to, artists or entertainers. Electroacoustic music generates a great deal of theoretical writing, so much so that academic peer-reviewed journals like *Organised Sound* and *Computer Music Journal* are devoted to it, as are numerous monographs, edited volumes, essays, and Web sites.

Although the approaches of electroacoustic-music institutions are distinct from one another and hardly interchangeable, a series of inspirational figures has shaped how electroacoustic musicians perceive themselves in relation to acoustic music. These figures include composers such as Milton Babbitt, John Cage, Pierre Schaeffer, Karlheinz Stockhausen, and Edgard Varèse. Schaeffer, inventor of musique concrète, considered himself an engineer first and a musician second and was committed throughout his career to forging connections among acousticians, performers, scientists, and composers. Because Schaeffer theorized so extensively, wrote so much, and taught so many students, his influence is easily traceable, and it is partially for this reason that I want to narrow my focus to electroacoustic music that has emerged in the wake of Schaeffer. This chapter considers works and theoretical positions of Luc Ferrari, Bernard Parmegiani, and Denis Smalley, all of whom studied or worked at the GRM, the institution founded by Schaeffer specializing in computer music research. I also include a discussion of Trevor Wishart, a self-taught electroacoustic composer whose works respond to many of Schaeffer's ideas. Post-Schaefferians diverge from Schaeffer on many issues, especially concerning the ability of listeners to ignore the perceived origins of sounds. Nevertheless, all composers influenced directly or indirectly by Schaeffer display an acute sensitivity to sound's capacity to refer to something beyond itself. Many regard sound in structuralist terms as a sign composed of a signifier (the raw acoustic phenomenon or, as Schaeffer might put it, the "sound object") that reflects a signified (a musical idea). Schaeffer's own writings, particularly his monumental *Traité des objets musicaux: Essai interdisciplines* (1966), demonstrate his familiarity with structuralism and the linguistic theory of Ferdinand de Saussure. In particular, Schaeffer regards music notation as a signifier whose relationship to the signified musical idea is arbitrary (1966, 35). As Nattiez's foundational discussion of music semiotics, *Music and Discourse* (1990), explains, Schaeffer also followed the structuralist task of distinguishing between compositional intention and listener experience.

Music and Discourse empowers scholars to discuss the semiotics of all music by means of a tripartite scheme consisting of poiesis, esthesis, and the neutral level, concepts that Nattiez borrows from semiologist Jean Molino. Poiesis refers to the creative processes that generate a work and can include authorial intentions; esthesis refers to the processes that receivers undertake when interpreting a work. Once the poietic and esthesic levels have been accounted for, there remains the neutral level, the trace or physical embodiment of the work that is accessible to the senses. For nonelectronic works, this trace manifests itself in phenomena such as live performances, scores, or texts (Nattiez 1990, 15). Nattiez devotes an entire chapter to musique concrète as it was first invented by Schaeffer and subsequently developed by his students at the GRM. In that chapter, Nattiez demonstrates that Schaeffer's texts parse all of electroacoustic music experience into either compositional intention or listener experience (92–96). (Interestingly, Nattiez notes that electroacoustic music collapses the third, neutral level into that of poiesis, which is admittedly true for Schaeffer and his students. Another electronic genre, the microsound movement considered in chapter 3 of this book, does, however, treat sound as an isolatable phenomenon that can be discussed separately from authorial intention or listener reception.) The present chapter enlists Nattiez's categories of poiesis and esthesis to examine post-Schaefferian electroacoustic discourse as a polemic between compositional intention and listener reception. Inherent in this conflict is the belief that in electroacoustic music, sounds function as signifiers for some underlying signified content, usually an extramusical idea, image, or even narrative. Frequently, the relationship between signifier and signified is mimetic: sounds are created and interpreted on the basis of their perceived ability to resemble something outside the musical work. This referential relationship is of central importance to my discussion, because it supersedes the presumption inherent in preelectronic music that musical structure and form are central to musical meaning. In post-Schaefferian electroacoustic music, while structure and form may be present in individual works, there are no generalized norms governing their use throughout the genre. The qualities of sound itself, such as its timbre and spatialization, are therefore primarily responsible for referring to the outside world. Post-Schaefferian electroacoustic music can thus be fruitfully understood as the product of clashes over whether music should stand apart from the outside world, as well as whether compositional intention can or should trump listener experience.

Before continuing, I should note that the ensuing discussion aims for a precision that might at times seem to impede this book's goal of making general observations about electronic music at large. The theoretical positions I outline in the following pages often differ from one another only on small points, but these details are important, especially when they are put into practice by theorists who also happen to compose. Nevertheless, readers looking for a quick summary of the basic concerns of electroacoustic music can jump to the section "Taking Stock of Post-Schaefferian Theory," which covers only the most essential theoretical issues before diving into the music.

POIESIS: PIERRE SCHAEFFER, REDUCED LISTENING, AND TREVOR WISHART

Schaeffer published his *Traité des objets musicaux* in 1966 after nearly twenty years of experimentation with musique concrète. Intrigued by Edmund Husserl's writings, Schaeffer adopted the phenomenological technique of reduction, "bracketing out" information external to the object of perception in order to describe the object itself. Schaeffer regarded the technologies of recording and radio transmission as acousmatic reductions, named after the followers of Pythagoras who supposedly listened to their teacher behind a curtain so as to avoid being distracted by his appearance or gestures. Radio and sound recording created acousmatic situations in which listeners could not see the sources of sound production. For Schaeffer, acousmatic reductions were potentially revelatory, because they allowed the listener to focus on the sound object (*objet sonore*). The sound object (Chion 1983, 34–35; Schaeffer 1966, 95) was Schaeffer's means of discussing sound material as separate from its notation, its means of production, and the listener's state of mind. It is the perfect acoustic encapsulation of the phenomenological object of contemplation, the sound in idealized form.

Schaeffer was pragmatic enough to know that acousmatic situations tend to provoke curiosity about the provenance of sound, which distracts from contemplating the pure sound object (1966, 93–94). In fact, he categorized hearing and listening practices into four modes, which parse out the varying degrees to which the listener interprets information. The first mode (*écouter*) concentrates on the objective qualities of sound and is intentional; Schaeffer describes this as "I listen to that which interests me" (1966, 113). Mode two (*ouïr*) refers to the purely physiological process of hearing sounds and entails no intention or interpretation. Mode three (*entendre*) describes hearing while attending to particular aspects of sound; Schaeffer describes it as "I hear, as a function of what interests me, from what I already know and what I seek to understand." Mode four (*comprendre*) constitutes an engagement with sound and its external references. We practice different combinations of these four modes depending on the object and purpose of our listening.

The nuances among these four modes may characterize how acousmatic situations affect listening. Schaeffer writes that acousmatic situations normally engage the first and fourth modes; because without benefit of visual cues, we listen to things that interest us and attempt to place them within a context of associations external to sound. Having explained how listeners perceive sound, Schaeffer's next step is to offer a prescription for how to listen better. Schaeffer takes up Husserl's concept of the transcendental-phenomenological reduction or *époché*, a bracketing out of knowledge about the external world in order to focus on the process of perception (1966, 263–265). Schaeffer calls this bracketing out reduced listening (*écoute réduite*). In order to access the sound object, Schaeffer thus conceives of a two-part reduction: the first acousmatic reduction takes place through the removal of visual cues, and the second takes place through the intentional disregard of the perceived sources and origins of a sound (Kane 2007).

Although they may seem highly theoretical at first glance, Schaeffer's recommendations were thoroughly grounded in empirical observations of turntable engravers. In 1948, when Schaeffer was working at Radiodiffusion Française (RDF), he developed a technique for isolating a specific sound by affixing it onto a disc that contained one locked groove (*sillon fermé*) in a complete circle rather than the normal spiraling groove.[1] An inwardly spiraling groove makes it possible for a disc to contain a substantial amount of material, enough to fit on numerous revolutions of decreasing diameter. A locked groove, by contrast, contains just enough material to fit on one revolution of the disc. Yet because the locked groove contains no bumps or barriers, the needle can repeat the recorded material indefinitely without pause. Among the many sounds that Schaeffer recorded on the locked groove was a bell sound whose attack was cut off, the *cloche coupée*. Schaeffer writes of these early experiments:

---

[1] The expression *sillon fermé* might seem to be better translated as "closed groove," but I refer to it instead as "locked groove," since this is how electronic dance music (EDM) turntablists refer to the same technique. See Butler (2006).

The locked groove certainly gave an object in the sense of *a thing* in some way stripped—in exchange for the destruction of another object. We have just recognized that this is a question not of an objective discovery, but rather of a new condition of the observer. . . . If we reunite the two experiments, that of the locked groove and that of the cut-off bell (both artificial, bizarre, unmusical objects), and open our ears, we begin to hear anything, whether a sound or music, in a new manner, thanks to the *reduced listening* which the experiment taught us through these two examples of rupture. (Schaeffer 1966, 391; emphases in original)

This "new condition of the observer" is a voluntary condition made possible by the locked groove and selective recording of an attackless pealing of a bell. Schaeffer acknowledged that reduced listening necessitates not only a choice on the part of the listener but practice, since listeners are conditioned to speculate on the origins of sounds (Schaeffer 1966, 270). With sufficient discipline, though, Schaeffer was certain that reduced listening was possible.

To what end did Schaeffer advocate these efforts? Schaeffer was keenly aware of the developments of electronic music in Germany, specifically in the radio studios of Westdeutscher Rundfunk (WDR), where Schaeffer's former student Karlheinz Stockhausen was perfecting techniques for synthesizing sounds out of pure sine tones. Schaeffer objected to the premise that music could be derived from abstract principles (such as serialist procedures) or abstract materials (such as sine tones). He instead advocated using concrete recorded sounds from which to abstract musical syntax and grammar that would be organically linked to sounds themselves (Dack 2002). Indeed, despite his prefatory remarks in the *Traité* that he was attempting an interdisciplinary exchange among performers, composers, scientists, and listeners, Schaeffer's recommendations seem most useful for composers alone. His advocacy of reduced listening is a call for composers to unlearn the associations of the sound objects they would extract from the outside world. Nattiez affirms this: "Schaeffer's 'concentrated hearing' is, contrary to his own implicit claim, essentially poietical in that it is in fact hearing *as experienced by a composer, who hears sounds with extreme attentiveness before integrating them into a work*" (1990, 95; emphasis in original). Listeners of musique concrète were not easily convinced, however. Pierre Boulez, who had enjoyed the use of Schaeffer's studio and even performed on some of Schaeffer's recordings, writes that musique concrète was "a sort of poetical parade" that perpetuated the "surrealist practice of collage" by presenting a "musical flea market" of sounds (1991, 226–227). Boulez objects to Schaeffer's use of concrete sounds whose preexisting associations force a "poetics without choice," a situation in which external meanings are imposed upon the work. Boulez continues, "To lend itself to composition, musical material needs to be sufficiently flexible, susceptible to transformation, and capable of generating and sustaining a dialectic." Lévi-Strauss echoes Boulez by noting that noises already possess external associations that interfere with any new grammar or syntax innate to a piece: "Musique concrète may be intoxicated with the illusion that it is saying something; in fact, it is floundering in non-significance" (1969, 23). As Taylor outlines, other contemporary critiques of Schaeffer were even less generous; many faulted him for not having formal musical training and for thus approaching composition as a dilettante or a technician (2001, 50–55). For these critics, musique concrète was too banal to be taken seriously as music. In his later years, Schaeffer himself admitted that his search for music within concrete materials was fruitless (Hodgkinson 1986), concluding that listeners are often too concerned with classifying sounds to be able to practice reduced listening.

Only a few composers today adhere to reduced listening as it was originally formulated. Schaeffer himself admits that before reduced listening is possible, the listener must "liberate [himself] from the conditioning created by [his] former habits, to pass through the challenge of the *époché*" (1966, 270). In contrast, Michel Chion, a GRM composer as well as an authority on film sound, writes extensively on ways in which causal listening or attention to the source-causes of sound can be encouraged to create illusion in cinema (1990, 96). Francisco López, a Spanish electronic musician and sound artist whose work I discuss in chapter 5, most faithfully echoes Schaeffer's calls for reduced listening, arguing that causal listening reduces the ability of music to communicate freely (López 1997).

As I illustrate below, post-Schaefferian composers have adopted Schaeffer's philosophy only selectively. While Schaeffer faulted German-led electronic music for relying on synthesis to generate abstract sounds rather than using what he felt were aesthetically rich found materials, many subsequent electroacoustic composers incorporate some manner of sound synthesis into their pieces; some also avoid using concrete materials at all. And as the name *electroacoustic* suggests, many of these works also incorporate traditional instruments. The decision to use acoustic instruments with recognizable timbres as well as musical notation with conventional rhythms, pitches, and gestures places post-Schaefferian electroacoustic music in a no-man's-land between the complete compositional freedom that Schaeffer envisioned and a musical discourse similar to that of nonelectronic contemporary art music. It is thus no surprise that reduced listening has endured considerable criticism within the post-Schaefferian camp. Pure reduced listening is virtually impossible when dealing with recognizable instruments and for many electroacoustic composers is unsettlingly ahistorical, although some advocate it as one component of a larger listening experience that simultaneously acknowledges the external associations of sound. Schaeffer's faith in the practicality of reduced listening allowed him to believe that a composer could exclude all unwanted associations of a sound. When post-Schaefferians reject reduced listening, they also reject the position that a composer can control everything about the listening process; this has led most post-Schaefferians to regard listening as an embodied, intentional activity rather than the reflective discipline Schaeffer imagined. Before elaborating this position, one championed by many of the composers associated with the GRM, I want first to consider Trevor Wishart's work, which presents an alternative attempt at poiesis. By using materials whose relationship to the outside world is manifest, the composer ultimately retains greater control over a work's materials.

Among British electronic composers who came of age during the 1960s and 1970s, Trevor Wishart is an anomaly. Unlike his peers, Wishart did not study in Paris with Schaeffer and is largely self-taught. He was briefly involved in the postpunk scene of Manchester, hosting during the 1970s a series of happenings and concerts that featured the likes of Joy Division and the Fall (Reynolds 2005, 119). Since then, he has assumed a place of distinction among British electronic musicians, and his writings, particularly his monograph *On Sonic Art*, are widely read. Wishart's best-known work "Red Bird" (1980) is an electroacoustic piece that contains sampled sounds as well as synthesized gestures bearing an unmistakable relationship to the outside world, namely to the shrieks of a political prisoner undergoing torture. This relationship is explicitly intended by the composer, who regards such sound symbols as means of conveying musical "myth." Wishart feels that it is impossible to separate sounds from their associations, so it is incumbent upon composers to acknowledge and work with sound references rather than to repress them: "In order to build up a complex metaphoric network we need to establish a set of metaphoric primitives which the listener might reasonably be expected to recognize and relate to, just as in the structure of a myth we need to use symbols which are reasonably unambiguous to a large number of people" (Wishart 1986, 55). Although Wishart clearly rejects the premise of reduced listening, he adopts a position similar to Schaeffer's in that he feels that the composer can control the listener's experience of the work.

Wishart here is applying structuralism, particularly as expressed in Lévi-Strauss's *The Raw and the Cooked* (1969), which demonstrated that musical compositions and myths share certain formal attributes. These attributes are effective organizational devices for guiding an audience's responses, because they also inform the stories many of us first hear during childhood. For Wishart, once those attributes have been detected and studied, the composer must utilize them if a musical work is to have any communicative success. Wishart's alternative to Schaeffer has won over many post-Schaefferians.

Although Field (2000) differs from Wishart in that he cautions against using both sampled and synthesized materials, he agrees that composers must cater to and anticipate the listening process rather than assuming that listeners will passively hear what the composer intended. Atkinson surveys the literature on musical semiotics to conclude that all sounds function as signs and that composers must acknowledge the extrinsic potentials of their materials while also allowing such materials to function musically. Atkinson goes so far as to call for the development of a "taxonomy (and thus theoretical framework) of how sound can 'stand for something,' i.e. function as a sign in semiotic terms" (2007, 113). Young (1996) exhorts composers to make the recognition of either actual or perceived origins of a sound central to their work.

Listening to electronic music demonstrates that reduced listening as Schaeffer conceived of it may be impractical, if not impossible. Yet Schaeffer nevertheless deserves credit for pinpointing what would become the key preoccupations of electronic musicians as well as scholars of electronic music, listening, and sound. This is not to say that many writers believe in or insist on reduced listening. In fact, most feel that reduced listening, if possible at all, can occur only under limited circumstances. Composers' efforts to dictate every aspect of the listening process are thus seen as futile. Post-Schaefferians tend to regard listening as a process necessarily determined by the listener; to cite Nattiez, we are talking about esthesis rather than poiesis. This is a different position from that taken by Wishart, who writes for the edification of the composer first and foremost. The composers and writers featured in the esthesis section below encourage listeners to nurture rather than repress their instincts concerning the sounds they hear in electro-acoustic music. These writers also admonish composers to accept that their materials do not lie entirely within their control.

ESTHESIS AND CRITIQUES OF REDUCED LISTENING

Schaeffer applied the phenomenological *épaché* to music with the objective of empowering composers to control the reception of their work; his methods are therefore poietic by definition. Reduced listening was for Schaeffer less a descriptive tool than a mechanism for substituting one set of preconditions (the external knowledge listeners might possess about sound) for another (the composer's desired interpretation of sound). Later phenomenological approaches to listening differ from Schaeffer's in that they claim to be descriptive rather than prescriptive and exhibit more caution in isolating one universal, perceptual experience that preempts culture and history. This caution is understandable given that the most common critiques of phenomenology insist on the impossibility of bracketing out culture and history.

For instance, Kane faults the phenomenological method, especially as Schaeffer applies it, for securing "an a priori ontological foundation, but the supposed benefits of such a foundation are attained at the expense of historically sedimented 'residual signification'" (Kane 2007, 22). I want to touch briefly on the reception of phenomenology as it is applied to music in general before discussing specific critiques of reduced listening and phenomenology in electroacoustic music.

In his book *Listening and Voice*, Don Ihde charts the debate over how much external knowledge can realistically be bracketed out. Ihde distinguishes between "first" phenomenology as described by Husserl and "second" phenomenology as forwarded by Heidegger. First phenomenology uses the *époché* to separate all external knowledge and cultural context from perception. Second phenomenology "understands that experience cannot be questioned alone or in isolation but must be understood ultimately in relation to its historical and cultural imbeddedness" (Ihde 2007, 20). Even more than Schaeffer, Ihde recognizes that a complete reduction of listening is exceedingly difficult:

> I can *focus* upon my listening and thus make the auditory dimension stand
> out. But it does so only relatively. I cannot isolate it from its situation, its
> embedment, its "background" of global experience. In this sense a "pure"
> auditory experience in phenomenology is impossible, but, as a focal
> dimension of global experience, a concentrated concern with listening is
> possible. (2007, 44–45)

A second critique of phenomenology argues that listening must, by definition, implicate the listener. Windsor puts it simply: "The sound object can, and does, point both ways, to a listener and to an environment, and only through accepting and exploiting this possibility can electroacoustic music give an immanent answer to those who revile its representation of the everyday as somehow unmusical" (1994, 91). Here, Windsor echoes statements by both Ihde—"Sounds are 'first' experienced as sounds *of* things" (2007, 59) and "To listen is to be dramatically engaged in a bodily listening which 'participates' in the movement of the music" (2007, 158)—and, ultimately, Merleau-Ponty, whose thesis in *Phenomenology of Perception* (2002) is that since all perception is necessarily bodily perception, one can therefore never speak of perception without also speaking of the perceiver's physical interaction with stimuli. The self-described postphenomenologist Jean-Luc Nancy formalizes this in his treatise *Listening* (2007) through his insistence that listening is always a self-reflexive act. Music for Nancy is "made to be listened to, but it is first of all, in itself, the listening of self" (2007, 27).

These various responses to phenomenology are consistent with trends throughout twentieth-century critical theory toward dethroning the author from his seat of power. Critiques of phenomenology teach us that perception amounts to more than the quotient of sensory input generated by an artwork, so creators must attempt to understand the experiences of their audiences rather than expecting audiences to submit uncritically to the artwork. These critiques inform the work of many electroacoustic composers, especially those profiled below.

The first composers to break with reduced listening themselves worked or studied with Schaeffer. In 1951, Schaeffer founded the Groupe de Recherche de Musique Concrète inside what was then called Radio-Télévision Française (Gayou 2007, 104). For the next few years, Schaeffer attracted numerous composers to his studios who were keen on studying musique concrète techniques; many of these composers were foreigners who would go on to introduce tape-music techniques to their native countries. In 1958, the name of this research group was changed to the Groupe de Recherches Musicales (GRM), a center specializing in research on sound and electroacoustic music. GRM composers have remained faithful to Schaeffer's initial mandate of researching the potentials of electronics, but even the most committed Schaefferians have approached reduced listening with reservations. Battier notes that Schaeffer's *Traité* coined the term *acoulogy* to refer to the "science" of reduced listening, an "act of isolating and of defining the musical characteristics of recorded sounds" (2007, 198). Yet Chion subsequently proposed expanding the notion of acoulogy to include the study of all aspects of hearing, including causal hearing. Luc Ferrari, a French composer who headed the GRM from 1959 to 1960, was the first Schaefferian to break publicly with the concepts of reduced listening. Although Ferrari wanted to retain the grammar of musique concrète, he did so while embracing the associations of his concrete materials, creating what he referred to as "anecdotal" music (Gayou 2007, 138). In his *Presque rien* series of pieces, Ferrari lets recorded sounds function simultaneously as music and as narrative tools. For instance, *Presque rien no. 1 ou le lever du jour au bord de la mer* (1967–1970) features the unprocessed sounds of a Dalmatian fishing village. Ferrari uses no formal method of organization, which encourages the listener to imagine the sound source and to derive a narrative to explain it. François Bayle, who headed the GRM from 1975 until 1997, has devoted his career to the semiotics in acousmatic music, particularly how different types of signifieds or "images" can be conveyed through sound (Bayle 1993). Many of the types of images that Bayle discusses are connected to a sound's perceived origins. Bernard Parmegiani, whom Schaeffer appointed as director of the music and image section of the GRM, has written numerous compositions featuring acoustic instruments and jazz idioms. The extent to which Schaeffer's students distanced themselves from Schaeffer's own positions indicates two things: Schaeffer encouraged healthy relationships with his students in which independent thinking was expected, and Schaeffer's theories came up short, even to those who looked to him for guidance.

Denis Smalley is a New Zealand-born electroacoustic composer and theorist who studied with Schaeffer and Bayle before eventually becoming the head of the music department at City University, London. Like both of his teachers, Smalley has written extensively on the process of listening to electroacoustic music. Following Nattiez (1990, 11–12), Smalley contends that music can be broken down into "intrinsic" or internally referent elements and "extrinsic" or externally referent elements. Smalley proposes spectromorphology, the study of sound changes and transformations over time, as a mechanism for attending to the intrinsic characteristics of a piece. Spectromorphology is "not a compositional theory or method, but a descriptive tool based on aural perception" (1997, 107). For Smalley, spectromorphological descriptions enable all listeners, not only practitioners or experts, to discuss their perceptions of electroacoustic music. Spectromorphology concerns itself with perceived reactions to sound rather than with the intentions of composers. As such, spectromorphology necessarily entails a component of reduced listening, since it disregards knowledge of any compositional preconceptions as well as the procedures through which sounds are created (1997, 111).

Smalley distinguishes between the sources of sounds and their references. In electroacoustic music, while "sound-shapes and qualities frequently do not indicate known sources and causes" (1997, 107), references are nevertheless patent:

> The wide-open sonic world of electroacoustic music encourages imaginative and imagined extrinsic connections because of the variety and ambiguity of its materials, because of its reliance on the motion of colourful spectral energies, its emphasis on the acousmatic, and not least through its exploration of spatial perspective. (1997, 110)

And while spectromorphology becomes a means of accessing and discussing the intrinsic elements of a work, attempts at completely bracketing out extrinsic associations are futile:

> The sounding materials within a composition cannot be solely or even primarily self-referential. The apprehension of musical content and structure is linked to the world of experience outside the composition, not only to the wider context of auditory experience but also to non-sounding experience. Approached from the multiple perspectives of life outside music, the materials and structure of a musical composition become the meeting-place of sounding and non-sounding experience. (Smalley 1996, 83)

Smalley's influence on the discourse of electronic music has been considerable, because he refines and formalizes distinctions already latent in Schaeffer's writings, making them practical for all listeners. Schaeffer himself distinguished between technicians' theories and the lived experience of listening to sound (1966, 26). Schaeffer felt, however, that all listeners could be trained to approach sounds in the way in which he trained his composition students. Smalley, by contrast, introduces a vocabulary for describing sounds independently of the outside world, all the while insisting that this perceived independence is only a heuristic device for accessing elements that might otherwise be overshadowed by sound references.

But unlike Schaeffer's recommendations for reduced listening, Smalley's listening theories combine prescriptive and descriptive elements. Reduced listening can thus be recommended as an analytic tool, but the ultimate results of listening are something to which composers must adapt, rather than something composers can control. Smalley's writings serve as a touchstone for electroacoustic composers, many of whom live in Britain and are associated with academic institutions. Chief among these is Simon Emmerson, a British composer who currently teaches at De Montfort University in Leicester and previously taught at City University, London. Emmerson edited *The Language of Electroacoustic Music* (1986) and *Music, Electronic Media and Culture* (2000), two seminal volumes of essays concerning the abilities of electronic music to signify. His own contribution to the former volume, "The Relation of Language to Materials," asserts that electroacoustic music can be characterized as having either aural (meaning abstract, self-referential) or mimetic (meaning representational, externally referent) discourse. The similarities to Smalley's intrinsic/extrinsic divide are obvious. Emmerson goes even further than Smalley in critiquing the collision between the ideal of reduced listening and the reality of musique concrète:

> The earlier works of Pierre Schaeffer's group in Paris (most notably Schaeffer's own *Étude aux Objets*) stubbornly refuse to relinquish this reference to the real world. The listener is confronted with two conflicting arguments: the more abstract musical discourse (intended by the composer) of interacting sounds and their patterns, and the almost cinematic stream of images of real objects being hit, scraped or otherwise set in motion. (1986, 18)

Speaking about electronic music in general, Emmerson argues:

> We can go even further perhaps risking the assertion: *sounds inevitably have associations.* So perhaps while the "source/cause" search might be suspended, the "association" of the sound, bracketed together with it by Chion (after Schaeffer), is certainly not. Some of these responses may

indeed be automatic and we may not have sufficient conscious control to "bracket them out." The unintended consequences of Schaeffer's puritan position were to be profound. (2007, 6; emphasis in original)

Emmerson regards these consequences as persistent attempts on the part of electroacoustic composers, from Ferrari and R. Murray Schafer to Luigi Nono and John Cage, to deal squarely with the external associations of sampled materials. Even synthesized tones, the supposed blank slates of electronic music, are for Emmerson rooted in reference (1986, 26).

One of Emmerson's colleagues at De Montfort University is the composer and editor of the journal *Organised Sound* Leigh Landy, whose writings have concerned themselves with how experimental composers can make their music more accessible to audiences at large. To that end, Landy designed the "Intention/Reception" project, which surveys listeners after they have heard a piece. The first set of questions is administered without providing information about a composer's intentions; the second set is given after listeners hear the composer speak (Landy 2007, 21–65). In emphasizing empirical data over theory, Landy surpasses Smalley in describing rather than prescribing the listening process. Landy concludes that electroacoustic music needs to offer the listener "something to hold on to" if it is to be at all rewarding; this "something" is usually material that patently refers to the world beyond the musical work.

The "Intention/Reception" project seems inspired, at least in part, by clinical acoustic and psychoacoustic research on recognition of the sources of sound. The presumption here is that empirical data trump any theorizing or philosophizing about the ways listeners classify what they hear. The reference for many writers on electronic music is the work of sociologist William Gaver, whose research indicates that listeners tend to identify sounds in terms of the objects and events that trigger them. Truly acousmatic descriptions of sounds occur only when their source events are unidentifiable, such as when musical sounds reveal little or nothing about how they are produced (Gaver 1993, 19). Gaver's research is central to the work of electroacoustic scholar Luke Windsor, who argues that electronic music encourages perception of the "probable" causes of sound even though the actual causes of sound might be quite different. (Windsor is also drawing on the ecological theory of perception as forwarded by J. J. Gibson; such an ecological approach to listening relates listening and listeners to the environment and takes into account sound sources as well as any meanings that might be attributed to them.) A synthesized sound of screeching might recall the sound of nails scraping a chalkboard, even though the true source of these sounds is the synthesizer itself. Windsor concludes that "Any structural description of acousmatic music *must* take into account the possibility that

Much of what we hear when we listen to anything is enhanced by information acquired through other senses. When all sensory faculties are working normally, hearing works in tandem with sight and, often, taste, smell, and touch to give a composite, integrated view of the world. But the proviso "when all sensory faculties are working normally" is stymied in much electronic music, because the acousmatic situation at a basic level thwarts our natural tendency to look for a visual cue to the sounds we hear. Hearing recordings (whether of nonelectronic or electronic music) is thus inherently odd, because we usually cannot pair a physical gesture with the sound.

Contrary to what Scruton (1997, 3) believes, most scholars maintain that it is not our first impulse to listen to any music (Western art music or otherwise) acousmatically. For anyone who has spent some time in Western societies, nearly all Western art and popular music is identifiable *as music* and therefore enmeshed within a whole web of associations about what music is and does. For listeners who possess a high degree of familiarity with musical works, that identifiability is made possible through harmony, melody, rhythm, form, and other typical musical attributes. But even for listeners who possess only a superficial awareness of musical syntax and grammar, instrumental timbre is a dead giveaway that what is being heard is music and not random noise. So, when listening to recordings of nonelectronic music, the full impact of the acousmatic situation is blunted by our tendency to imagine the instruments and even gestures that trigger musical sounds. We hear a recording of a symphony, and we can easily envision some sort of orchestra, or even the synchronized upward and downward movements of the violin and viola bows that would normally create this sound. This is not to say that we always think of instruments and their movements when we listen to recordings of symphonies, only that we often have at ready disposal an easy target to which to attribute the causes of symphonic sound.

The same is clearly not true for electronic music. In recorded form, the acousmatic situation in electronic music is truly acousmatic when there are unrecognizable sounds at play. And in live performance, recording, playback, and sound synthesis technologies drastically change the experience of watching a performance for two reasons: many electronic instruments function as "black boxes" that render sound creation invisible, and the definition of liveness has been put into question by the technologies of live playback, when something recorded in the past is reanimated during the present. The case of the theremin, the device created by Russian inventor Léon Theremin in 1919, is an early example of the "black box" effect. The instrument was notable for many reasons: its eerie timbre, its strange appearance (just two antennae and two frequency oscillators), and, above all, the way it was played. The theremin was the first instrument that did not require direct contact from the performer. Sounds are generated when the performer moves his or her hands near the antennae; changing the distance between the hands and the antennae changes, respectively, the frequency and amplitude of the sound. A theremin performance was thus inherently mysterious to watch, because there was no vibrating resonator and no visible site of sound production. Audiences, introduced to commercially available electrical power only some forty years previously, were confronted with a new experience: a phantasmagorical musical instrument that seemed to hide the creation of sound.

The strangeness of electronic instruments persists to the present day. Consider what happens in a typical concert of electronic music. Assume that this concert features performers rather than just loudspeakers onstage. We might see players with synthesizers, sequencers, turntables, or other various devices. Or we may see performers with acoustic instruments that interact in some manner with electronics, like the routine scenario of an acoustic instrumentalist who performs with live effects managed by the software Max/MSP. Some of these electronic devices have interfaces that resemble conventional instruments, such as the synthesizer whose keyboard is modeled on the piano. Other instruments, such as the laptop computer or the RCA Mark II Sound Synthesizer famously used by Milton Babbitt, are utterly dissimilar to any preexisting musical instrument and seem better suited to an office or a laboratory. And still others, such as the theremin, are in a class by themselves, resembling nothing that has come before. The point is that even if electronic music contains sounds that are attributable in an abstract sense to some source, the experience of *watching* that sound being performed often reveals a gestural synapse between the performer's actions and the sounds he or she produces, as well as a temporal synapse (if the effect is prerecorded) between the present and the past moment in which the sounds were first created. As Croft (2007, 61) succinctly writes, "we expect the sound to have a more or less transparent relation to the properties of the sounding body we see before us."

Emmerson offers a provisional set of criteria for defining what liveness means in contemporary electronic music. The first requirement is that a human performer be present who makes decisions that change the outcome of the performance *at the time of performance* (what he elsewhere calls "real time"). This performer produces sound on instruments that can operate mechanically or on electronic instruments that mimic mechanical instruments through requiring the performer to make some performative gesture. But this performer can also control the outcome of the piece through mechanisms that call for no such performative gestures; laptops are the obvious example (Emmerson 2007, 90).

The current discourse on the ontology of liveness in the era of the computer (Auslander 1999; Croft 2007; Emmerson 2007; Smalley 1996) can be summed up as a concern with how performances of electronic music are destroying the frame that has traditionally encased music. I want to shift my focus here from anxiety about the concept of liveness to what I perceive as the true object of confusion: how the nature of performance in electronic music affects its ability to signify. If the definition of liveness is murky, it has been for some time, because it was recordings, not electronic music, that first introduced the possibility of performances of preexisting material. After nearly one hundred years of phonographic technology, listeners have become savvy enough to accept a "live" performance of sounds clearly not originating in the present, so long as other criteria for a performance are met. The true issue here is how electronic music is dismantling the various cultural and aesthetic habits that frame a performance as separate from the outside world.

Let's revisit what constitutes performance. In almost any musical culture in existence today, performances occur when listeners attend to musicians giving a public rendering of music. Often, that rendering takes place in a specifically apportioned space like a concert hall or a stadium; on other occasions, that rendering occurs in settings like subway stations or street corners. Some traditions, such as Western art music, govern the behavior of both musicians and listeners: musicians must dress in black and adopt a solemn expression; listeners must refrain from applauding between movements and sit quietly in their seats. In popular traditions, listeners sing and dance in accompaniment to the music, and musicians verbally and physically encourage this participation.

The differences among various musical genres notwithstanding, all types of nonelectronic performance frame the musical act as separate and distinct from the outside world. Staging, lighting, costumes, and formal behavior all underscore the status of performance as an event containing a special type of acoustic discourse that is separate or aesthetically distant from the other sounds we hear in daily existence. In other words, live performances of non-electronic music are both in this world and not of it. Performances take place thanks to the gestures of live human beings whose efforts are visible as well as audible. These efforts ground the performance in the here and now, in the same physical space as the audience, so in this sense, listeners experience the presence of music. Similarly, electronic-music performances *can* delineate music from daily life, but they need not do so. As the cited authors have stressed, the mechanisms through which electronic sounds are produced can confuse or obscure the visual cues that announce a traditional performance. Gestures that musicians make to trigger sounds may be absent, as may musicians themselves if sound is being diffused exclusively by machines. But these absences are parenthetical to the real issue: how electronic music sounds themselves can disassemble the frame between music and daily life.

The uncertainty of the "liveness" of prerecorded sounds, or of sounds generated by loudspeakers or humans at laptop computers, amounts to doubt about how to reconcile music with its surroundings. To recall Goehr (2007), cited above, Western aesthetics since the classical era have made the case for music's legitimacy among, and even superiority to, the plastic arts. One means of claiming this legitimacy was to impose cultural practices that frame music in a metaphorical sense, so that listeners could contemplate works in a way similar to how museum goers contemplate works of art. Electroacoustic music can be seen as wreaking havoc with preelectronic music's rituals through its use of unmusical sounds as well as its destruction of liveness; this is the same sort of havoc that twentieth-century art movements, from Cubism to minimalist sculpture, wreaked with their destruction of the frame. Cage began the deconstruction of this barrier with the silent piece "4'33." In exposing the ideal of silence as unattainable, Cage redirected attention to all sounds, musical or otherwise. In a sense, all subsequent experimental works have constituted reactions to "4'33" insofar as they raise unmusical sounds for contemplation. This is most apparent in electronic music that veers toward the category of sound art. When the language of music ceases to be separate from the outside world and starts to resemble base phenomena that could be heard at any moment in time, the factor distinguishing music from sound or noise becomes irrelevant.

Most post-Schaefferian works, even those by Smalley and Wishart that sound very little like music, nonetheless adhere to the conventions of the live performance of music. When these works are experienced live, audiences sit quietly, just as they would at a concert of acoustic music. Smalley and Wishart discuss their works as music even if they also employ alternative terminology such as "sonic art" and do so in venues and media that identify clearly with music rather than sound art (see more on this subject in chapter 6). The resulting friction here is not negligible; even the most radical works in terms of form and sound content still identify themselves as music through the rituals in which they are experienced, creating a schizophrenic condition in which electroacoustic music is simultaneously music and something other than music, such as sound art.

The music considered in chapter 2, electronica, exists in a similar situation of embracing generic norms, but these are the norms of popular dance music rather than experimentalism or avant-gardist academic music. In both electronica and electroacoustic music, artists generally have faith that sound is meaningful. For electronica, sound materials acquire meaning over time through association with particular themes such as space or science fiction, actions such as construction or destruction, and even instants in time, whether the distant past or the future. Now that we've pondered how composers and listeners argue over signification in post-Schaefferian works, we can examine the metaphors that guide the listening experience in electronica.

2

Material As Sign in Electronica

Chapter 1 argued that a nagging preoccupation in much electroacoustic music concerns whether the listening experience can be controlled and enhanced. This discussion, oddly enough, often avoids technical descriptions of how sounds are created, sticking instead to how sounds are received. A chief distinction between the discourse surrounding institutional electroacoustic music and that surrounding electronica is that the latter discourse concentrates on sound *material* rather than the acts of composing or listening. What I mean by material here amounts to the objectified, audible phenomena in electronic music, from notes and rhythms to sound grains, clicks, timbres, and even silence; it is, as Adorno puts it, "what artists work with" (1997, 147). Material necessarily refers back to its own generation, and so any discussion of material must include the actions and devices involved in its creation. My usage of *material* is thus distinct from Schaeffer's formulation of the *sound object*, which Schaeffer insisted is separate from its modes of production and the media on which it is affixed (Schaeffer 1966, 76). Material also needs to be distinguished from the listening theories detailed in chapter 1, for while those theories offered prescriptive or descriptive accounts of perception, electronica's materialist discourse focuses more on the perceived objects themselves. *Material* is admittedly not a term that all of the artists considered in this chapter would use to describe their sounds or musical building blocks. But as a concept, *material* may encapsulate the dual concerns of sound itself and sound generation, concerns that, as I demonstrate, are traits held in common among many electronica genres.

In particular, I want to focus on material generated through three activities central to electronica: the construction, reproduction, and destruction of sound. For now, I'll put forward some admittedly naive definitions for these three terms, with the understanding that electronic music is rarely as neat and tidy as these initial demarcations suggest. *Construction* refers to the creation of new material and often happens by means of synthesis. *Reproduction* refers to the use of preexisting recordings within a new work, particularly by means of digital sampling. *Destruction* pertains to the perceived disintegration or disfiguring of sound and occurs thanks to digital signal processing, as well as any number of "analog" activities, from feedback to mutilating recorded media. There will naturally be some overlap among construction, reproduction, and destruction. Consider that many synthesizers available today construct their sounds from raw materials consisting of samples, or reproduced material. Similarly, samples often consist of preexisting sound that was itself synthesized. Sound destruction is a particularly subjective category, since what sounds like destruction to one listener may sound like construction to another. These technicalities notwithstanding, the gamut of electronic-music instruments suggests this type of tripartite structure.

My discussion is complicated by the fact that various forms of treatment and processing may distance the perceived sound source from the actual sound source. A synthesizer may render what sounds like the gushing of a waterfall, although the actual sound source is the synthesizer itself. But technical slippages are only the beginning; more to the point is the fact that synthesized and sampled sounds can bear either direct or distant resemblances to their models. The raw content of a sample can be blatantly recognizable or totally obscure. Signal processing can make a sample sound old when it is new or make a sample sound new when it is actually quite dated. Synthesis methods, meanwhile, have attained a level of sophistication such that many devices can now generate flawless imitations of acoustic instruments. Yet legions of electronic musicians still prefer the warmth and buzz of older analog synthesizers that sound nothing like their supposed acoustic models. In other words, the ontological status of a sound as sampled or synthesized, "real" or "fake," is no longer as relevant as it was during the 1950s, when the technical processes that generated sound were patently audible. More important, rather, is whether a sound *seems* old or new, artificial or natural. Put simply, electronic sounds can lie about whether they are constructions or reproductions.

This chapter considers examples culled from various genres of electronica, a catchall term for everything from electronic dance music (EDM) to avant-garde and even certain works of hip-hop. Record labels began to circulate the label "electronica" during the early 1990s to lure consumers to an increasingly disparate collection of electronic dance music and ambient works (McLeod 2001, 67). Some electronica is manifestly popular in that it is marketed to large audiences and is intended for dancing or as background music for parties. Other electronica works possess extremely small audiences and are not particularly accessible. While it would be naive to offer a single theory to explain every facet of every electronica genre, I want to talk about how listeners and practitioners hear electronica's sounds as metaphors. These metaphors can link a particular work with a web of external concepts such as the history of other musical works, outer space, the past, or the material on which sound is encoded. Electronica's sounds, in other words, are always heard in relation to something beyond the works in which they are housed, but these linkages to the outside world tend not to be mimetic as do the sounds in post-Schaefferian electroacoustic music. In electronica, the relationship between signifier and signified is not based on simple resemblance but rather on conventions that over time have paired a sound with an exterior concept.

CONSTRUCTION

Construction and reproduction were central in the debate that polarized early electronic music, that between French musique concrète and German *elektronische Musik*. In the early 1950s, there was a seemingly irreconcilable division between sounds that were entirely new and synthesized from the "pure" raw materials of sine tones and those that were extracted from the outside world through recording. This distinction was underscored by the fact that musicians who synthesized their sound materials congregated at the studios of Westdeutscher Rundfunk (WDR) in Cologne, while musicians who recorded their materials worked at Radiodiffusion Française (RDF) in Paris. The principal researcher at WDR, phoneticist Werner Meyer-Eppler, analyzed the human voice in order to derive methods for reconstructing it artificially. Meyer-Eppler's work was particularly useful to the composer Herbert Eimert, a committed twelve-tone composer who wanted to expand serialism's control of musical parameters to sound and timbre themselves. RDF's Pierre Schaeffer, meanwhile, was an avid reader of symbolist poetry and, like the symbolists, wanted to create art that played with the internal music of words and found sounds, irrespective of their meanings. The philosophical and geographical distances separating these two studios seemed to suggest that synthesis and sampling were incompatible.

The chasm between WDR and RDF was first bridged by Karlheinz Stockhausen, who studied musique concrète with Schaeffer before assuming a privileged research position at WDR. Stockhausen's experience with both synthesis and sampling methods made him uniquely qualified to reach a compromise between the two. After initially rejecting concrete composition in favor of the complete control afforded by synthesis, Stockhausen composed *Gesang der Jünglinge* (1955–56), a piece built on the affinities between a boy's recorded voice and synthesized sounds. The critical success of *Gesang der Jünglinge* provided compelling evidence for subsequent composers that synthesis and sampling were not mutually exclusive but could together be harnessed to generate meaningful sound worlds.

The main figures at WDR would probably never have dreamed that frequency oscillators and their digital progeny, tools for sound construction, would by now have accrued cultural associations. A testimonial to the domestication of synthesizers is the 2008 album by Benge (Ben Edwards) entitled *Twenty Systems*. Benge, a self-described enthusiast of antiquated electronics, recorded twenty ambient tracks on twenty synthesizers that were produced between 1968 and 1987. The tracks are arranged chronologically such that the album begins with the 1968 Moog Modular 3C and ends with the 1987 Kawai K5M. In the intervening tracks, the listener tours sounds generated by models of the ARP, Oberheim, Roland, Fairlight, and Yamaha. The simplicity of the compositional material, pared down to repetitive patterns played at slow tempi, allows the characters of these devices to emerge. *Twenty Systems* appeals to a niche market of audiophiles and electronic-music fans. The disc comes with a fifty-page booklet containing a foreword written by electronica musician Scanner (Robin Rimbaud), who cites Baudrillard and Deleuze/Guattari to remind us of how strange and unique synthesizers are, not only for musicians but for society at large.

Rimbaud writes that synthesizers always expose the absence of the instruments they are supposed to imitate:

> Synthetic production presents cultural artifice, the sign, the map of
> recognition, as a substitution for the real, an alternative vernacular, "as
> signs of the real for the real itself" as Baudrillard argued. The erasure of
> historical reference points within this imagined synthetic universe has
> developed into simulacrum, which differentiates itself from representation
> in the sense that a simulacrum marks the absence, not the existence, of the
> objects it is supposed to signify. (Rimbaud 2008)

Rimbaud is correct, but we shouldn't go so far as to assume that the musicians who play synthesizers are somehow complacent enough to settle for an imitation violin even though they would prefer a real one. In fact, electronic musicians have relished the differences between acoustic and electronic instruments. Robert Moog dismissed electronic instruments intended as imitations of traditional instruments, praising instead tape recorders and voltage-controlled instruments for their ability to revolutionize composition (Moog 1967). Wendy Carlos's watershed 1968 recording *Switched-On Bach*

introduced the Moog synthesizer as an instrument in its own right, not simply a substitute for a piano or a harpsichord. Analog-synthesizer innovator
Tom Oberheim noted in 1977:

> The equipment that's available now only approximates what acoustic
> instruments can do. We've got oscillators, filters, very crude envelope
> generators. Not that it's important to synthesize sounds of real instruments,
> but what makes real instruments interesting is that they've got very
> complex sound structures. And that's what I want to see in synthesizers—
> machines that will produce magnificent sounds. (Oberheim 2000, 80)

Digital-synthesizer manufacturers who followed in the 1980s might have
marketed their devices as reasonable imitations of orchestral instruments,
but musicians employed them precisely because they did *not* sound like the
instruments they supposedly were emulating but rather appeared new and
alien (Cateforis 2000, 181). The continued popularity of vintage synthesizers
(as well as their software facsimiles) and the very existence of Benge's vintage
synthesizer compilation speak to the fact that synthesized sounds are more
than clumsy approximations of a symphony orchestra.

Rimbaud's argument makes sense only when considered within this historical context. Some constructed electronic sounds are desirable because
they are *approximate* imitations of acoustic instruments rather than faithful
reproductions. The amplified electric guitar is still a guitar, and when it is
played with a minimum of amplification, it is clearly related to its acoustic
cousin. And even with feedback and distortion, the strumming and particular timbre of electric guitars still flag them as guitars. Many works of electronica cash in on the friction created through electronic treatment of an
acoustic instrument. In Christian Fennesz's "The Colour of Three" from his
2008 album *Black Sea*, an electric guitar is subjected to a type of distortion
that creates and maintains transients around the core pitch content. These
transients make the guitar resemble a bowed cello. But this virtual cello can
produce sounds no normal cello could, tones that are at once granular and
legato.

Sometimes, though, electronica musicians and listeners like to talk
about constructed sounds on their own terms, as something other than
rough facsimiles of traditional instruments. This poses a significant challenge to analysis. Since the earliest experiments with frequency oscillators
in WDR's studios, it has proved notoriously difficult to discuss the qualities
of electronic sound, particularly synthesized sound, because musicians lack
a universally recognized vocabulary with which to do so. Statements by
electronica musicians and producers reveal two common strategies for discussing sound construction. The first strategy relies on descriptions of the

equipment and methods used to produce sound. Inherent in this discourse is the assumption that an informed listener will know, for instance, how a particular synthesizer sounds and how it is different from other synthesizers. In a 2003 *Keyboard* feature on industrial music, interviewees described their compositional process almost exclusively in terms of equipment. Grothesk (Stephan Groth) said:

> The goal is of course to come up with new sounds that haven't been heard before. I run stuff through as many plug-ins and as much hardware as possible. I start out with a sound from my Kawai 100F, my Korg MS20, or some other analog synth and then record it into Cubase or Pro Tools through a TLA FatMan compressor. (Preve 2003, 29)

The sharing of information concerning the methodology of sound construction is common among electronica artists but less so among institutional electroacoustic composers, who seem to guard their sound-production methods as something approaching a trade secret. This is not to suggest that institutional composers are not interested in describing how they produce sounds—far from it. Rather, this sort of discussion tends to be relegated to the classroom or sequestered conversations among colleagues or friends. In terms of publicly available discussions of sound generation, the best sources are textbooks such as Curtis Roads's *The Computer Music Tutorial* (1996) and *Microsound* (2001).

The second strategy for describing constructed sound material relies on its associations with extramusical subject matter. This type of discourse is less satisfying for those looking for technically specific terms but is more accessible to those who may not have an exhaustive knowledge of electronic instruments and software. Among electronica musicians and listeners, a perennial trope is that constructed sound is otherworldly, futuristic, and even alien, like nothing else that has ever been heard before. These links were forged thanks to film soundtracks that use synthesized sound to conjure alien worlds. From Louis and Bebe Barron's *Forbidden Planet* (1956) to Wendy Carlos's *A Clockwork Orange* (1971) and Vangelis's *Blade Runner* (1982), synthesized sound has been a preferred means of depicting the flight of spacecraft and the technological dystopias envisioned in postapocalyptic fiction. Numerous popular-music concept albums, from Jean Michel Jarre's *Oxygène* (1976) and Tangerine Dream's *Phaedra* (1974) to Air's *Moon Safari* (1998), have capitalized on these associations to evoke the cosmic and extraterrestrial. Even when film soundtracks enlist synthesizers to perform older compositions (as the *Clockwork Orange* soundtrack does with its Moog renditions of Beethoven and Purcell), the strangeness of the synthesizer timbres makes familiar works seem foreign.

In EDM, the futuristic associations of synthesis have embedded themselves in the very language of techno and house, even if lyrics (if present at all) do not mention futurism. One popular method for making sounds spacey is the emphasis of their various partial harmonics. This is easily done without electronics; simply sing a constant pitch and change the shape of your mouth and lips, and you have modulated a note to bring out its different partials. Over the past few decades, the sound of synthesized partials has gradually become synonymous with futuristic technology. The output of Juan Atkins (one of the Belleville Three "inventors" of Detroit techno along with Derrick May and Kevin Saunderson) is replete with images of space travel and UFOs. When Atkins records under the name Model 500, his tracks are named after stars on a constellation map. The relentless "M29 Orbit" (1995) contains a spare bass-drum pulse and intermittent, modulating synth chords. American techno artist Joey Beltram uses a mercilessly spare language in "Energy Flash" (1990), whose "melody" consists of a single note, the tonic, which is repeated with what sounds like phase distortion that succeeds in making partials sound as distinctive as separate pitches. Like Model 500, British ambient-house group the Orb frequently calls up space imagery in its tracks, particularly in "Earth (Gaia)" (1990), which features undulating chords set atop samples from what sounds like a low-budget sci-fi film of the 1960s. These three examples all contain a minimum of melodic material, but that material is treated to processing, usually modulation, that now seems perfectly at ease alongside robots, spaceships, and computers.

What constituted futurism in the 1970s or 1980s has become nostalgia for contemporary electronica listeners. Taylor (2001) has explored how 1950s-era futurist easy-listening music was recuperated in 1990s-era nostalgic pop by groups such as Stereolab. Another symptom of this technological revivalism is the deliberate use of outdated and obsolete audio devices (Sterne 2003, 285). Vintage-audio fans hear in older analog equipment a warmth that they find lacking in digital devices. The Scottish duo Boards of Canada seizes upon this tendency as the underpinning of the 1998 album *Music Has the Right to Children*. Band members (and brothers) Michael Sandison and Marcus Eoin Sandison have explained their interest in nostalgia, particularly in the educational television programs they watched as children (Boards of Canada biography). Unlike digital-synthesizer preset sounds that supposedly imitate a violin or an oboe, analog synthesizers require that the performer decide what components go into creating a sound. The output of these devices can (with some effort on the part of the programmer) approximate acoustic instruments, but the Sandisons give them a monolithic, grainy quality that aims less at replicating a particular instrument than at recalling a particular moment in time when such sounds were commonplace. On the consecutive tracks "Bocuma" and "Roygbiv," the antiquated timbre of the synthesizers counterbalances the tracks' familiar, infectious grooves. "Bocuma" is a single monophonic, fanfare-like melody with no bass line, set to heavy reverb. As "Bocuma" fades out, "Roygbiv" enters at a slightly slower tempo, a thick walking bass line that paves the way for another repetitive, arresting theme. The artwork for *Music Has the Right to Children* gives clues to the intentions behind these tracks, depicting children with 1970s-era bell-bottoms, T-shirts, and feathered hair, whose faces have been digitally erased. The sounds and groove of "Bocuma" and "Roygbiv" place us stylistically sometime in the 1970s, but the absence of clear quotations exudes vague nostalgia rather than directed longing for a specific instance in time.

In identifying synthesis as an act of sound construction and in asserting that sound construction entails the creation of new sounds, I have set up an expectation for a tabula rasa listening experience that can perhaps never occur. Although synthesis might technically be defined as the creation of new sounds, listeners inevitably compare what they hear with preexisting sounds and categorize new sounds according to the type of equipment that might have produced them. This conclusion might at first seem merely to confirm what we know instinctually: we make sense of sensory perceptions on the basis of what we have already lived. Constructed sounds, no matter how much they might be intended as new, are ultimately experienced as metaphors likening the unknown to the familiar. Adorno (1997, 145) diagnoses this impossibility of constructing an entirely new type of material. For him, modern art consistently works with two types of materials: those that imitate empirical reality and those that are newly constructed. Imitative materials mimic the outside world through techniques such as collage and quotation. Constructed materials, however, are not spontaneously created from nothing but rather mediate empirical reality through technology, alienating (or, literally, making strange) what was initially familiar.

The casual generalization so often made about electronic music, that it enables the creation of any type of sound, thus needs to be reexamined. Both institutional electroacoustic music and electronica proceed under the assumption that sound is a sign pointing beyond itself toward something familiar. And in electronica especially, it is often impossible to hear the difference between constructed and reproduced sound. If synthesized sound constructions are heard on the basis of how they imitate what we have already heard, then what distinguishes sound constructions from sound reproductions? This question is especially daunting when directed toward contemporary reproductions of antique methods of sound construction. Musicians today can call upon a host of vintage-synthesizer imitations. For example, the Korg keyboard company in 2003 launched its

Legacy Collection, applications that reproduce the sounds of vintage keyboards on the home computer (Anderton 2004). What's odd about these devices is that they use sampling methods to reconstruct the sound of an original synthesizer; this is the acoustic equivalent of taking thousands of tiny snapshots of a sound in order to rebuild it. Many of these applications produce sounds that are indistinguishable from their prototypes. But whereas the original impulse behind synthesis was to struggle for a new language, sampled reproductions of synthesis objectify that language into just one more reference in a sea of musical quotations and allusions. A preliminary answer, then, to the question above could be that while sound constructions might loosely recall other similar sounds, sound reproductions underscore their own status as citations. Reproductions, in other words, explicitly display the frame enclosing a sound, a frame that identifies a sound as originating from another place or time.

REPRODUCTION

In 1960, Vladimir Ussachevsky, one of the founding members of the Columbia-Princeton Electronic Music Center, was commissioned by a radio enthusiast club to write a piece that commemorated the birth of wireless radio transmission (Beaudoin 2007). By that time, Ussachevsky had gained a considerable reputation as a composer of electronic music. On October 28, 1952, he and mentor Otto Luening had staged a concert of their works at the Museum of Modern Art in Manhattan, and although the critical response had been unsurprisingly less than warm, Ussachevsky did nonetheless garner adjectives such as "novel," "original," and "experimental" (Taubman 1952). But while his earlier works consisted entirely of newly composed materials, Ussachevsky's 1960 commission, *Wireless Fantasy*, was a bold departure, consisting of the sounds of Morse code signals and shortwave radio, as well as a recording of Richard Wagner's *Parsifal*.

Ussachevsky chose *Parsifal* as a nod to inventor Lee De Forest, who selected the opera as the first piece of music ever to be broadcast over radio. Perhaps realizing that many listeners might be unaware of the importance of *Parsifal* in radio history, Ussachevsky filtered his *Parsifal* recording to make it sound as though it were being broadcast through one of De Forest's shortwave radios. The result was perhaps the first example of what would become a fruitful combination in elements in post-1980 electronic music: a carefully chosen borrowing paired with carefully crafted sound editing.

Wireless Fantasy was a visionary piece, but it was by no means the first to rely on preexisting recordings as sources for its own musical materials. In July 1956, Dickie Goodman released an audio collage of rock-and-roll songs entitled "The Flying Saucer," a comedic pastiche reminiscent of Orson Welles's 1938 radio play version of H. G. Wells's 1898 novel *The War of the Worlds*. Goodman also drew inspiration from radio disc jockey and impresario Alan Freed, whose programs of upcoming hits, interviews, and Freed's own commentary contributed to the craze surrounding rock and roll. Goodman followed Freed's cue in constructing a musical play that seemed to narrate itself through the era's most successful recordings. And a decade before "The Flying Saucer," Schaeffer was laying the groundwork for musique concrète, the first music to rely exclusively on recorded materials.

To label these three instances of musical creativity as sampling is admittedly anachronistic. The term *sampling* came into popular usage in the 1980s to describe digital devices that played prerecorded materials, and only later was it applied to other means of reusing recordings in new works (Davies 1996). During Ussachevsky's era, more fitting descriptors for *Wireless Fantasy* might be the prosaic *tape music,* or else a term borrowed from the visual arts, *collage,* literally meaning any work consisting of pasted-together materials. Nevertheless, I will refer to the use of any materials recorded in the past, whether discrete or inchoate sounds or entire musical pieces, as sampling. This choice of terms foregrounds the aesthetic affinities among turntables, Mellotrons, and digital samplers, devices that traditional discourse would keep separate.

A certain indifference to the processes and techniques behind sampling allows us to view more clearly the traditional explanations of sampling in musicological scholarship. The most basic explanation is utilitarian: sampling broadens an artist's palette and allows for sonic combinations impossible to re-create in live performance. Many musicians do sample for precisely this reason, and there is no deeper significance to their actions. A second explanation interprets the meanings behind samples, meanings that could be intended by the artist or constructed independently by the listener. This explanation regards sampling as a means of intertextual commentary between one work and another. Beaudoin thus argues that the *Parsifal* excerpt is intended as an homage, not to Wagner but rather to De Forest. Likewise, Goodman's collages are explained as celebrations of their source materials, whether early rock and roll or later soul and funk (Rockwell 1975). In both cases, sampled materials are "read" as texts whose original meanings and associations contribute to the meaning of the new composite work. It is only natural that this sort of interpretive strategy exists for sampling, because a great deal of the training that music scholars undergo consists of identifying and interpreting borrowings between works and composers. Indicative of the connection between literary and musical intertextual studies is the fact that musical borrowings are often referred to as quotations. Kristeva (1980, 66) argues in her christening of intertextuality that "any text is constructed as a mosaic of quotations; any text is the absorption and transformation of another." Irwin (2004) observes that intertextuality advocates open-ended and multiple connections among texts, so much so that the idea of a single privileged interpretation of a text is disallowed.

Intertextuality within the field of musicology has taken a different tack in emphasizing a single definitive interpretation contingent on accurate identification of quotations, a practice amounting to quotation connoisseurship. In Western art music in particular, where notated scores often embody the definitive version of a piece, it is relatively easy to determine when materials from one source are being reused in another. The underlying assumption in most scholarship on musical borrowing is therefore that the listener hears a similarity between two works, a similarity that can be verified by examining the scores of the two pieces (Bicknell 2001; Burkholder 2007; Metzer 2003). Yet the flaw of intertextual analysis in musicology is that it assumes the presence of an ideal reader (or listener) equipped to recognize the borrowing. Once scholarship begins the act of classifying and identifying references, whether in a Shakespearean sonnet or a hip-hop hit single, the end result is a contest of connoisseurship in which the assumed reader is an idealized, thoroughly educated, and primed one who identifies and translates references on command. This ideal reader is virtually synonymous with the author, since it is assumed that all quotations are intentionally included.

The blame for quotation connoisseurship can hardly be placed on academics alone. Many works of art actively encourage connoisseur-based decoding, not least of which sample-based genres such as hip-hop that elevated informed listening to an art. Since the mid-1970s, hip-hop has frequently sampled from black popular genres such as funk, soul, and disco. The better hip-hop DJs were able to excerpt portions from songs, often the break sections in which vocals and melody drop out to leave the rhythm section, and with these fragments constructed new collages. As hip-hop gained audiences and commercial appeal during the early 1980s, sampling grew more sophisticated in terms of both procedures and materials. Digital samplers allowed producers to excerpt specific portions of a song, like the bass line, allowing for more targeted appropriation of sounds. Producers and DJs expanded their sampling palettes to encompass previously untouchable genres such as rock and singer-songwriter pop in order to appeal to white teenage listeners. Meanwhile, copyright lawsuits against unauthorized sampling became increasingly common. By the mid-1990s, the prosecution of illegal sampling and the cost of legally licensing samples chilled what once had been a free-for-all of sampling. In this newly litigious environment, a great deal rode on the identity and provenance of sound material, underscoring what had already been an active interest among hip-hop DJs and listeners in the origins of samples (Demers 2006).

Hip-hop's fixation on the pedigrees of samples has conditioned hip-hop scholarship and criticism, which tends to interpret recognizable samples as social or cultural commentary. My PhD thesis and first published article deal with the sampling of blaxploitation soundtracks in gangsta rap, which, I argued, was a strategy for making hip-hop seem more politically engaged (Demers 2002; 2003). One song I frequently teach in lectures on hip-hop is Dr. Dre's "Let Me Ride" (1991), which "samples" (technically, reperforms) portions of Parliament's "Mothership Connection" (1975). Dre's lyrics and musical quotations demonstrate that he is subverting the Afrofuturist optimism of the Parliament original, transforming it into gangsta boasting. In a similar vein, Elflein (1998) describes the inclusion of traditional Turkish music in German hip-hop as a way for Turkish-German musicians to celebrate their ethnic identity, and Yang (2000) reads the sampling of Western classical music in hip-hop as an appeal to intelligence, morality, and upward mobility. Quotation-based readings of hip-hop samples can be useful and intriguing when balanced with attention to other qualities such as the flow of rap lyrics, but the approach is sometimes overused as a sort of Rosetta stone that promises to explain every facet of a song's meaning. The habit is not strictly the purview of academia; many hip-hop DJs and artists view sampling as a means of insider communication with their fans, a way of conveying messages to the select few informed enough to identify quotations. The fact remains that this mode of listening to music hinges on connoisseurship: if we grasp the reference, we assume that we have grasped the meaning of the music. As Bourdieu (1987) points out, in reality, we have simply proved our cultural competence with the particular codes of the work. If we don't catch the reference, we conclude either that the text is not sampling anything or else that the samples are obscure since we don't recognize them.

Recordings freeze moments in time and make them available for repeated contemplation. Simply put, recordings change the ontological status of sound from fleeting and impermanent to eternally present. Sample-based music thus affords the possibility for a mode of communication impossible in all previously created music, for samples can convey not only their underlying sonic or musical content but also the surrounding sounds of recording mediation that signify age. Many samples stand out from the texture of a work thanks to recording-mediation sounds such as pops, scratches, or the manipulation of tape-playback speed or direction. Tantalizingly, however, samples in much recent electronica do not necessarily reveal their age. Sound-editing technologies have made it possible to hide all traces of recording mediation, allowing a sample to sound contemporaneous with materials performed in the present. Conversely, samples can be made to sound older than their true age through the addition of artificial recording mediation (such as the *Parsifal* sample in *Wireless Fantasy*). Samples, in other words, can lie about their age, identity, and origins.

It would be unjust to lambaste hip-hop scholars for their attention to the identity of samples; turntablism is, after all, often a game of identification and one-upmanship between DJs and audiences. But a great deal of electronica has taken a different approach toward samples that deemphasizes the actual provenance of samples in favor of other sonic qualities such as perceived age. In such cases, the listener may be aware of the existence of samples but need not recognize where they come from or how they are created. The strategies that have thus far worked well enough for connoisseur-based genres such as hip-hop are of limited use for other forms of electronica.

By way of example, I want to consider the Swiss-American artist Christian Marclay, who has worked for the past thirty years as both a visual artist and an experimental musician. Many of Marclay's visual works display a clear indebtedness to Marcel Duchamp and the "ready-made" or found object (such as a bicycle wheel or a urinal) imported from the outside world into the artwork. Marclay is famous for being one of the first non-hip-hop artists to work with turntables when he began using damaged records in the late 1970s. Ferguson (2003, 40) notes Marclay's "realization that recorded music could be treated as a form of readymade," producing sample-based recordings that neither repress nor emphasize the identity of their samples. Marclay's strategy is to approach the identity of his samples in an oblique manner. When he moved from Switzerland to the United States as a young adult, Marclay was shocked to find stray records thrown in the street:

> If I had grown up in the U.S., I wouldn't have thought twice about seeing a
> record on the street. That's what surprised me about American culture: its
> excess, the prevalence of so much waste. When I first came to the United
> States, it was a common sight to see broken records on the street. It took
> away the preciousness of the object. I grew up always taking very good care
> of my books, whereas here everyone was underlining all their books,
> scribbling things on the book itself. When there is excess, when there are
> thrift stores filled with books and records that are 25 cents apiece, it makes
> you think about objects differently. (Kahn 2003, 19)

For Marclay, the redundancy and abuse of records detract from their "preciousness," a term recalling Benjamin's aura that imbues one-of-a-kind artworks with a sense of distance and poignancy (1969). Most artists would respond to this deficit with the expected gesture of reinvesting the artwork with aura. Marclay instead embraces the emptiness of disposable music. He goes on to describe picking up one such record from the street, a children's recording of music to accompany the "Batman" story. When he played it on a turntable at home, Marclay became transfixed by the skipping and noises that tire damage had produced on the vinyl. Those phonographic vestiges would go on to characterize Marclay's turntablist music for the next two decades.

The "Batman" anecdote coincides nicely with other moments in the history of experimental music. A musician notices that damaged artworks yield serendipitously interesting results and then proceeds to reproduce that damage intentionally. As John Cage did with his tape piece *Williams Mix* (1952), Fluxus artist Milan Knizak did with reassembled records in *Destroyed Music* (1963–1979), and glitch group Oval would do in the 1990s with compact discs, Marclay crafted the sounds of the damaged phonographic medium into a coveted property. His approach is to break or mutilate records by stacking them without sleeves, cracking and then reassembling them with glue, exposing them to dirt and dust, and inviting listeners to walk on them before playing them back on more or less functional turntables. What distinguishes Marclay from other avant-gardists is that he works with found objects rather than his own original sound materials. Interestingly, the identity of those objects is of little consequence to him:

> I do not remember specifically which records were used on most of these mixes; to my ears they were only sounds, very abstract and detached from their original sources. They lost their identity and became fragments to be mixed—a loop, a texture, a transition, a beat, an intro, a word. (Marclay 1997, 4)

This equivocal approach toward samples is apparent in a track like "Smoker" (1981), which begins with a loop of a woman speaking the phrase "long tube on the end of his smoker." These words begin clearly enough but gradually become submerged into a crescendo of a guitar and the drone of crickets. Even the crickets dissolve into the structure of the piece, initially standing out as sounds from nature but then becoming mechanized and repetitive thanks to looping.

The interest in a work like "Smoker" has less to do with the samples themselves than with what happens to those samples through the course of the work. The connection between the woman's smoker story and the subsequent cricket noises is unclear, but as Marclay suggests, both samples are valuable for their innate qualities as sound objects as well as any semiotic value they might once have possessed. Another work, "Dust Breeding" (1982), features a typical Marclay gambit: a reference that acts as a red herring rather than a semantic key to the work. "Dust Breeding" is named after the Man Ray photograph *L'élevage de poussière* (1920), which captured the underside of Duchamp's bizarre glass-and-dust composite *La mariée mise à nu par ses célibataires, même* ("The Bride Stripped Bare by Her Bachelors, Even," 1915–1923). The Duchamp work provided Marclay with the inspiration for his first musical group's name, the Bachelors (Ferguson 2003, 33). These details might seem to hint at an explanation of Marclay's "Dust Breeding," but they do not deliver on the promise. The track begins with what sounds like a single record whose needle is regularly dropped and then lifted, so that the music plays, stops, and then begins again in the same place. This record's material emits primarily from the left channel, and its materials are utterly abstract, consisting of what sounds like a bass clarinet playing extended techniques. The right channel then enters with a classical string recording that at first stops and starts in time with the left channel record, but gradually, the two fall out of synchronization. The right channel then changes to what sounds like Romantic-era piano music and plays without interruption, while the left channel filters in abstract, frenetic piano music. "Dust Breeding" hobbles on like this in its own internal tension. There is the initial sense of balance created by the stop-and-start flow and noises created perhaps by dust accumulating on the record needle. This balance is soon interrupted as left and right channels diverge, but then, within the last ten seconds, the right channel seems to reconcile itself with the left by disintegrating into a fast loop whose material sounds as abstract as that of the left channel. Another artist might have taken the more predictable tack of demonstrating the affinities between the abstract materials of the left channel and the more conventional materials of the right. Marclay does the opposite in "Dust Breeding" by allowing the supposed order of classical music to disintegrate into the noise of its surroundings.

It is one thing to argue against intertextuality using a Marclay work that places so little stock in the practice. It is quite another to argue against intertextuality in the music of Girl Talk, which engages so directly with the conventions of hip-hop sampling. By all rights, Girl Talk (the stage name for Gregg Gillis) and his label should already have been sued out of existence; the *New York Times* gleefully labels this music "a lawsuit waiting to happen" (Walker 2008). Like other mash-ups and turntablist collages, Girl Talk's work is exciting because of its improbable combinations of different artists and genres. It puts together sounds that were not meant to go together and does so in a way that displays obvious affection for its source materials while simultaneously relishing the complete control that it exerts over them.

The samples that appear in Girl Talk songs are elided together admirably. Materials that might have different tempi, rhythms, or keys are mixed in such a way as to make their combination seem necessary, almost inevitable. His technical skill notwithstanding, Girl Talk is in most ways simply rehashing the original principle of mash-ups, a genre that began to appear in the 1990s. Mash-ups followed up on the promise of hip-hop turntablism, which popularized the extraction of portions of individual songs in order to create a new work. But hip-hop DJs typically extract a small portion of a work, whether a drum break, a synthesizer riff, or a vocal line, and, in the early days of hip-hop, played that portion by itself with few added sounds. Digital signal processing as afforded by programs such as Audio Mulch now allows users to pinpoint a specific track, even a specific sound, within one song and then import that particular portion into whatever new environment they choose. This technology has engendered progeny such as 2ManyDJs' "Smells Like Booty" (2001), a conflagration of Nirvana's "Smells Like Teen Spirit" with Destiny's Child's "Bootylicious."

The formula in many Girl Talk songs, especially those on *Feed the Animals* (2008), is to superimpose the vocals of a rap tune onto the hooks of Top 40 hits dating from the 1970s through the present. All materials are sampled from preexisting songs; none is created by Girl Talk himself. Unlike earlier mash-ups that pit only two well-known songs against each other, Girl Talk features several combinations within one song. Most combinations contain two songs, but occasionally, the elements from three or even four songs occur simultaneously. Consider "Hands in the Air," which begins with the unlikely pairing of the hip-hop group Tag Team's party anthem "Whoomp! (There It Is)" against early-1980s Scottish rock band Big Country's "In a Big Country." The climax of this first face-off occurs when the title words for "Whoomp!" are synchronized with the fist-pumping hook of "In a Big Country." Girl Talk's talent is for pushing through such moments of listening pleasure rather than celebrating them. Here, after only a few bars of Scottish hip-hop, the mix intersperses the electro classic, Afrika Bambaataa's "Planet Rock," itself a strange combination since it matches early-1980s b-boy rapping to Kraftwerk's "Trans-Europe Express." Bambaataa provides the transition to the next pairing, of the Cardigans' "Lovefool" with Hot Chip's "Ready for the Floor."

Girl Talk songs draw from a relatively small collection of popular songs, which suggests that the goal of this music is not to rediscover obscure tracks but rather to recontextualize famous songs in novel, even awkward surroundings. And what makes these surroundings so awkward is the perceived mismatch of genre and cultural context. Since its early days, hip-hop has touted its separation from the white mainstream. Tracks such as Run-DMC's "Walk This Way" (1986) or anything from Dangermouse's *Grey Album* (2004) mash-up of the Beatles and Jay-Z, where hip-hop samples from other supposedly white genres such as rock, classical, or country play on the tension between white and black music; they are cases where the repressed has become the repressor, where hip-hop colonizes outside itself. Girl Talk's pairings work because they seem to flout unspoken conventions dictating the relationship between music and race.

But the baiting in Girl Talk song combinations should bring up some questions. For whom is this music intended? An initial response might be music geeks, listeners who have heard enough different types of recordings to be able to recognize hits and appreciate the humor of unholy song combinations. It's difficult to imagine how Girl Talk songs might work with listeners unfamiliar with any of the source materials. For less informed listeners, this music would attract attention based on its other attributes, namely its relentless tempo and danceable beats. But if Girl Talk is for specialized listeners only, why is this music currently so popular, especially with college students born well after many of these songs first appeared? Not all of the listeners in this age group are music geeks; many of them possess only the most general awareness of popular music styles. Yet even the most casual listeners know that gangsta rap carries around heavy baggage, the bad press that fairly or unfairly links it to criminality, racism, and misogyny. Forcing gangsta to play nicely with progressive rock is an act of transgression, not only of race but of genre as well. As Girl Talk practices it, sampling works as an unnatural act of violence to generic conventions.

DESTRUCTION

With the ever-expanding palette of materials available to artists comes a commensurate broadening of taste. Undergraduate music majors are routinely indoctrinated into the "beauty" of hitherto "ugly" or at least aesthetically neutral sounds, everything from sirens, sine waves, and bowed sheets of metal to insect chirping. One recent trend in electronica consists of sounds that repulse or sicken the listener, because repugnant sounds are the last unmusical ones available. The San Francisco-based electronic duo Matmos constructs beats from materials that inspire either humor or physical dread: rat cages played with violin bows, noises from liposuction and LASIK surgery, and the electrical impulses measured by an acupuncture meter. Matmos has become one of the most visible electronica groups in recent years, thanks partially to their production of two Björk albums, *Vespertine* (2001) and *Medulla* (2004). Press coverage on Matmos has also focused on the group's interest in the sounds of body and medicine. Their 2001 album, *A Chance to Cut Is a Chance to Cure*, features materials culled from plastic surgery (member Drew Daniel's parents are plastic surgeons). Reporters and interviewers alike relish the pun that runs along the lines of "Matmos surgically abstracts sounds from the operating room to make beats for the dance floor." The requisite example is a track like "Lipostudio . . . And So On," which begins innocuously enough as lounge-inflected techno but introduces the jiggling whine of fat being sucked from thighs and stomachs.

"Lipostudio . . . And So On" works very well as background music and would hardly attract undue attention in a bar or at a party from those unaware of the sources of the samples. An interviewer asked Daniel whether Matmos is tapping into 1970s-era conceptual art that treats the body as a medium for protest. Daniel's response acknowledges the influence of that work on his compositions but finds that the shock in body art is contingent on its visual element:

> We're using sound rather than image, that's the big cut-off, that we aren't
> relying on the experience of recognition you have when you see a perfor-
> mance of someone doing something extreme to their body. Instead, you are
> hearing it as sound and I think that changes it quite a bit . . . how your
> imagination completes it. (Tobias V 2001)

But Daniel's denial of any sensationalism runs counter to the titles of Matmos tracks, which give clues to the origins of their samples (e.g., "L.A.S.I.K.," "California Rhinoplasty"). Spectacle is difficult to avoid when artists disclose the origins of a potentially horror-inducing sound. The imagination completes the sound with an image, and that image accrues greater force because it is gruesome rather than prosaic or mundane. Whether Matmos admits it or not, it has seized upon grotesque sounds as a last frontier in a landscape where the thrill and outrage of unmusical samples is quickly vanishing.

Lest Matmos be seen as a fringe case in an otherwise sober community of sampling musicians, let's return to the basic premise of sampling. Sounds are abstracted, literally cut, from their original context. Those sounds are then spliced into a new recording. The process easily invites metaphors with sewing, surgery, or even Frankenstein-like experimentation: the artist sutures together disparate sounds into a new being.[1] This is not fanciful language; for American experimental composer Steven Takasugi, sampling reminded him of visits to his biologist father's laboratory at UCLA, which housed embalmed specimens of animals, plants, and human body parts. Takasugi regards his samples as sound specimens culled from their natural environment and subsequently embalmed in containers of other sounds or pure silence (Takasugi, personal communication, February 12, 2006). The quality of these sonic containers thus becomes as important as their contents. In Takasugi's *Iridescent Uncertainty* (1999), a work for sampled koto, *shamisen*, and cello, the perceived spatial dimensions of individual sounds are manipulated so that some seem to emanate from a stereophonic field (or a voluminous container), while others seem to originate impossibly from a

---

[1]Wlodarski (2007) also uses "suture" in connection with samples in Steve Reich's *Different Trains*.

monophonic source (or an impossible space lacking depth or breadth) (Takasugi 2004). (◐ Audio example 1: Takasugi's *Iridescent Uncertainty*.)

Another metaphor involving the physicality of sampling links the practice to breaking apart sound into fragments. In his *Strange Autumn* (2003–2005), Takasugi uses a computer algorithm to "pulverize" sound samples into tiny fragments (Takasugi 2005). English experimental composer John Wall speaks in terms of organic development to describe his works, which sample avant-garde composers such as Xenakis, Birtwistle, and Nono, as well as newly performed sounds. Wall explains his process as looking for potentials of growth between different sounds:

> I could listen to a CD for half an hour, barely interested in what was going on, then a sound would jump out, and if it seemed manipulable, loopable, I'd proceed from there. Composition works its way out of this situation, but very slowly and always intuitively. One sample leads to another and the kernel of a structure begins to suggest itself. (quoted in Marley 2005, 195)

But Wall resists being classified alongside other sampling artists such as John Oswald, who use fragments of easily identifiable pop songs to critique intellectual-property law. Wall continues:

> I don't deny the value of that approach, but in my own work these concerns remain implicit. To avoid this misunderstanding [being labeled a Plunderphonicist alongside John Oswald], but more importantly for musical reasons, I began to use smaller and smaller samples, slivers of sound, micro-samples that couldn't be identified. Now I almost never sample from CDs. I generate nearly all of the sounds myself. (quoted in Marley 2005, 200)

For Wall, these ever smaller cuttings destroy whatever continuity might have existed in the original materials, freeing them to cohere into a new whole.

What Matmos, Takasugi, and Wall share is a materialist approach toward sampling, a natural consequence of a musical environment where all sounds are viewed as objects. The three artists acknowledge that samples necessarily bring to new works associations from their original environments. The three artists have developed solutions to manage those associations: Matmos flatly invites horror and fascination by disclosing its sources, Takasugi underscores the process of sample extraction and encasing to emphasize the abstracted quality of his sounds, and Wall breaks down samples into nearly untraceable minutiae that can serve as the fodder for new meanings.

If the previous few examples seem too extreme to be worth any notice, consider that many artists and commentators have noted an unsettling quality inherent in sampling. Mtume, the percussionist who worked with Miles Davis during the 1970s, refers to the practice as "artistic necrophilia" (quoted in George 1998, 96). Countless musicians, lawyers, and music-industry personnel have argued that sampling is akin to theft. Part of the disquiet in sampling naturally involves issues of intellectual property. Yet conflicting values of originality and authorship fail to explain the more basic sentiment that sampling is a fundamentally unnatural phenomenon. And that unnaturalness stems from listeners' awareness that sound collages do what no regular piece of music can do in stringing unlikely sounds together.

Paul Virilio's essay "Art and Violence" condemns various artworks of the twentieth century for defiling the human body. He contends that artistic processes and subject matter reflect societal attitudes about the relative importance of human life. Cultures that respect human life produce art that cherishes the human body. Post-World War II art fragments the body and even aestheticizes torture and mutilation because those taboos have long been broken in real life. As Virilio sees it, technology is complicit in art's barbarism:

> In the end, "modern art" was able to glean what communications and
> telecommunications tools now accomplish on a daily basis: the *mise en
> abyme* of the body, of the figure, with the major attendant risk of *systematic*
> hyperviolence and a boom in pornographic high-frequency that has
> nothing to do with sexuality. (2003, 35)

The argument that artistic subject matter sheds light on the values of a society is far from new, but Virilio reveals the more insidious side of modern art, even that which does not explicitly celebrate violence. Digital technology itself, with its ability to abstract material and its reduction of data to ones and zeros, dehumanizes:

> The demise of the relative and analogical character of photographic shots
> and sound samples in favour of the absolute, digital character of the
> computer, following the synthesizer, is thus also the loss of the poetics of the
> ephemeral. For one brief moment *Impressionism*—in painting and in
> music—was able to retrieve the flavour of the ephemeral before the *nihilism*
> of contemporary technology wiped it out once and for all. (2003, 48)

Adorno arrives at similar conclusions in his discussion of the give-and-take between material, which draws originally from nature, and form, which is the structure the artist imposes. By definition, form inflicts violence on material, and for Adorno, attempts to remove this cruelty from art would be tantamount to disabling art's ability to reflect critically on itself and the world around it:

> [A]rt's own gesture is cruel. In aesthetic forms, cruelty becomes imagination. Something is excised from the living, from the body of language, from tones, from visual experience. . . . If in modern artworks cruelty raises its head undisguised, it confirms the truth that in the face of the overwhelming force of reality art can no longer rely on its a priori ability to transform the dreadful into form. (1997, 50)

But is digitization really a tool of "undisguised cruelty"? In the case of Aphex Twin's "Mt. Saint Michel's Mix + St. Michael's Mount" from the album *Drukqs* (2001), certainly. The track spends some seven minutes constructing an ambitious blend of impossibly fast break beats with voices and synthesized chords. In the last forty-five seconds, however, this mixture suddenly seems to be devoured from inside out. Small chunks of sound begin to disappear from the track even though the rhythm is constant. This process resembles what might be described as an acoustic strobe effect, where islands of sound appear amid a growing void of silence. As time goes by, these chunks grow in size, so that by the end of the track, silence seems to have devoured the track from the inside out.

William Basinski's work counts among the most direct manifestations of sound destruction in all electronica. During the early 1980s, Basinski laid down a large amount of synthesized material, mostly tonal, consonant melodies, onto reel-to-reel tape. Inspired by the tape pieces of Steve Reich, he used five- to ten-second loops taken from these old tapes as the basis for extended tracks. When in 2001 Basinski began to archive this material onto digital media, he witnessed the destruction that time and preservation both visited upon his music. The passing years had so damaged the tape that the mere act of replaying it scraped away the magnetized particles that encoded the sound. Time, and the effort to save his music from time, destroyed Basinski's music; he promptly realized the serendipity and released his finds as a four-disc set entitled *Disintegration Loops* (2001–2005).

As I discussed above in relation to Christian Marclay's music and will discuss in chapter 3 with regard to glitch, many artists have made the sounds of phonographic damage central to their work. What distinguishes Basinski is that he regards this damage as decay, as a retreat from some earlier, more perfect condition to a compromised place of mourning. This melancholy (Basinski named one of his other albums *Melancholia*) is a music of bereavement for life that has expired and cannot be resurrected. Christian Fennesz also touches on the impossibility of returning to the past in his album *Endless Summer* (2001), whose tracks evoke carefree surf rock if heard through the lenses of digitization and middle age. Fennesz's signature sound subjects conventional acoustic or electric instruments, often the guitar, to heavy distortion that can be likened to listening to music through a waterfall or an ocean. *Endless Summer*'s title suggests that it derives from the classic surf film directed by Bruce Brown, although I wondered initially what an Austrian like Fennesz would know about the search for the perfect wave. Apparently, he knows a lot, because Fennesz is able to capture the fragile beauty of the Sandals' soundtrack theme without quoting a single line of it. The first half of the track "Caecilia" contains a melody that sounds as if it is being performed on a xylophone; at the end of each phrase, this melody becomes bogged down in an undulating pitch bend, as if it is being played through a curtain of splashing water (◐ audio example 2: Fennesz's "Caecilia"). This first section ends with some glitch and distortion sounds and then suddenly cuts to what is one of the most beguiling moments in electronic music. What sound like a guitar and a bass guitar deliver a melody reminiscent of the Beach Boys' "God Only Knows," a tune so innocent and affirmative that it seems too precious for this world. It repeats several times, each time dogged by more static and distortion. What Basinski does literally in his music in demonstrating time's destructive force Fennesz does metaphorically. Not only is it impossible to reanimate a work from the past, but attempts to do so inflict further injury on the corpse.

Let's take a step back to see what all of this means. Electronica concentrates heavily on the construction, reproduction, and destruction of sound material and, as the examples above suggest, has invented elaborate metaphors to impute meaning onto sound material. These individual examples all confirm a general tendency within electronica, that material *itself* functions as a metaphor. The definition of musical material is slippery at best. If we rely on Adorno's definition, which I cited at the beginning of this chapter, it is "what artists work with," but if the art in question is music or sound art, that unnamed something is sound, or ephemeral air vibrations. Yet contrary to Adorno and the many others who have used the term, *material* as a physical, tangible, or repeatable object simply does not exist in music. Every musical sound is distinct and one of a kind, even those supposedly captured on recordings, because what are captured are not sounds themselves but the traces they leave in other media as sympathetic vibrations. But musicians for centuries have found it revealing to talk about sound material as a way of linking the transience of sound with more stable concepts. When electronica musicians construct, reproduce, or destroy material, they are perpetuating one of the grandest metaphors in all of music history, that electronically produced vibrations not only exist as objects but also can carry with them associations and references. In terms of physics, we know that such transportation is impossible. Sounds can no more carry ideas than they can carry anything else.

Perhaps in reaction to this cherished belief in electronica that sound material exists and is meaningful, there are other electronic music practices that deny sound's ability to bear meaning. Chapter 3 considers one such movement, microsound, and its repudiation of the musical sign in favor of the sound object.

PART II

Object

3

Minimal Objects in Microsound

Minimalism refers to such a large cross-section of artistic activities that the term has lost much of the usefulness it might once have possessed. Like other catchphrases, *minimalism* now functions more as a placeholder, a word that facilitates conversation through the assumption that everyone understands it in the same manner. Yet in varying contexts, *minimalism* could refer to artworks displaying simplicity and lack of adornment, repetition, gestalt wholes as opposed to composite assemblages, or nonreferential materials. Appearing first in 1960s visual arts, where it pertained to sculpture featuring large, nondescript found objects such as fluorescent lighting tubes and steel girders, *minimalism* was only later applied to music. By many accounts, Michael Nyman was the first to write about minimalist music; he did so sometime in the early 1970s before the publication of the first edition of his *Experimental Music: Cage and Beyond* in 1974 (Warburton 1988, 141). In the intervening years, minimalist music has become synonymous with predominantly American music featuring rhythmic and melodic repetition, tonal harmonies, and textural transformations that unfold slowly through a process of accretion.

The links between 1960s minimalist visual arts and minimalist concert music are thus already tenuous. To muddy further an already confused situation, electronic musicians use the term *minimalism* to describe subgenres ranging from drone music to techno to ambient music. So it would seem that anything resembling either Young's multiple-hour meditations on a single pitch, or Reich's *Drumming*, or Brian Eno's *Music for Airports* counts as minimalist. And as the shadow cast by minimalism grows, justifications for continued comparisons with minimalist visual arts lose validity and at times seem suspiciously akin to what Licht (2007, 211) has called "playing the art card," the habit among musicians of claiming cultural capital through association with galleries and exhibitions instead of concert halls and performances.

My task here is not to revise the definition of minimalist music as a whole but rather to investigate one particular type of recent electronic music known as microsound. Critics and record labels frequently depict microsound as a type of minimalist, post-techno ambient music. This description exists, no doubt, because a great deal of microsound employs repetitive, four-on-the-floor dance beats with little, if any, melodic development. This vision of microsound as minimalist is the sanctioned one, the well-known syllogism linking repetition to minimalism. But we should demand a more thorough excavation of the term. This chapter explores how strategies among microsound artists for creating and manipulating material echo the discourse of "objecthood" that minimalist artists and their critics generated during the 1960s. Often, this resemblance is intentional, since many microsound practitioners identify themselves more as artists than as musicians or composers. Microsound is thus minimal not in the sense of its belonging to a larger minimalist movement but rather because it uses the smallest, most minimal particles of material to nullify external referentiality, converting sound into raw objects. My point here is not merely to demonstrate literal affinities between minimalist music and minimalist visual arts. Music and the visual arts are different media. Claims (Bernard 1993; Potter 2000) that the flatness of a paint texture or sculpture material resonate with the perceived flatness of a musical sequence or orchestration smooth over the significant distinctions between auditory and visual faculties. But hearing microsound as a manifestation of objecthood reinvigorates a genre that might otherwise be categorized and thus dismissed as just another type of electronic dance music (EDM) and also casts a spotlight on a resurgence of the polemics of reduced listening.

Chapter 4, the companion to this chapter, is titled "Maximal Objects," which might suggest either the opposite of minimalist music, such as "New Complexity" works, or Louis Andriessen's statement that he prefers to be considered a maximalist rather than a minimalist (Johnson 1994, 758). But in chapter 4, as in chapter 3, I reject established definitions of minimalism by considering works that in some way seem to attain a sense of surfeit and overabundance. And while the associations among drones, repetition, and minimalism will no doubt persist, my task here is to offer an alternative set of categories for understanding electronic music. Drones and repetition are ubiquitous in recent electronic music, but the manner in which these processes are executed distinguishes a work of microsound from, say, a work of noise music. Together, chapters 3 and 4 point to two opposite tendencies in recent electronic music, the former toward restricted objects, the latter toward excessive objects.

Microsound describes recent electronic music that treats sound as collections of infinitesimally small particles. The word defines both a set of compositional procedures and a musical aesthetics. The procedural definition of microsound refers to the use of the smallest elementary particles of sound to build compositions. Microsound procedures can be found in academic, popular, and independent electronic music. The most visible exponent of academic microsound is Curtis Roads, professor of media arts and technology at the University of California, Santa Barbara. Roads published the authoritative treatise *The Computer Music Tutorial* (1996), as well as the definitive textbook on microsound (2001). According to Roads, microsound was invented by Xenakis, who wrote the first pieces featuring granular techniques (Roads 2001, 64–65). One such piece is "Analogique B" (1959), made up of small fragments called "grains" of sine tones. (As its title suggests, "Analogique B" is the timbral analog to "Analogique A," in which the same gestures and rhythms are performed by strings.) "Analogique B" is striking in that it resembles neither synthesized music nor musique concrète. Although it technically is closer to the former because it uses sine tones to construct new sounds, its treatment of those sine tones as malleable, plastic material was unprecedented in electronic music. "Analogique B's" musique concrète cousin was "Concret PH" (1958), a granular synthesis treatment of a recording of the sounds of burning wood. Together, these two pieces demonstrated the potentials for using minimal, abstract sounds as elementary particles, the building blocks for new sounds.

Practitioners like Roads often rely on metaphors comparing granular synthesis with subatomic physics. Until the twentieth century, it was generally assumed that sound was a wave phenomenon. Thanks to hypotheses by Albert Einstein and Dennis Gabor, it has been accepted today that sound, like light, exists simultaneously as waves and as particles. In granular synthesis, a sound is split apart into particles or grains lasting between one-thousandth and one-tenth of a second. These elementary particles exist on the microtime scale, meaning that they are so brief that they are barely perceptible. But when combined, grains can construct previously unimaginable textures and sounds. Microsound is thus the reassembly of sound at its most basic level, yielding new composite sounds that would be unthinkable if working with longer, macro levels of perception.

The aesthetic or stylistic definition of microsound pertains to a subset within the larger community of musicians who use microsound compositional procedures. Here, *microsound* refers to what is often described as minimalist, ambient techno and electronica that began to appear in North

America, Europe, and Japan during the mid-1990s. Microsound musicians of this ilk are usually not associated with research or academic institutions and in many cases have no formal music training. Instead, they gravitate toward visual arts and design and may consider themselves affiliated with the intelligent dance music (IDM) movement that evolved from the techno and house scenes of the 1990s. This type of *microsound* is sometimes used interchangeably with the term *laptop music*, but since so much music is performed on laptops these days, that term is too vague to be of much use. For the sake of clarity, I will refer to this variant of microsound as the independent kind to distinguish it from institutional microsound. Independent microsound has thrived as a niche genre of electronic music since the late 1990s and has generated cult-following compilation albums such as *Clicks + Cuts* (2000) and *Microscopic Sound* (1999).

Like institutional microsound, independent microsound is "micro" insofar as it relies on software applications that can analyze, edit, and process sound at the elementary level. But unlike institutional microsound, which is too disparate to possess any defining stylistic traits, the distinguishing characteristic of independent microsound is its preponderance of digital noise, so much so that microsound is often synonymous with the genre of minimalist posttechno known as glitch. The glitch is noise, the sound of the mistake in digital recording and playback, such as the skipping sound that a scratched compact disc makes. The use of scratched or damaged recorded media is not new; students of performance art will know that Milan Knizak used damaged phonographs in the 1960s and 1970s (Stuart 2003), and, as discussed in chapter 2, Christian Marclay elevated scratched vinyl to the status of art object during the 1980s. In the 1990s, acts like the German group Oval recuperated the newest version of phonographic failure, the sound of digital skipping and scratching, transforming the sounds of dysfunction into something musical. Oval's "Textuell" (1996), for instance, repeats a brief skipping sound in a regular rhythmic pattern, producing the basic beat for a track that is otherwise draped with a hazy drone and intermittent synthesizer figuration (⊙ audio example 3: Oval's "Textuell"). "Textuell's" treatment of the glitch sound as a rhythmic unit is typical, recalling early hip-hop tracks in which DJs scratched records to create new rhythms on top of those already present in the music they replayed.

Fans might want to chime in at this point and say that glitch and microsound are not the same. Let me preempt this by saying that the terms often overlap and are used interchangeably by listeners, musicians, and record labels. Some writers have gone so far as to explain microsound as simply the academic version of glitch (Gard 2004), although this statement incorrectly reduces all microsound compositional procedures into mechanisms for producing digital noise. Likewise, some popular microsound contains no glitch sounds. The important issue here is not the ontological status of *glitch* and *microsound* but rather how these labels are used. Independent microsound, for better or worse, is usually synonymous with glitch and, therefore, noise. This perception gelled with the 2000 publication of the unofficial manifesto of glitch and microsound, Kim Cascone's article "The Aesthetics of Failure: 'Post-Digital' Tendencies in Contemporary Computer Music," which appeared in the academic periodical *Computer Music Journal* (Cascone 2000). Cascone is probably the most famous microsound artist in the world. He worked during the late 1980s and early 1990s as a sound editor and Foley artist, most notably for David Lynch's *Wild at Heart* and *Twin Peaks* pilot, before leaving Hollywood film to pursue a career as an independent electronic musician. Cascone's activities during the late 1990s as a creator, critic, and scholar of the burgeoning microsound scene made him particularly well qualified to write a reflection on the movement. His essay has been anthologized in Cox and Warner's *Audio Culture* reader (2007) and stands as the most important writing on glitch/microsound to date. In "The Aesthetics of Failure," Cascone argues that musicians have become disillusioned with technology and are now using digital signal processing to zoom in on the errors and glitches in sound reproduction. These sounds of failure are evocative because they allow musicians and listeners to demystify technology, which otherwise threatens to become ubiquitous and therefore unquestionable. Glitch noises, in other words, force listeners to reassess the definitions of admissible and inadmissible sound in the musical work.

Cascone's assertions are unimpeachable, but the enthusiasm that his article has generated has distracted from what is another equally striking aspect of independent microsound: its propensity for extremely quiet volumes. This trait is so common that it sometimes leads to the mistaken impression that the word *microsound* refers to microvolumes. To make matters more confusing, the microsound musician Miki Yui refers to her work as "small sounds" or "quiet music." Although the *micro-* in *microsound* pertains to microtime scales or the minuscule durations of the smallest grains of musical sound, duration and volume are nonetheless intimately connected. Roads (2001, 22) notes that at the microtemporal scale of reference, short sounds must be greater in intensity to be perceptible. In other words, the processes for creating microtemporal events also happen to make sounds quiet.

I focus here on independent microsound music that is very quiet and that treats its materials as minimal, elementary units divested of any external significance or reference. This includes ambient and glitch works of music and sound art, particularly those appearing on the record labels Mille Plateaux, Trente Oiseaux, 12k, and 12k's subsidiary label LINE. This body of work has attracted considerable scholarly and journalistic interest, which focuses exclusively on the significance of glitch sounds. But next to nothing appearing from either academic or trade presses has addressed the signifi-cance of silence, that is, the true digital silence and quietness in microsound. I want to ask the following questions: How does quiet microsound affect the listening process? Is microsound simply rehashing the attitudes toward silence put forth by composers such as John Cage, R. Murray Schafer, or Morton Feldman? What can we make of the seeming contradiction between the quiet volume of microsound and its reliance on glitches? I will conclude with some thoughts about how these very specific observations of microsound pertain to more general discussions of electronic music at large.

SMALL SOUNDS

Quiet microsound is recorded at soft volumes, so much so that playback at what one usually considers a normal volume is often inaudible. Turning up the volume does not necessarily help and may in fact hinder the listening process, because a loud volume can produce speaker hiss that competes with the recorded sounds. Miki Yui, the abovementioned Japanese microsound artist, refers to her works as "small sounds."[1] In the liner notes to her album *Lupe Luep Peul Epul* (2001), Yui writes: "please play at trans-parent levels in different atmospheres." A track on this album, "Torli," con-tains what sounds like a modified sine tone whose volume and pitch swell gently before climaxing in a small popping sound leading to a separate rat-tling sound (● audio example 4: Yui's "Torli"). This pattern continues with slight modifications throughout the piece, constantly accompanied by a softly undulating low drone. The combined effect of these various sounds suggests that "Torli" is replaying in a large, resonant space, with the sine tone, pop, and rattle sounds occurring near the listener's ears and the drone sounds taking place at some distance from the listener. But the most striking aspect of "Torli" and the other tracks on *Lupe* is that they contain no con-ventionally musical materials such as melodies or rhythms. Some, such as "Torli," feature inscrutable synthesized material, while others are made of field recordings. In many cases, these materials lack incisive attacks or tim-bres, making them virtually inaudible when played at the low volume Yui requests. As Yui describes it, her process is to begin with personally signifi-cant materials that she then transforms into universally poetic sounds (per-sonal communication, June 16, 2009). Making sound universal in a certain sense means divesting it of particular meanings. But Yui calls this "defo-cused" rather than reduced listening. The difference here amounts not to

---

[1] The German sound artist Rolf Julius has used a similar term, "small music," to describe his works that rely on close miking to capture soft sounds (Licht 2009, 5).

insisting on the meaninglessness of sound but instead to balancing whatever personal meanings it might have had for her with the impressions it cultivates in others.

The American microsound artist Richard Chartier indicates that his *Series* album of 2000 and *Decisive Forms* album of 2001 are "for quiet amplification" and/or "headphone use." Track one from *Series* showcases what may be the most Spartan use of quiet volume anywhere in electronic music (◐ audio example 5: Chartier's "Series 1"). In what is otherwise a track completely void of sound, a faint digital fluttering occurs in the left channel (the left loudspeaker or left headphone) for a fraction of a second before flitting to the right channel. This event lasts for perhaps a second and is followed by several seconds of silence. The nature of this fluttering is itself hard to apprehend; the sounds are so brief that they resist classification as conventional tones and instead invite analogies to tactile sensations such as the tickling of a hair as it falls down one's neck. Shortly after the one-minute mark, tiny pops and static begin to punctuate these fluttering sounds, grains of glitch noise that can easily be mistaken for the sound of earphones shifting slightly on the listener's ears. But this glitch pop originates from the recording itself—an intentional sound. At around 2:50, a barely perceptible swishing sound replaces the fluttering, as if of an insect's wings beating in slow motion or a helicopter from very far away. Along with the swishing occurs a subliminally low buzz like the kind heard when speakers are left on but no recording is playing. At around 4:30, this drone fades to make way for what sounds like small objects being dropped in a cavernous room. This dropping sound contains an initial attack followed by a small decay and is eventually joined by the tiny glitch snags from earlier in the recording.

The liner notes in Yui's and Chartier's albums direct the listener not to do what would come naturally: to turn up the volume enough to create an immersive experience, or at least enough that the recording is somewhat audible. Quiet microsound thus asks listeners to submit to a rather frustrating set of conditions. The desired outcome of this discipline, as Chartier describes (Boon 2002), is one in which the listener has learned to hear differently, to become more sensitive to phenomena usually ignored in our noise-laden world. But as many fans can attest, using headphones does not guarantee a pristine listening experience. Even under the calmest circumstances at home, noises external to the living space, such as a car alarm or a plane flying overhead, can overwhelm such fragile sounds.

How can one make sense of the seeming contradictions between quiet recorded materials and the directives to listen to them in less than immersive conditions? The work of ethnomusicologist Lorraine Plourde, who has conducted fieldwork in the *onkyō* experimental music scene in Tokyo, offers a point of departure. *Onkyō*, as Plourde explains, is "an extremely minimal, improvisatory musical style and performance approach that pays particular attention to sound texture, gaps, and silences" and is "often performed at barely audible levels" (Plourde 2008, 270). Much *onkyō* is performed on laptops or samplers that atomize sound into grains. Plourde notes that traffic noises and other sounds from beyond the concert space often permeate performances of quiet music. Given the disciplined quiet that is common in *onkyō* performances, one might understandably conclude that participants adopt a Cage-like acceptance of all sounds, both those intended by the musicians and those that occur naturally or accidentally. As Plourde explains, this is not the case in *onkyō*, because musicians still expect silence and decorum from their listeners.

One might try to connect quiet music (whether in *onkyō* or other variants of microsound) to Western notions of Japanese culture, particularly Zen mysticism. But as Plourde points out, this conclusion is facile and misleading: the muted volumes of *onkyō* have less to do with a Zen sensibility than with Tokyo's densely packed buildings and virtual lack of soundproofing. And, like Plourde, I also want to avoid easy connections among microsound; Zen; the phenomena of noise, silence, and quiet; and the person inevitably mentioned in tandem with those phenomena, John Cage. It is certainly true that Cage is a touchstone in any discussion of microsound. A brief survey of the musicians considered in this chapter speaks to the importance of Cage's legacy: Kim Cascone cites him as the fountainhead for recent electronic music (and even named his son after him); Brian Eno considered him a mentor and went on to invent ambient music, which is how many microsound artists describe their own music; 12k founder Taylor Deupree borrows from Cage's friend Robert Rauschenberg in designing album covers that are monochromatic and devoid of figuration. Cage is a requisite name to drop in the scholarship on microsound, particularly in articles by Phillips (2006), Stuart (2003), and Thomson (2004). And Cage's influence on the techniques for producing microsound is undeniable. Cage's 1975 work *Child of Tree* uses close miking to capture the sounds of cactus needles being plucked, sounds that would be nearly inaudible to the naked ear. Similarly, the principle behind glitch microsound is that the roving ear of the microphone and headphone renders what were initially minuscule sounds into miraculously audible sound objects.

While these affinities are important, to overemphasize them would err in making microsound seem like just one more Cageian exercise in stretching our tolerance for unusual sounds and noises. Comparisons to Cage obscure a fundamental and distinctive trait of microsound: its use of what practitioners and listeners consider to be nonreferential, precultural sounds. One obvious divergence from Cage's music is that in microsound, there is a difference between noises interior to the music, such as glitch sounds, and noises exterior to the music that may interfere with hearing performances or recordings. Cage wrote in "The Future of Music: Credo" that music in subsequent years would have as its "point of disagreement" the tension between "noise and so-called musical sounds" (1961b, 4). Cage's statements about his celebrated visit to the anechoic chamber at Harvard and the silent piece *4'33"* indicate that for him, silence did not exist and that throughout Western music history, musical sounds garnered attention while undesirable "noise" was stigmatized and suppressed. Cage urges us to listen dispassionately, without intention, so that we might appreciate the richness of all sounds. Quiet microsound does not accept its noisy surroundings as unconditionally as Cage does. Chartier, for instance, describes his work as a reaction to environments in which soft sounds are drowned out by noise (Boon 2002). Chartier's liner notes call on the audience to listen *through* noise rather than *to* noise. The difference between Cage and Chartier amounts to whether noise is a worthy object of contemplation or merely an obstacle to overcome. In fact, a better point of orientation might be the composer and acoustic ecologist R. Murray Schafer, whose book *The Soundscape* (1994) envisioned and even hoped for a technological disaster that would return to society to a quieter, preindustrial landscape. For Schafer, technology can potentially reveal the subtleties of natural soundscapes but instead too often produces noise and extracts local musics in a process he terms "schizophonia." This analogy to Schafer has only limited applicability to microsound, because, unlike Schafer, microsound musicians do use noise in an applied manner, noise of their own creation. Unlike Schafer and his followers, microsound composers express little interest in preserving or protecting natural sound environments.

These preliminary considerations of Cage and Schafer and their relevance to microsound underscore the tension in most microsound works between quietness and the noises that exist within the musical work. Most scholars working in the fields of contemporary music or sound studies feel the need to interpret these noises, which would indicate that these noises do indeed signify something. A quick survey of the writings on noise in contemporary music, writings generated by both practitioners and theorists, reveals unanimous agreement that the use of noise within music leads not to meaningless gibberish but rather to an overabundance of meaning (Attali 1985; Emmerson 2007, 19–20; Hegarty 2007; Kahn 1999). Link (2001), for instance, writes that phonographic noise renders everything in past tense. And Collis (2008) points out that in acoustics, noise adds information to any communications system rather than being simply undesirable detritus.

Whatever meanings noise might contain, many microsound practitioners regard quietness and silence as means of neutralizing noise, of rendering it meaningless. Chartier states:

The advent of digital audio has greatly increased what composers can do in terms of using the aspect of silence as a compositional element. Where it really is silent, not an analog silence that has that hiss. With digital silence, there's nothing. An absolute zero—no code. My work is really a process of removal. . . . That's what I like about working with sound as opposed to paint and canvas: especially working on a computer, you can take away sound until there's really nothing left. (Boon 2002)

Other statements confirm Chartier's feeling that both noise and silence are inert materials. Cascone writes:

Many glitch pieces reflect a stripped-down, anechoic, atomic use of sound. . . . This is a clear indication that contemporary computer music has become fragmented, it is composed of stratified layers that intermingle and defer meaning until the listener takes an active role in the production of meaning. (2000, 17)

Electronic musician and music critic Philip Sherburne writes of the glitch sounds in 12k releases: "[N]otes, pulses, and textures bear no immediate relation to the world around them, to a language of melody or tonal narrative" (2002, 171). Mille Plateaux founder Achim Szepanski writes of his label's glitch releases:

Music does not function as a carrier of messages but offers nothing but empty signification and resists any attempt for decoding. So it more or less allows any form of interpretation. Its only content is that of its own sound and the sound of a reality existing outside. More precisely, music should be referred to as a function which is crossing different units and forms a transversal whose expression does not refer to references or meanings. (2002, 226)

The thread running throughout these statements is an attention to the material qualities of sound and silence. Chartier's silence is not the same as the pregnant silences in Cage's music, full of ambient, neglected sound, but is rather completely blank, empty space. Cascone views microsound processes as methods of "deferring" or deflecting meaning. Sherburne states simply that the sounds featured on 12k releases bear "no immediate relation" to the outside world. For these writers, sounds function less as placeholders for meaning than as blank objects that can be added to or removed from the texture of a work.

MATERIALISM

Rather than looking to Cage or even Schafer for orientation, we can better situate independent microsound amid key moments in the discourse of materialism surrounding visual-art movements of the twentieth century. Materialism is the focus on material, the physical stuff of artistic creation and life itself. Material has long been marginalized in Western philosophy and aesthetics, harking back to the Platonic belief in the schism between an ideal and its form. For much of Western history, philosophers regarded material as incidental to the truly worthy objects of contemplation: ideas and essences. Materialism emerged at various moments in the past several centuries as a repudiation of idealism. There are a few materialist anteced-ents worth mentioning that have no direct bearing on microsound but help point the way toward the movement that arguably did: minimalist visual art. Writer and critic Georges Bataille broke away from former surrealist col-league André Breton's Marxist-indebted historical materialism to propose "base materialism." This type of materialism identifies an aesthetic experi-ence that fixates on formless, taboo materials such as urine, excrement, and blood. Bataille believed that disgusting, profane objects are not weighed down with the associations linking normal artistic materials to some higher spiritual or religious plane. Material for Bataille is only material, no matter how ugly or forbidden:

> Most materialists, although they want to eliminate all spiritual things, have
> ended up describing an order of being which, in so far as it involves
> hierarchical relations, is characterized as specifically idealistic. . . . It is
> time, when the concept of materialism is involved, to refer to the direct
> interpretation of raw phenomena, *excluding all idealism*; and not to some
> system based on fragmentary elements of an ideological analysis, devel-
> oped in the name of a religious analogy. (Bataille 2002, 483–484)

The relevance of base materialism to microsound is admittedly limited. Although it does claim to use what is elsewhere considered to be the ugly or forbidden sounds of digital audio, microsound certainly has no gripe against religion or taboo. Yet microsound does claim to strip sound of its associa-tions, leaving only the sound itself. More fundamentally, base materialism helps explain microsound's utter lack of sentimentality with regard to its materials. With sampling, synthesis, and digital signal processing, sound can be created from scratch or else be transformed from recognizable mate-rials to something beyond recognition. Bataille's other writings, particularly *The Story of the Eye* (1987), demystify eroticism by focusing on the raw flesh and substance of the sexual act, leaving no hint of spiritualism. Microsound, by exerting utter control over every aspect of sound, similarly divests sound of any ancillary musical function.

A second inspiration for microsound's materialism is Morton Feldman, the interlocutor between abstract expressionist visual art and avant-garde music of the 1950s and 1960s. Clearly, many of Feldman's works challenged performers to produce extremely quiet sounds. Wong (2008) discusses how Feldman approached his sounds the way that he felt painters approached their paints: as objects capable of assuming shapes and forms but not as conveyers of narrative, metaphor, or origin. Throughout his career, Feldman made statements to this effect: "leave the sounds alone; don't push them" (quoted in Villars 2006, 28); "Most music is metaphor. . . . I am not metaphor" (quoted in Villars 2006, 35–36); "Part of my musical thinking is to have the sound sourceless. . . . I like the instruments to play in the natural way; they become anonymous" (quoted in Villars 2006, 48); "I feel that I listen to my sounds, and I do what *they* tell me, not what I tell them" (quoted in Villars 2006, 55); "Everything is a found object. Even something that I invent is a found object. . . . And in realizing that, you must lose your vested interest in ideas" (quoted in Villars 2006, 195). Simply put, Feldman was a sound materialist, relishing the internal characteristics of sounds rather than their semantic potential.

Bataille and Feldman indicate a general migration in modernist aesthetics away from material as transcendent and spiritualized to material as hermetically sealed from the outside world. Minimalist sculpture from the mid-1960s intensified this push through its use of large, voluminous objects that seem to chafe against the framing devices traditionally separating artworks from the outside world. I will now provide an extended discussion of minimalist sculpture in order to illustrate its sway over microsound.

OBJECTHOOD AND REDUCED LISTENING

One of the givens of Western art of the past four hundred years has been the perceptual gap between the world of the artwork and that of the viewer. Perspectival treatment of the art subject requires a set of illusions, conventions understood by both artists and viewers suggesting that the world depicted in the artwork is in a separate but realistic plane of existence. In painting, the underpinning of these conventions is the conversion of a two-dimensional canvas into a three-dimensional realm. Thus, successful painting since the Renaissance has generally demonstrated mastery of techniques for creating the illusion of depth despite the obvious flatness of the canvas. In sculpture, illusion is created through the use of alternative scales, both of the object at large and of its constituent parts. We accept that a one-foot-tall sculpture of the Virgin Mary is at least somewhat of a realistic representation, just as we overlook disproportions among her body parts in order to accept as realistic the larger whole of her form. Beginning in the early twentieth century, the boundaries between art and viewer began to fall under attack, and the chief object of that attack was the premise of illusion. Picasso was one of the first to dismantle illusion in sculpture, with his *Guitar* (1912), a chimera combining elements of the ready-made, sculpture, and collage that threatened to undo the cordoning off between art object and its surroundings (Foster et al. 2004, 37).

American art critic Clement Greenberg wrote in 1960 that what distinguishes modernist art is its focus on the elements inherent to a particular medium. Modernist painting, for example, does not try to create the illusion of three-dimensional perspective so common in earlier painting but instead emphasizes the flatness of the canvas and the materiality of paint and brushstrokes. In so doing, modernist painting renounces any attempt at emulating sculpture, focusing instead on its own "area of competence" (Greenberg 1982). Many subsequent artists, especially those who would later be called minimalists, perpetuated this critique of illusion. Minimalist sculptor Donald Judd's manifesto "Specific Objects" championed the creation of "three-dimensional art," works that were neither illusionistic like premodernist painting nor piecemeal composites like traditional sculpture:

> Half or more of the best new work in the last few years has been neither painting nor sculpture. Usually it has been related, closely or distantly, to one or the other. . . . The new three-dimensional work doesn't constitute a movement, school or style. The common aspects are too general and too little common to define a movement. . . . Three-dimensionality is not as near being simply a container as painting and sculpture have seemed to be, but it tends to that. But now painting and sculpture are less neutral, less containers, more defined, not undeniable and unavoidable. They are particular forms circumscribed after all, producing fairly definite qualities. Much of the motivation in the new work is to get clear of these forms. (Judd 2003, 824)

Hal Foster explains "specific objects" as follows:

> By radically reducing the elements in a work to such a degree that all would connect self-evidently to the unitary shape, Judd hoped not only to cancel composition but also to eliminate the other aspect of the a priori, namely the sense of an idea or intention that exists prior to the making of the work in such a way so that it seems to lie inside the object like its

motivating kernel or core. Eradicating illusionism is thus part and parcel of ridding the work of this motivating idea, this sense of a *raison d'être* that the resulting object clothes or expresses. (Foster et al. 2004, 493)

Judd's statement was thus nothing short of a reassessment of the responsibilities of art, a renunciation of illusion and embrace of the characteristics specific to the medium of sculpture.

Despite their shared interest in dispelling illusion, modernist painting and minimalist sculpture were in other ways irreconcilable with each other. Greenberg's disciple Michael Fried published in 1967 the famous essay "Art and Objecthood," which condemns minimalist (or what Fried calls "literalist") sculpture. For Fried, minimalist sculpture functions as theater, an experience that simultaneously confronts and isolates the viewer. Minimalist sculpture is not art, because it lacks a frame that separates itself from the viewer. Its incorporation of everyday objects creates the sense of a living presence that occupies the same space as the viewer. Modernist painting, on the other hand, recuses itself from the world thanks to its framing and the limits of a two-dimensional canvas. At stake in minimalist sculpture is a shift in ontology, away from art that identifies itself explicitly as art and toward an objecthood that at times makes serious claims for its status as nonart. What galls Fried is the presence of solid, voluminous objects such as cubes, steel girders, and two-by-fours, objects that "extort . . . a special complicity . . . from the beholder" (Fried 1998, 155). Such objects demand "that the beholder take [them] into account" *as* objects, which for Fried is an unforgivable lapse for an artwork because it demands self-reflexive absorption on the part of the beholder.

The analogy with minimalist sculpture does not explain everything in microsound, nor is it meant to. As an art form that enfolds over time, music is obviously antithetical to sculpture, which is fixed or frozen in time. What for Fried constitute objecthood in sculpture are integral shapes and forms that cannot be broken down into constituent parts, while objecthood in microsound entails the use of sound materials that cannot easily be registered as musical, as well as the distillation of sound to its most basic materials in order to discourage decoding or interpretation. Despite these divergences between visual arts and music, objecthood provides a compelling alternative paradigm to the theories that thus far have driven criticism and analysis of recent electronic works.

Microsound espouses a sort of reduced listening, but the means through which listening is divested of its external associations are more radical (through the use of extremely small grains of sound) than in traditional musique concrète, where the reduction occurs through the listener's own sheer will. The affinities between objecthood and Schaefferian aesthetics are patent. There is the etymological proximity between objecthood and sound object, which is more than superficial: Judd's "specific objects" are not piecemeal assemblages of parts but integral elements, just as Schaeffer's *objet sonore* is similarly defined as "an organized totality that one can assimilate into a 'gestalt'" ("*un ensemble organisé, qu'on peut assimiler à une 'gestalt'*"; Chion 1983, 34). Objecthood departs from the rules of discourse that determined the course of art for centuries, which Foster refers to above as the "a priori . . . idea or intention" that determines how objects function within a work of art. A similar set of rules also supported the existence of illusion in music, but here, the illusion consisted of the belief that musical units (i.e., phrases, melodies, chords, etc.) could function as a semiotic system that generates internally or externally referent meaning. Implicit in this sort of illusion is a constant awareness of the *separation* between music and non-musical sound. Schaeffer's description of the sound object, like Fried's and Judd's encapsulation of objecthood, proposes an object that is stripped of its external associations. Fried observes that minimalist sculpture's cubes, girders, and tubes "do not represent, signify, or allude to anything; they are what they are and nothing more" (Fried 1998, 165). Similarly, minimalist forerunner Barnett Newman spoke of the art object as a pure object rather than a symbol for something outside itself (Bernard 1993, 91), and Frank Stella famously described his work as follows: "My painting is based on the fact that only what can be seen there *is* there. It really is an object. . . . What you see is what you see" (Battcock 1968, 158).

Likewise, in microsound, the sparse, quiet noises that interrupt an otherwise pristine digital silence are intended to eschew any associations to the outside world. Many independent microsound artists work to achieve abstract, premusical sound, sound so stripped of any external meaning that it is a blank slate. For instance, Kim Cascone's *Cathode Flower* (1999) begins with a single grain of sound that appears to occur very close to the listener's head (◐ audio example 6: Cascone's *Cathode Flower*). After a few seconds, this almost complete void is somewhat filled when an ambient hum gradually emerges. The rest of the track is propelled by the tension between the grain and the drone, between sounds that seem very close to the listener's ears and those that come from far away.

We now touch on the other common stylistic trait (other than soft volumes) that characterizes independent microsound: its reliance on seemingly near and distant sounds perpetuating the illusion that we are listening in a large, voluminous space. The Cascone, Chartier, and Yui examples all employ very similar means (grains and drones) to achieve this effect. The semantic function of these grains and drones is minimized; it matters less what type of grain we hear than the fact that it suggests a listening space that is much larger than us and almost certainly larger than the space our bodies actually occupy at the time of listening. These sorts of sound objects are markedly different from the unanchored *objets sonores* Schaeffer envisioned. They are physical objects suggesting density and volume, collections of sounds whose placement communicates the perceived dimensions of the acoustic space in which they resound.

CRITIQUE

Two issues warrant critique in glitch microsound: its intentions and its means of achieving those intentions. With regard to the former, microsound artists aspire toward a monumentality that preempts any deciphering, explaining, or decoding art. But the effort to strip sound down to its basic, precultural building blocks is itself a gesture intimately tied to culture and history. As demonstrated in chapter 1, a great deal of the institutional electroacoustic music to emerge in the past sixty years has rejected reduced listening. Notable apostates include Schaeffer-protégés Luc Ferrari, who used musique concrète collage techniques but with recognizable sounds to create narrative pieces, and Michel Chion, whose compositions and academic writings affirm listeners' tendencies to speculate on the origins of sound. The reasons for this rejection are, above all, practical; empirical data and common sense both indicate that the recognition and classification of sound are integral aspects of the listening process and cannot easily be discarded. But another reason for the general antipathy toward reduced listening is that it strikes many contemporary listeners as a resuscitation of the rhetoric of absolute music, the belief that instrumental music can communicate directly through pure emotions and ideals, without representation, reference to the real world, or narrative program. Adorno attacked the premise of absolute music throughout his career, arguing that artworks simultaneously demand critical interpretation even as they evade facile decoding of their sociopolitical affiliations:

> There are artworks in which the artist brought out clearly and simply what he wanted, and the result, nothing more than an indication of what the artist wanted to say, is thereby reduced to an enciphered allegory. The work dies as soon as philologists have pumped out of it what the artist pumped in, a tautological game whose schema is true also of many musical analyses. (1997, 128–129)

> The claim that there is nothing to interpret in [artworks], that they simply exist, would erase the demarcation line between art and nonart. (1997, 128)

More recently, musicologists such as McClary (1991) and Hoeckner (2002) have discredited absolute music as a vehicle for keeping art separate from culture and, in so doing, rendering invisible power relations that have kept women, homosexuals, and non-Europeans at a disadvantage. In writing about electroacoustic music, Windsor (1996) argues that sampling and collage techniques necessarily invoke the associations of their source materials. Similarly, Fink (2005) faults American minimalist music for its insistence on its own abstraction despite its being a cultural practice inspired by the repetition of advertising. In short, any suggestion that music or sound can stand apart from the outside world is highly unpopular these days.

Or, at least, it is highly unpopular in academia and any other type of writing influenced by Marxist criticism. While much of the scholarship devoted to electronic and electroacoustic music theorizes the communicative abilities of music and sound, many microsound artists persist in the belief that sound can, to quote Cascone, defer meaning. It may well be true that, from a listener's perspective, the associations of sounds are inescapable. But we would be missing half the story if we did not also attend to the intentions of electronic musicians, many of whom are still striving for sound that precedes culture and history.

The second critique has to do with how microsound artists execute their ideas. The most ambitious gambits toward reduced listening in microsound are those that least resemble music of any kind. The Cascone, Chartier, and Yui tracks described above demonstrate this; when sound is incredibly quiet, stripped of the trappings of music such as rhythm or melody, and made to resemble nothing in the outside world, reduced listening seems more attainable. But note the crutch I lean on to discuss these tracks: metaphor. In relying on written and spoken words to communicate, humans must at some point use metaphor to describe and explain sounds. Thus, I liken Yui's mysterious sounds to sine tones, pops, and drones, and Chartier's barely perceptible sounds become flutters and loudspeaker hums. Extremely quiet and esoteric sounds can evade meaning, but they cannot trump it altogether once listeners begin the process of explaining what they hear.

Yet when microsound works enlist the rhythms and syntax of EDM, something strange happens. Predictable rhythms and other conventional devices make some microsound "musical enough" so that metaphors are no longer necessary for explaining the provenance of sound. The *Clicks + Cuts* and *Microscopic Sound* compilation albums, the most representative collections of microsound, contain almost exclusively tracks that are based on the template of techno: a repeated 4/4 bass-drum beat adorned with interjections in the higher registers. Admittedly, some of these tracks count as microsound only on a superficial level: they may feature brief sound grains akin to those on a Chartier recording but also contain sounds of longer duration and even those taken directly from identifiable instruments such as the electric guitar. Some tracks are recorded at low volumes, but others are not. These idiosyncrasies notwithstanding, if we consider all of these tracks as microsound, the question remains of what a regular meter and the trappings of EDM do to the listening process. My response is that the nonreferential qualities of microsound are actually abetted by dance rhythms; that is, when listeners hear a standard techno rhythm, they are less prone to be curious about the origins or provenance of individual sounds. The repetitive rhythms of dance genres constitute the frame that identifies microsound as music and distinguishes it from the outside world. When, on the other hand, such rhythmic markers are absent, as in the Cascone, Chartier, and Yui examples, the identification of sounds takes on heightened urgency. Paradoxically, once a track identifies itself as music, our curiosity about its contents is sated.

An awkward compromise between the abstraction of Yui and Chartier and the referentiality of EDM is Ryoji Ikeda's 1996 album +/−, widely considered to be a definitive work of independent microsound. Ikeda identifies himself as both a musician and a sound artist, and his works frequently feature sounds that travel through the stereophonic field. (As will be elaborated in chapter 5, sound art often purports to be distinct from music on account of its emphasis on space and location, although it arguably takes more than playing with stereophonic panning to accomplish this. Not coincidentally, Ikeda is one of the musicians Licht accuses in the comment cited above of "playing the art card.") The back cover of +/− explains the album's engagement with psychoacoustics: "+/− has a particular sonority whose quality is determined by one's listening point in relation to the loudspeakers." This note refers to the fact that much of the album consists of a single sound (a sine tone, a grain, a moment of static) that seems to travel back and forth between left and right channels. Much of +/− thus seems demonstrative, exploring the listening process through a highly repetitive and restricted sonic language. The album contains two sections: "Headphonics," made up of three pieces built roughly around a techno beat, and "+/−," featuring several tracks containing individual pulses (featured in the plus-containing tracks "+," "+.," and "+. .") and their polar opposite, sustained tones (featured in the minus-containing tracks "−," "−.," and "−. ."). The section culminates with the album's title track, "+/−," suggesting a synthesis of opposites through its barely audible volume, short duration, and reliance on the faintest gossamer sound grains (🔊 audio example 7: Ikeda's "+/−").

Ikeda's album certainly suggests affinities with EDM, especially in its first section, but it ultimately operates less according to the conventions of dance beats than to its own rules governing sequential rhythms and spatialization configurations. This is especially the case in its second half, where the track titles inform listeners that the recording explores two antithetical types of material before reaching some sort of compromise position between the two. Even though +/– may ultimately buck the generic constraints of EDM, Ikeda's use of repetition situates these microsound works within musical discourse. Regular rhythm, in other words, exerts a nearly irresistible pull on the material, making what seemed abstract and inscrutable sound, ironically, musical. And musical sound, as Scruton (1997, 3) states it, encourages perhaps the only practicable type of reduced listening: since we know that what we are listening to *is music*, we cease to attend to its source-causes.

I want to throw a challenge back to those who would dismiss reduced listening and its intellectual progeny in microsound. It may be exceedingly difficult to ignore the perceived origins of sound, and it may well be impossible to create a sound that has no associations to the outside world. But the vehemence with which various writers have proclaimed this impossibility would suggest that humans are capable of only one type of perceptual experience. Lived experience tells us a different story. Although listeners may not be able to banish all associations of sounds all the time, they can and do choose to focus on some aspects at the expense of others. When we hear a musical work performed by a less than competent musician, depending on how generously we are disposed toward the work and the performer, we can overlook a great deal of technical mistakes in order to attend to the musical work itself. We can similarly listen to microsound works simultaneously as works of music and as abstract objects.

The fact that listeners can practice a modified form of reduced listening has, in fact, galvanized some microsound artists to critique the ideal of abstraction. I want to conclude with two manifestations of such a critique. The first pertains to a particular work, Alva Noto's *Xerox No. 1* (2007). Alva Noto, the stage name of German glitch musician Carsten Nicolai, rivals Kim Cascone for the position of the world's most prominent microsound musician. His work appears on both the *Clicks + Cuts* and *Microscopic Sound* compilations, and he has recorded extensively as a solo artist as well as with Ryuichi Sakamoto and Ryoji Ikeda. Alva Noto's sound in the late 1990s and early 2000s epitomizes glitch microsound: barely audible shimmering effects that click away with robotic regularity. This music is quite different from Richard Chartier's, where pulse is mostly absent and volumes are defiantly low. But, like Chartier, Alva Noto loves to work with inscrutable sounds. Yet *Xerox No. 1* is different; unlike nearly all microsound recordings, it contains a program of sorts. Its liner notes invoke Baudrillard and Benjamin in talking about copies and reproductions as disconnected from their purported sources. The album's tracks are built on samples that have been transformed. The emphasis here is no longer on sphinx-like glitch sounds but rather on sounds that bear a ghostly resemblance to something heard in the past.

A second critique of abstraction in microsound was present in a thread on an electronic discussion list devoted to microsound during the first few weeks of January 2009. Shortly following an outburst of violence between Israel and Hamas in the Gaza Strip, a participant named Charles Turner asked microsound list participants to consider whether they could "learn" anything from an attached link to a YouTube video for a folk song, "We Will Not Go Down (Song for Gaza)," accompanied by a slide show of still photographs depicting Palestinian casualties (Microsound list archives). Turner complained that microsound music avoids explicit engagement with politics, which Turner took as evidence that experimental musicians often perceive themselves as "above" having to deal with everyday themes in their music. A few list participants responded that the microsound list was intended as a platform for aesthetic issues only, which only confirmed Turner's point. But for Turner and the many other respondents on the list who agreed with him, the idea that art can divorce itself from its situation within culture and history is a fallacy.

To be fair, those microsound composers who disagreed with Turner might not have been insisting on their art's complete detachment from the outside world but rather on the way in which "We Will Not Go Down" chose to address the situation in Gaza. The combination of photographs of destroyed buildings and shattered families with a conventional folk tune can seem maudlin to even the most sympathetic listeners. So, if we want to avoid demonizing Turner's detractors, the real issue here might not be whether microsound *should* address politics but, rather, how it does so. This issue will sound familiar to listeners of nineteenth-century Western art music, where the debate between absolute and programmatic music camps was not a debate on whether music was meaningful but rather on whether music should rely on written or spoken language to convey its meaning. Absolutists like Eduard Hanslick (1986) maintained that musical material itself contained meaning and that programs or extramusical explanations were therefore superfluous.

In chapter 1, I referred to Nattiez's tripartite schema for levels of music semiotics. The first two levels describe what composers and listeners bring to the business of interpreting music. The third level is what Nattiez terms the "neutral" level, describing what meaning is present in the notation, recordings, and other material traces left by the act of making and hearing music. These trace elements could, according to Nattiez, be perceived as language in and of themselves, not beholden to written or spoken explanation but capable of conveying ideas with immediacy. It is not difficult to sympathize with the desire to locate a neutral level in music and therefore not difficult to understand why practitioners of reduced listening and microsound might want to demarcate sound from the outside world. Once music relies on written or spoken language, it becomes subject to interpretation and misinterpretation, fates that befall any language. If, on the other hand, music is heard as being separate from conventional language, its meaning becomes simultaneously more difficult to understand and more resistant to mistranslation and devaluation. Microsound might thus represent less an effort to avoid signification altogether than an idealistic attempt to preserve music's ability to signify. In the next chapter, we visit electronica works that aspire toward an alternative mode of signification rooted in the body rather than the intellect. Just as musical objects in microsound use brevity to evade meaning, musical objects in chapter 4 use their large scale to transcend meaning.

4

Maximal Objects in Drone Music, Dub Techno, and Noise

Microsound is minimal in terms of the duration and volume of its materials and, in the work of artists like Richard Chartier, also because of the scant amount of activity in the pieces. Other microsound works are downright busy, calling to mind images of quiet little machines that chug along with mechanical precision. And yet little in the way of material transformation occurs even in the most eventful microsound works. Microsound is minimal, in other words, because it effects no particularly great change on its environment or itself.

Here and in chapter 3, I discuss the treatment of sound in electronic music as an object, but the means by which microsound and maximal music set about this task couldn't possibly be more different. Microsound aspires to a reductive absence of meaning, as if atomizing sound can divest it of its residual signification. After their meaning has been removed, grains in microsound exist as mute objects. The works profiled in this chapter, by comparison, have not given up on the belief that music can signify but have rather abandoned faith that signification occurs through intelligible units of a musical language. In drones, dub techno, and noise, the use of stasis and noise runs counter to habitual expectations for how elements of musical syntax interact with one another. These elements last too long and are too loud, and they disrupt the sense that music functions as a language by calling attention to physical aspects that music usually asks us to ignore. The liminal qualities of this music—the stresses it places on the body and the attention span—all wrest music out of a reasoned, ordered plane and thrust it back into the world of objects and raw materials.

This chapter profiles pieces that seem to change their surrounding environments and, especially, our own bodies. They are powerful, exerting their will to alter the way we listen. Their long durations and loud volumes test our limits of concentration and, in some cases, our tolerance for pain. These pieces confine their materials to drones, noises, and repetitive rhythmic patterns and often studiously avoid any other types of sounds that might distract from these elements. The three subgenres that I call maximal music—drones, dub techno, and noise music—are distinct practices, and I do not mean to collapse them, but one aspect they all share is a quality of excess, something appreciable only after long stretches of time. Therefore, this discussion will entail an investigation of what perceived long durations and stasis do to the listening process. (I say "perceived" because there is nothing inherently static or timeless in music; sound waves are by definition in motion and proceed along the space-time continuum just like any other phenomenon.) Maximal music generally avoids development according to the conventions of nonelectronic Western art music, yet it also avoids the sort of nondevelopmental variation and contrast that occur in other types of experimental electronic music such as microsound and soundscape. Most of the pieces in this chapter are classified as minimalist, but as chapter 3 explains, the category of minimalism refers to too many types of music to be of much use. Whereas the pieces in chapter 3 aspire to concision and meaninglessness, maximal music posits a space of euphoric or utopian excess. The corporeal effects of maximal music are direct and immediate, and although these sounds can be and are interpreted for their individual meanings, what is more pertinent here is the extent to which they signify general surfeit. Noise, duration, and the purity of a single tone or chord all test our ability to concentrate and perceive the passage of time.

We'll begin with some examples of drone and electronic dance music (EDM) that are static and repetitive. Despite this stasis, however, these works are also dominated by tension between stasis and action, or between limitlessness and constriction. Maximal music is appreciable as maximal only in the presence of boundaries, when we know that the music will at some point come to an end. In the second half of the chapter, we'll revisit conceptualizations of the sublime by Kant, Adorno, and Bataille while considering how the sublime in maximal music leads to "negative beauty." The maximal dimensions of much electronic music—its long durations, seeming avoidance of change, and noise—ultimately reinforce traditional notions of beauty and form. Drones and dub techno might seem static compared with music whose materials are constantly evolving, but the scarcity of materials in these genres ensures that even subtle changes assume great significance. Likewise, while Attali (1985), Hegarty (2007), and Kahn (1999) interpret noise as political or social critique, inherent in this critique is the regret that noise is unacceptable. As beauty's opposite, noise reinforces the ideal of beauty. We'll close by asking why so much electronic music, and in particular so much maximal music, is, for lack of a better word, beautiful. Why, in the midst of a vigorous avant-garde tradition, does maximal music rely on tonality and consonance?

STASIS

We tend to think of stasis in music as the opposite of teleology. Static music goes nowhere, achieves no goals, does no work, and sounds the same three hours into the work as it did when the work began. These truisms have explained what distinguishes Western art-music warhorses from non-Western music as well as the post-1945 avant-garde. But it is not enough to rest here, for the simple reason that so much electronic music is nonteleological. The definition of static music does not need to remain a negative one in the sense that it only describes an absence or failure. Static music is not only music that avoids conventional harmonic or melodic goals but also music that takes specific steps to obscure any sense of the passage of time. We can hear these aspects of stasis in drone music and dub techno, two subgenres that clearly differ from each other in terms of presence or absence of pulse yet share important affinities in terms of how they manipulate sound and silence.

It is exceptionally difficult to write about drone music. I say this as a person who likes a lot of it, so I lack the prejudices often seen in print about drone music being "boring" or "like listening to a dentist's drill." Technical descriptions of drones take only a few words to state that one tone or chord lasts minutes or hours, leading to a rather sizable imbalance between the minimal number of words required to describe a drone and the maximal amount of time a drone takes. We also lack specific terminology for conveying exactly what goes on during a drone. "Sustained" and "held for a long time" are practically our only means of communicating what drones do, even though drone activity is often more complicated than these descriptions let on. Another approach would be to reflect on the ways in which drones affect the listening process. Drones impose a kind of sensory deprivation through effacing the variation we take for granted, the ebb and flow of acoustic data that occur not only in music but in daily life as well. Like other types of sensory deprivation, drones eventually sharpen other modes of perception by refocusing the listener's attention on the subtle fluctuations in timbre or pitch that accrue greater importance against an otherwise static background.

One of the more remarkable aspects of drone music is its surprising variety, both within individual works and among works across the subgenre.

Despite this variety, there is little written about drone music outside of ethno-musicology, and ethnomusicologists tend to discuss only specific case studies of drones rather than attempting cross-cultural comparisons (Kaeppler 1994). The work that has been done on drones in art or popular music centers almost exclusively on La Monte Young, and much of that work concentrates on tuning systems (Gann 1996). Apart from Young's work, however, drone music seems to be studiously avoided. The work of Éliane Radigue quickly puts to rest suspicions that all drones sound like Young's. Radigue is a French electronic-music composer who studied with Schaeffer and Pierre Henry in the 1950s before trading musique concrète for a musical language resembling that of Terry Riley. Radigue had long been interested in combinations of drones with improvised melodies. But her conversion to Tibetan Buddhism in the 1970s exerted a deep influence on subsequent compositions, whose stasis and enormous proportions draw on her experience with meditation. Until recently, Radigue has worked exclusively with tape and the ARP 2500 modular synthesizer, and these instruments figure in her massive *Trilogie de la mort* (1998), a three-movement work that Radigue was composing at the time of her son's death in an automobile accident. "Kyema," the first movement of the *Trilogie*, begins with the fading in of two sustained but undulating pitches, a root and its fifth. At around 1:30, a third line enters, a simple melody whose tonic is one octave above the root of the piece. This melody spins out pitches of a major scale, with no particular rhythm, trajectory, or development. This section continues with little variation until around 5:45, when two new sustained tones enter. By 6:45, all other pitches have begun to fade out except for the new low tonic. Like the preceding section, this new one spins out a slowly moving melody an octave above its root, with each line pulsating at a different rate.

I hear eleven discernible sections in all of "Kyema," and almost all of them progress in a manner similar to the two sections described above. Their structure consists predictably of one or more undulating drones paired to a simple melody, with each section fading out as another one fades in. The one exception to this rule takes place in the sixth and seventh sections. The sixth section begins at around 28:00 with a drone. After about a minute, what sounds like a tape sample of an orchestral work enters, a brief, looped fragment lasting only a few seconds. This material is accompanied by what sounds like a recording of wind blowing (or windlike sound effects).[1] This section continues for several minutes like this, only fading into the new seventh section at around 37:20. The seventh section consists of quiet electrical static and intermittent low pulses of a single pitch. It is unclear from my

---

[1] Gann (1996) states that all sounds on *Trilogie de la mort* are produced by analog synthesizers, but I have been unable to confirm this. In any event, these sounds *seem* like samples and wind effects.

compact-disc recording whether this static sound is intentional or the result of extraneous noise when the work was transferred from analog tape.

What I have just described seems like an eventful piece, and it is, but only if one listens very carefully. There are other ways to hear Radigue's music: the soft roundness of these sounds is pleasing and even lulling. It is easy to fall asleep to this music, although I mean this as a compliment rather than a criticism. Even when listening while fully awake, I often let these sounds wash over me without attending to the relationships among different sections, and I might only barely register that there are any sections at all. The more attentive mode of listening I employed in writing the analysis above may be able to discern specific traits of the piece such as the orchestral and windlike sounds. But all listening experiences, from those that are highly observant to those that lead to sleep, register the two most striking aspects of Radigue's works: their pitting of stillness against movement and their sheer length.

Although nominally a drone work, Jim O'Rourke's *Long Night* (1990) is so different from Radigue's *Trilogie* that I hesitate to refer to the two works by the same generic designation. "Kyema" is sectional and episodic, with a climax of sorts occurring approximately two-thirds of the way through the piece, with the sounds resembling an orchestra and the wind. *Long Night* avoids any hint of increasing tension or climax, maintaining the same glacial pace throughout its longer than two-hour duration. The process driving *Long Night* is simple: the piece begins with one single pitch (played on what I presume is an analog synthesizer) to which other pitches are gradually added. As the piece unfolds, some pitches fade out as others fade in, meaning that the piece effectively modulates from one chord to the next. Fast-forwarding on a compact disc player or an iPod generates a "digest" format in which material lasting longer than two hours is compressed into a recording lasting only a few minutes. Yet fast-forwarding also confirms that these modulations are only ancillary to the listening experience, because they attract much less attention at normal speed. The time between modulations is so great that it becomes difficult to track the progression between adjacent chords, let alone the overall harmonic trajectory of the work. Although O'Rourke occasionally allows some of these pitches to spin out into tiny melodies as Radigue does, the importance of these melodies seems secondary. These noodles are not improvisatory riffs like those in Terry Riley's music, attracting notice on the basis of their status as melody. They play at a modest volume and function as filigree rather than as the main attraction.

Phill Niblock's drones are distinct from both Radigue's or O'Rourke's. In his "Harm" (2006), the drone consists of a single note played on the cello (● audio example 8: Niblock's "Harm"). In fact, this is not a single note but rather one pitch that is subjected to slight microtonal manipulation such that in the resulting recording, there are several pitches chafing against one another in a tone cluster. In the liner notes to *Touch Three*, the album on which "Harm" appears, Niblock states that all sounds were produced by acoustic instruments and microphones; no electronic manipulation occurred. This assertion is somewhat inaccurate given that any recording, and especially one containing microtonal manipulation, depends on electronics. "Harm" is as much an example of electronic music as anything containing synthesized or sampled materials. But Niblock's desire to identify this work as nonelectronic points to an undercurrent among many drone musicians, starting with La Monte Young, that drones are somehow a more primal and universal music because they draw from ancient practices present in musical traditions around the world.

Charlemagne Palestine's drone works are rituals, especially when he performs them live in his customary fashion amid dozens of stuffed animals and the scent of clove cigarettes. A work such as *Schlingen-Blängen* (1979) for organ lasts more than seventy minutes and contains one chord that alters only very slightly and infrequently. What few timbral changes do occur are brought about through the manipulation of organ stops. It may be simply a result of the inherent reedy qualities of the organ, but there is an urgency to this drone work that makes it utterly distinct from works by O'Rourke or Radigue, an energy that suggests not lack of movement but constant, unabated movement.

These four examples of drone music are unarguably distinct in terms of structure as well as means of sound production. The quality they do share is an absence of pulse, which obscures the passage of time in drone music. Articulations, if present at all, occur at wide intervals, such as with the sections or episodes interspersed through Radigue's "Kyema." The lack of pulse in a drone work contributes to the impression that it also lacks trajectory or propulsion, even if the work does contain contrasting materials. So on this basis alone, EDM would seem to run counter to every trait in drone music. EDM contains a constant pulse, and many EDM tracks incrementally add or remove sounds to create anticipation for the next section or the next track. Examples of this technique are too numerous to count, but one well-known case is Manuel Göttsching's proto-techno work, *E2-E4* (1984). Like most techno, *E2-E4* is built on a rhythmic ostinato. Over the course of an hour, synthesized chords and guitar riffing intermittently join and then disappear from this basic rhythmic pattern. The inspiration behind such layering owes a great deal to minimalist works like Steve Reich's *Drumming* or Terry Riley's *In C*, in which the scaffolding of a basic rhythm serves as the foundation for extenuated figuration in higher registers. This compositional approach is teleological and sequential because it marks time with a procession of drum beats and intersperses mileposts of different musical events along the way.

If left to Göttsching's *E2-E4* and other automaton-like works by Kraftwerk and the Belleville Three (Juan Atkins, Derrick May, and Kevin Saunderson), EDM might have continued chugging along like a well-oiled machine, with dry attacks clicking away with watchlike precision underneath muted synth pads. But EDM underwent a crisis of sorts beginning in the late 1980s and culminating around 1992, as frenetic rave music began to alienate listeners and musicians (Reynolds 1999, 180–195). Subgenres such as chill-out, ambient house, ambient techno, and dub techno fragmented what had already been a disparate collection of house, acid house, and techno. These newest subgenres drew listeners in part because they provided a respite from relentless dancing but also because they fleshed out the sparseness of straight-ahead techno and house. In particular, dub techno replaced EDM's mechanization with a way of muffling the sense of time's passage, despite the persistence of the four-on-the-floor beat. Sound in dub techno appears to linger thanks to processing techniques that make it seem as if a clearly defined pitch or drum attack is traveling through a large space before dissipating several moments later. With this reverberance, dub techno approaches the endlessness of drone music.

To appreciate the shift from the sharpness of early techno to the blurriness of dub techno, let's return to one of the Belleville Three, Juan Atkins. The sound of Atkins's early group Cybotron, particularly on tracks like "Clear" (1990), is metallic, brittle, and robotic, the textbook definition of techno. "Clear" resembles Afrika Bambaataa's "Planet Rock" (1982) with its electro beat, robotic arpeggios, and synthesized melodies. In "Clear," the attacks are crisp, parroting the cybernetic movements it seeks to emulate. Around 1993, however, Atkins changed his sound after starting work in the Basic Channel studios of Berlin with Moritz von Oswald. Oswald and partner Mark Ernestus ran the techno group and recording label Basic Channel, which was gaining prominence for its minimalist dub techno, a pared-down response to Detroit techno with bare-bones percussion and irregular modulating synth chords. If, as Derrick May famously stated (Butler 2006, 42), techno was born when Kraftwerk and George Clinton got stuck in an elevator together, one could say that dub techno appeared when King Tubby or Lee Scratch Perry attempted to rescue the elevator occupants. The dry, precise attacks of first-generation techno are softened with echoes, as if the sounds are traveling through water.

Atkins, who by the mid-1990s was performing as Model 500, recorded several tracks with Oswald as engineer, among which "M69 Starlight" (1995) stands as one of the most highly regarded techno tracks. Like other Model 500 tracks, "M69 Starlight" associates its synthesized sounds with space flight and science fiction. The track begins with a four-on-the-flour bass-drum pattern to which are added synth-pad syncopations just before the third beat. This rhythm remains steady throughout the work. There is no conventional melody to speak of, so these syncopations function like a melody, because they seem to fit on top of the rhythmic underpinning of the track. But the syncopated material is not melodic, instead consisting of reiterations of the same single pitch whose timbre is varied through modulation. These controlled gestures make "M69 Starlight" an early example of dub techno, "dub" thanks to its thick reverb and modulated synth chords. "M69 Starlight" and other dub-techno tracks scrupulously avoid any sense of trajectory or anticipation.

German electronica artist Wolfgang Voigt's work as Gas has generated some of the most influential ambient techno albums of the past ten years, especially *Gas* (1995), *Zauberberg* (1997), *Königsforst* (1999), and *Pop* (2000). These four albums were rereleased in 2008 as a box set called *Nah und Fern*, an apt title given that these works immerse the listener in a forest of near and distant sounds. A typical Gas work contains a dance beat, although many do not. This beat, however, is not crisply articulated as it would be in most other techno tracks but rather sounds as if it was replayed on failing analog equipment. It lies submerged in a smeared mess of synthesized chord clusters and intermittent figuration, usually only three or four notes. The untitled second track of Gas's eponymous album provides the template: a muted drum track running about 120 beats per minute sits below synthesized, wordless choral singing that repeats a collection of perhaps five or six pitches. The rates of repetition here are not synchronized, so the choral material begins at a new place along the rhythmic pattern each time. What distinguishes Gas from other techno acts is the murkiness of its production. Most techno by definition embraces its technological underpinnings, its reliance on sequencers and synthesizers that emit razor-sharp attacks and clockwork-like rhythms. And most techno also contains a good amount of empty silence into which perfectly chiseled beats fall into regular patterns. Gas rejects this paradigm by using constant, unrelenting walls of sound that bleed into one another, what might have happened if Phil Spector had produced an EDM album. There are no clear timbres or easily audible melodic phrases here, and the monotony of materials combined with their irregular cycling in relation to one another suggests that these tracks simply exist without any development.

Returning to dub techno and Moritz von Oswald, his work with Mark Ernestus as Basic Channel popularized a paradoxical static trajectory in which the only changes are shifts in volume or modulation of synthesized materials. Basic Channel tracks are otherwise totally static, usually recycling the same few figures from start to end of a track. In "Quadrant Dub I" (1995), the track's materials are separated into different strata on the basis of their perceived distance from the listener. An ambient drone with a slight hiss lurks in the background, while pitched bass-drum attacks, first on the root followed by the fifth, occupy the foreground. A straight 4/4 pitchless drum beat later enters the foreground, followed by some synthesized, syncopated figures with reverb that hide in the background. The use of foreground and background materials, combined with the fact that those materials are quite simple and do not mutate over the course of the track, creates the impression that these sounds have solidified into inert objects promising no future growth or evolution.

Let's take a step back to reconsider these various examples of stasis. My language in discussing drones and dub techno echoes several examples of musical analysis that are perhaps too generous in accepting the perceptions of listeners uncritically. According to Kramer (1981) and Rowell (1987), traditional Western music treats time as a linear phenomenon. Musical works possess clear beginnings and endings and employ tonality and rhythm to create the expectation for organic development, climax, and denouement. As tonality's importance began to wane during the twentieth century, alternative approaches toward the organization of time began to appear, especially those claiming some affinity with non-Western musical traditions. Drones and other types of static music avoid development through repetition of one tone or one set of tones for long periods of time. Listeners and scholars hear in these works an alternative sense of time, what Kramer calls "vertical time," a timelessness in which the work could continue indefinitely without start or finish.

The tendency to pit teleology against timelessness in twentieth-century music studies is deeply ingrained. It has become so commonplace to think of classical music as goal-oriented and minimalist music as circular, immanent, or static that we tend not to give it a second thought. Even Adorno, usually reliably contrarian about clichés, toes the line in diagnosing the aesthetic experience of conventional art, which he argues amounts to awareness not of the essence of materials but of how materials interact with one another over time. He writes, "Analysis is therefore adequate to the work only if it grasps the relation of its elements to each other processually rather than reducing them analytically to purported fundamental elements" (1997, 175). This statement describes how we perceive the artwork, how we believe artworks grow and develop. For Adorno, our perception fixates on the artwork's "becoming" rather than "being"; the distinction refers to whether we see artworks as static, preformed objects or as living beings.

However, Adorno isolates a distinction elsewhere overlooked in discussions of musical time: the difference between aesthetic time and empirical time, or between how we *think* artworks behave over time and how they actually behave:

> Once a text, a painting, a musical composition is fixed, the work is factually
> existent and merely feigns the becoming—the content—that it encom-
> passes; even the most extreme developmental tensions in aesthetic time
> are fictive insofar as they are cast in the work in advance; actually, aesthetic
> time is to a degree indifferent to empirical time, which it neutralizes.
> (1997, 107)

That is, artworks become objectified the moment they are inscribed onto some medium, so our impression that their elements grow organically to become something else is simply that, an impression or illusion.

I want to infuse Adorno's sensitivity to the empirical time of art into the discourse on trajectory and stasis. When Adorno was writing *Aesthetic Theory*, he had in mind artworks for which stylistic conventions expected, even demanded, organic development. For music, this would entail notation of the work before its performance, as well as the expectation that a performer would adhere to the notation as closely as possible. Adorno's high-modernist favorites, the works of Schoenberg and Webern, contain figures and motives that, for him, seemed to grow and mutate to become something other than what they were at their inception. By contrast, most accounts of drones and dub techno speak in terms of inertia rather than forward motion. Maximal music is thus the counterpart to developmental music: immanent rather than transcendent, finished rather than developmental. But Adorno reminds us to attend to the physical realities of artistic experience, the fact that listening to notated, classical music in effect means listening to an event that has already been determined. Admittedly, different performances of a particular work can vary in terms of how they execute what is written in the score. But this does not change the fact that precomposed (or prerecorded or preplanned) musical materials are finished.

From the point of view of a philosopher or a physicist, there is no ontological difference between the sounds heard in teleological music and those heard in static music. In both cases, sounds happen but do not engender one another: contrary to what a Schenkerian analysis might argue, the opening chords of Beethoven's *Eroica* Symphony do not physically generate the ensuing exposition. Scruton (1997, 19) states that this sense of inevitable growth characterizes what he defines as "tone," but even Scruton would acknowledge that this causality is in the mind of the listener, not an objective reality. Yet the illusion of organic development in Western art music is nevertheless important because it drives both the creation and the reception of these works. When we listen to teleological music, we fall into the habit of attributing agency and volition to sounds. But static works confound our experience of aesthetic time, because they renounce any claims toward organicism or development. Instead, they highlight our experience of the empirical time of the artwork, the sometimes uncomfortable, sometimes heavenly length of time it takes to sit through a long drone work, the seemingly arbitrary duration of a techno track. Static works remind us that their materials are not fertile seeds poised to grow but rather inert objects. Two examples can help illustrate this point: a dub track produced by Augustus Pablo and an ambient track by Sawako.

Dub provides the most accessible acoustic example of this objectlike quality in static music. Dub reggae in the 1970s was one of the first genres to elevate the producer above the musician. In an album such as *King Tubby Meets Rockers Uptown* (1976), for instance, the musicians play straight-ahead reggae songs, but producer Augustus Pablo scatters and disassembles those songs, removing some tracks, treating others with heavy reverb or echo, and looping other materials. The strange moments on this album occur when a dub effect overtakes the underlying material, when a background singer's shout is made to echo and fade away while the percussion continues untreated at a consistent volume. In flaunting their acoustic artificiality, these sound effects alienate what was reassuringly musical material. Dub treatment renders sound awkwardly present and long-lasting, no longer camouflaged inside the frame of the track. Similarly, dub techno uses echo and reverb to mitigate the reassuring clip of the bass-drum beat. Thus, Basic Channel and Gas work a sleight-of-hand on the EDM template, showing that the automatism typical for a dance track can no longer be taken for granted. In dub techno, our experience of time is Adorno's empirical time, where listeners are attuned to the unnaturalness of the dissipation of sound.

"August Neige" (2007) by the ambient electronica artist Sawako contains several loops that repeat at different rates, producing something akin to a solar-system model whose planets rotate about their sun at varying speeds (⬤ audio example 9: Sawako's "August Neige"). The track begins with the sounds of plucked instruments that outline a major triad plus the sixth; this chord never modulates. The faint, repetitive scratching of a phonograph needle that occurs when a record finishes spinning marks time in what is otherwise a static cloud of sonorities, to which the sound of half-whispered, half-sung words contributes from time to time. At one moment before the two-minute mark, the sound of a speeding vehicle races across the stereophonic field from the right to the left channel. This recording shimmers and hangs suspended in time, calling to mind perpetual-motion machines that could supposedly click and churn indefinitely. Because each strand of material has its own rate of repetition, events do not line up or synchronize regularly, meaning that Sawako probably created these sounds separately without determining any particular alignment. The comparison with perpetual-motion machines is apt, because we can listen to "August Neige" as well as drones and dub techno differently from the way we normally listen to music. This type of listening is predicated not on expectations about what musical works do but rather on attention to the material qualities of sounds, how they linger and finally decay. Static music—music that is maximal in terms of its duration and repetition—engenders a condition that is unmusical: the absence of development, of growth, of organicism. Because there are no expectations regarding the ways in which materials will interact with one another, the duration of these works is arbitrary; a drone or dub work that lasts fifteen minutes is no less legitimate than one that lasts five hours.

We now turn to another curiosity in maximal music: the tension between noise and beauty. This polemic furnishes another example of how maximal electronic music exists in a dialectical relationship with conventional music. Noise music seemingly does everything it can to avoid conventional notions of beauty, which can be interpreted as resisting the idea of music altogether. But this resistance is an ambivalent gesture, for the very act of thwarting beauty by creating ugliness in fact reinforces the idea of beauty.

NEGATIVE BEAUTY

It is no coincidence that the titles of many works examined in this chapter allude to extremes of nature. There are the many references in drone music to the sun: the drone metal band Sunn O))); John Cale's album *Sun Blindness Music* (1965–1968); the album cover of clarinetist Anthony Burr and cellist Charles Curtis's performance of several Alvin Lucier drone pieces (2005), which features an infinite promulgation of sound waves that could easily be mistaken for a depiction of sun rays. Even Phill Niblock's "Valence" (2006) refers to radiation, except that here it involves the level at which electrons orbit the nucleus of an atom. Drone music also features nocturnal references, such as Jim O'Rourke's two-hour drone work *Long Night* and Model 500's techno hit "Starlight." If we are generously metaphorical in interpreting the sun as a symbol of warmth and therefore life, its antipode would be Radigue's *Trilogie de la mort*, a three-movement drone rumination on Tibetan Buddhism's interpretation of death.

What these works and many others like them share is a sense of extremity, of excess, of long duration, and of testing the limits of endurance. This is not a new sensation: Kant famously classified these traits as constituting the sublime, which, he wrote,

> is to be found in a formless object, so far as in it or by occasion of it
> *boundlessness* is represented, and yet its totality is also present to
> thought. . . . Therefore the satisfaction in the one case is bound up with the

representation of *quality*, in the other with that of *quantity*. But the other
[the feeling of the Sublime] is a pleasure that arises only indirectly; viz., it is
produced by the feeling of a momentary checking of the vital powers and a
consequent stronger outflow of them, so that it seems to be regarded as
emotion,—not play, but earnest in the exercise of the Imagination. (Kant
2000, 101)

Sublime objects are impossible to encase within a frame because of their sheer
scale. They inspire within the viewer a sober respect and awe that Kant describes
as a "negative pleasure," whereas beautiful objects elicit unambiguous pleasure
thanks to their adherence to perfect, universally recognizable forms.

Yet the paradox in maximal works by Alva Noto, William Basinski,
Fennesz, Tetsu Inoue, and the many rock bands influenced by My Bloody
Valentine, is that their materials might be considered conventionally beautiful if heard without electronic amplification or processing. These works
contain a great deal of noise, and we can hear them as sublime objects
because they contain an admixture of beautiful and dreadful elements:
simple tonal language submerged in pure noise or extreme dissonance, loud
volumes, and long durations. The noise in these works has hardly gone by
without notice. Noise is one of the most popular subjects in electronic and
contemporary music studies today, and thanks to Hegarty's work (2007;
2008), we now have a critical vocabulary and historical frame in which to
contextualize (or fail to contextualize, as Hegarty would see it) noise works.
The facet I want to explore here is not noise per se but rather why so much
of noise music is, underneath its deafening volumes, distortion, and feedback, so traditionally beautiful. Beauty here is obviously in the ear of the
beholder, and I make no claims regarding the aesthetic value of these works.
Yet amid devices and imagery that point to the pushing of physical, physiological, and psychological limits, these works use consonance and tonality,
foundations of the language of Western art music. Electronica artists usually
posit themselves as avant-gardist in terms of both their methods and their
position within music history. Why, then, would they employ aspects of an
older musical language that have become so suspect?

Tonality and consonance might well have vanished from late-twentieth-
century experimental music. The efforts on the part of the Second Viennese
School composers to wrest musical language from cliché targeted consonance and functional harmony for being reactionary, for having outlived
their expressive capacity. Integral serialism and mid-century experimentalism further insisted on the avant-garde's alienation from conventional
expression, spurred on by statements from Adorno such as "Loyalty to the
image of beauty results in an idiosyncratic reaction against it. This loyalty
demands tension and ultimately turns against its resolution" (1997, 53).

Adorno and many composers associated with the Darmstadt summer courses condemned the language of conventional beauty for offering false consolation, the empty promise that an artwork could provide closure and order in a world that had resoundingly rejected such comforts. For this brand of modernism, art could remain faithful to the ideal of beauty only through rejecting facile attempts at beauty. Easily consumable features of musical language such as tonality, catchy melodies and rhythms, and sentimental themes turn music into a commodity, allowing it to be sold piecemeal for the fleeting pleasure it offers to listeners. For Adorno, the presence of such commodifying elements cheapened music and rendered it a mass-culture product, so contemporary art music had to reject these elements if it was to retain any claim of integrity.

The recuperation of tonality and beauty into the language of experimental music is largely the work of non-Europeans, particularly American minimalists such as Steve Reich and Philip Glass, as well as non-Westerners such as Toru Takemitsu. Their works freely blend elements of high and popular culture, asserting that accessibility and expressivity are not incommensurate. This having been said, Adorno's critique of beauty still exerts considerable influence. There remain serious reservations even on the part of popular musicians about beauty's connections to naiveté and commercialism. For some, the way around this potential stumbling block is the pairing of beautiful writing with noise, static, interference, and the placing of these elements in situations that demand concentrated listening over long stretches of time. Beautiful melodies and recurring consonances can thus destabilize a work, making it excessive, voluptuous, and decadent. Noise and beauty might initially seem like opposites, but in combination, they dismantle the musical frame that used to maintain a healthy distance between the artwork and the outside world.

In other words, beauty and noise in electronic music can conspire to produce a sense of excess, a concept that Bataille explores in some detail. Bataille's idiosyncratic theory of economics holds that excess rather than scarcity drives markets, cultures, and physical bodies. Excess results when gifts are given without the expectation of reciprocity or when living beings consume more than they need to maintain basic vital functions. With excess consumption arises the problem of what to do with the surfeit; it can be stored as fat, given away, or sacrificed. In looking at Aztec culture, where sacrifice—particularly human sacrifice—was routine, Bataille argues that excess consumption subverts the belief common in modern Western cultures that the future must trump the present:

> If I am no longer concerned about "what will be" but about "what is," what reason do I have to keep anything in reserve? I can at once, in disorder,

make an instantaneous consumption of all that I possess. This useless consumption is *what suits me*, once my concern for the morrow is removed. And if I thus consume immoderately, I reveal to my fellow beings that which I am *intimately*: Consumption is the way in which *separate* beings communicate. (Bataille 1989, 58)

Gaillot applies Bataille's theory of excess directly to techno, arguing that its endless dance beats and nonteleological structures "can, of course, only express [techno's] opposition to the fact that existence is ordained exclusively on this sacrifice of the present with a view to the future" (1999, 25).

Within maximal electronic music, excess often leads to discomfort or even pain. Drone music places great physical demands on the listener: to tolerate one or a very small number of static sounds that are often monotonous or even grating and to remain still while the work takes many minutes or even hours to unfold. The assault of a Merzbow or My Bloody Valentine concert forces listeners to brace themselves for volumes that can cause nausea and permanent hearing loss. Even in recordings or live performances of EDM that reside safely within healthy decibel levels, the repetition of seemingly endless beats that do not culminate in any appreciable sort of climax can seem stifling.

And yet many people enjoy listening to these types of music. The pain and tedium of hearing a long, loud single pitch can be accompanied, even eclipsed, by something resembling ecstasy. In his excellent description of watching My Bloody Valentine perform an extended noise section from their song "You Made Me Realise," McGonigal (2007) relates how the band's choice to turn *all* speakers, even monitors, to face the audience led to mayhem. Many fans simply ran out of the concert space; others swayed in confusion and pain. And then the epiphany happened, the transcendent moment when surreally beautiful overtones and harmonics seemed suddenly to descend on a bed of deafening noise. This moment acquired mythic status among My Bloody Valentine audiences and was reproduced at dozens of concerts, to the point where fans expected and even demanded it. According to MBV leader Kevin Shields, though, the epiphany was not brought on by any particular action or event but was rather a psychoacoustical quirk, the moment when excessive volume and pain trigger auditory hallucinations. Nothing changed objectively in the band's playing, nothing was added, and certainly nothing was taken away; it was rather the nature of the listening experience that suddenly embraced with quasi-religious fervor what it had resisted only moments before.

Experiences of the sublime in art often assume the dimensions of religious epiphany. These moments are transactions, trade-offs in which the compensation for agony, imprisonment, or the deprivation of the senses is enhanced appreciation of other sensory faculties. Bataille again proves instructive, especially through his fascination with a 1905 photograph of a Chinese assassin who is tortured to death through the famous *leng chi* or "slow-slicing" method. The torturers cut away portions of the assassin's flesh while keeping him alive and conscious through administering opium. The photograph captures the assassin's upturned face at a moment (one hopes) shortly before his death; he is almost smiling while looking up at the sky, so far beyond the threshold of pain that he is delirious and even joyful (Smith 2001). Bataille and, in the present day, Merzbow mention the sense of liberation that occurs paradoxically through bondage. This explains Merzbow's professed interest in sadomasochism and, as Hegarty (2007, 155–165) explains, his use of noise as an instrument of bondage and discipline. I want to apply these concepts to some static works, not all of which deal with pain or suffering but which do participate in the same sort of transaction, where the limiting of certain musical parameters leads to the enhanced appreciation of other parameters. Or, as the back cover of the SunnO))) album *Black One* puts it, "Maximum volume yields maximum results."

Mechanization, excess, dread, and *delight* should sound familiar, because they are the adjectives used to describe the *technological sublime,* Leo Marx's term for the moment when machines and industrialization began to be perceived as aesthetically legitimate objects rather than mere tools (Marx 2000). Many electronic musicians recycle the discourse of the technological sublime in their work. Cascone's diagnosis of the aesthetics of failure, synth-pop musicians' fidelity to analog instruments, and the importing of the sounds of machinery from rail cars to water-treatment plants in musical works all showcase the simultaneous attraction and repulsion of modern technology. But in the examples just listed, conventional beauty is often lacking. Schaeffer's *Railroad Etude* features the sounds of trains looped into rhythmic patterns but to the exclusion of melody or harmony. Cascone's microsound compositions are usually abstract and certainly avoid anything as commonplace as a consonant chord or cadence. And so the choice of simple, consonant melodies in maximal works is not one we can take for granted. Hegarty (2007) points out that industrial acts such as Merzbow, Nurse with Wound, and Throbbing Gristle perform noise *as noise,* as something dissonant, ugly, and painful. Hegarty is correct with regard to these particular artists, but this observation runs the risk of suggesting that all noise and distortion are necessarily intended as friction or signal jamming that thwarts traditional aesthetics and notions of beauty. In cases where some vestiges of conventional harmonic or melodic beauty linger, the role of noise, repetition, stasis, and distortion shifts to negative beauty, a pleasure that does not conform to Kantian standards of balance and semblance but nonetheless aspires to the condition of beauty. The sublime and the beautiful are thus not so much opposites as they are different destinations along the same trajectory.

Noise in rock music is arguably intrinsic to the medium. Feedback, the assault of a drum set, and the seditious messages of many rock lyrics all seek to subvert the norms for seemly and compliant behavior. But this cliché errs in emphasizing the ugliness of noise over its aesthetic potential. The first act to make noise central rather than peripheral to music was the Velvet Underground. It is important to keep in mind that the two creative forces behind the band were Lou Reed, whose previous job was as composer for a bubblegum pop songwriting factory, and John Cale, whose forays into the New York avant-garde scene included collaborations with John Cage and La Monte Young. Reed brought a rock–and–roll sensibility, while Cale brought drones and extended jam sessions. These two elements were not as diametrically opposed as one might think. The aching quiet of "Candy Says" (1969) is similar to at least the beginning of "Heroin" (1967), but "Heroin" gradually swells in volume until it becomes a screeching roar. Nico's voice complemented the band so well because it was an amalgam of these two tendencies, a soft contralto that could be soothing or strident depending on how much Nico pushed it.

The many bands that derived inspiration from the Velvet Underground tend to borrow more heavily from the noise end of the band's repertoire. Sonic Youth, the Jesus and Mary Chain, and My Bloody Valentine are famous for overloading their tracks with feedback and distortion and playing at extremely loud volumes. But even at their loudest, these bands often play melodies that are at their core consonant. Fennesz provides the best example of this, especially with his 2001 album *Endless Summer*, whose "Caecilia" I discuss in chapter 2. "Caecilia" and other tracks on this album pit the innocence of surf rock against glitches, white noise, and distorted electronic and acoustic instruments. Even more so than *Endless Summer*, Fennesz's earlier album *Plus Forty Seven Degrees 56' 37" Minus Sixteen Degrees 51'08"* (1999) uses bluntly simple materials: cascades of static that threaten to overwhelm a simple sustained major chord. Whereas Cascone might diagnose glitch sounds on their own as signs of frustration with the recorded medium and its failures, when these sounds of failure occur alongside sounds conforming to traditional ideas of beauty, something different is at play: not the critical deconstruction of the boundaries that have marginalized noise from musical language for so long but rather the desire for a return to conventional aesthetic language mixed with the knowledge that such a return is impossible. What makes Fennesz's music so heartbreaking is that it knows that carefree beauty is naive and inaccessible.

Kevin Drumm's reputation as a noise musician is certainly warranted, thanks to sonic assaults such as *Sheer Hellish Miasma* (2002), an album containing unremittingly hostile sounds whose provenance is far from clear. (Drumm is famous for his prepared guitar playing as well as for being able to create seemingly new sounds from conventional instruments and techniques.) His album *Imperial Distortion* (2008) stands out as a surprise and perhaps a return to form, given that his earlier works were generally quieter. *Imperial Distortion* features spare drones that slowly fade in and out of existence. There is virtually no rhythm or even regular pulse to the piece, just a series of ghostly isolated pitches and, from time to time, a sustained chord. This reductive approach continues almost for two entire compact discs, that is, until the last several seconds of the appropriately titled "We All Get It in the End," when Drumm unexpectedly cuts to the type of searing electronic noise typical in *Sheer Hellish Miasma*. This cut is totally unprepared and might well be a joke at the expense of listeners who might have been lulled or even bored by the placidity of the album's previous two hours. Where Fennesz gilds his consonant sounds with noise and distortion, Drumm takes a purist approach; his consonances are spare and unadorned but also unfettered by noise. *Imperial Distortion* can, of course, be heard on its own merits, but its effect is more dramatic when heard with the knowledge of the types of sounds Drumm is capable of producing and indeed *does* produce in the last few moments of the album. Drumm demonstrates that violence and illness (the first track on the album, "Guillain Barré," is named after a debilitating syndrome involving paralysis) are the inevitable companions of beauty.

The examples of consonance and beauty considered here employ rudimentary materials, usually a repeating scalar motive or a sustained note or chord. Moments of beauty and consonance rarely exceed these simple means, probably because to have more complicated melodies or harmonies would distract from the presumed aim of winnowing down musical expression to a few elements that play for long stretches of time. The maximal qualities or excesses in these works stem from how these minimal elements are deployed, eliciting what many listeners describe as an experience like listening from underwater, where sounds reach the ears only through considerable mediation. Negative beauty is a way of mitigating the horror of both noise, which is by definition supposed to be alienating, and consonance, which in its own way can be just as horrific, considering what its presence confirms or denies about the inherent goodness, beauty, or order of the outside world. These examples reveal the world for the dark, oppressive, and yet hope-inspiring place that it is.

Still, such combinations of horror and beauty do not represent all of electronic music. In some extreme variants of electronic music, such as the famous *Filament 1* album as well as some recordings by Merzbow, there are no gestures toward conventional beauty, no consonances or cadences. But unrelenting noise is also absent. Rather, these works present a sort of hermetic purity, a scarcity of materials whose constant repetition underscores the textures of the sounds. *Filament 1* was a 1998 collaboration between Japanese experimental musicians Otomo Yoshihide and Sachiko M. Their album consists of very little besides tiny record snaps and crackles, sine tones, and digital fluttering. It flatly refuses to give listeners anything vaguely musical to grasp. But this refusal paradoxically makes the album eventually emphasize the sensuality of hearing. The minute details in its tiny sounds become beautiful because they are allowed to emerge from an otherwise blank canvas. Merzbow's album *Merzbuddha* (2005) achieves a similar sort of sensuality in listening situations where it is not played at an extremely loud volume, but this is a provision worth mentioning, because Merzbow's concerts often are deafeningly loud. *Merzbuddha*'s sounds are predictably atonal, irregular, and looped, but there is sensuality here, too: throbbing bass ostinatos, occasional record-player cracks, and hiss in the high treble give the listener contrasting textures that offset what might otherwise simply be heard as noise.

Readers might object that I have used the terms *beauty* and *noise* as if they have an a priori definition. This is a reasonable objection, but let me approach the issue in a different manner. Many, if not all, of the musicians I consider here possess a sophisticated knowledge of many types of music, so much so that they are aware of the historical implications inherent in any invocation of tonality. In contemporary art music, it would be considered naive to hear any consonance uncritically, as merely an isolated instance without connection to the rise and fall of functional harmony. This does not mean that we need to hear these works as engaging in a dialogue with Schoenberg or Boulez but only that we should hear them as one might hear a contemporary writer who employs Shakespearean English: as a purposeful use of a language that has in some sense already died.

Now that we've spent some time with works that bristle against interpretation or decoding, we can return to electronic music that does conceive of sound as meaningful. But unlike the works detailed in chapters 1 and 2, those in chapter 5 locate meaning less in the structure or syntax of musical language than in the ways sound can evoke ideas of space, place, or location. The final part of this book, "Situation," attends to two different concerns: how sound is enmeshed in a site and how electronic-music aesthetics emerge from the discourse surrounding genre, distinction, and experimentalism. Chapters 5 and 6 discuss sound as always tinged by its physical and cultural surroundings.

PART III

Situation

5

Site in Ambient, Soundscape, and Field Recordings

We are accustomed to thinking that electronic music, even more than non-electronic music, is concerned with *space*, a quotient of acoustics and spatialization. There are strong justifications for this association, including the numerous works that engage with space as a formal parameter like timbre or structure. Alvin Lucier's *I Am Sitting in a Room* (1969) is one of the most frequently mentioned examples of electronic music's interest in space or, specifically, in how the acoustic properties of a room can alter sound. But space in this work ultimately refers back to listening. It is not enough to know that *I Am Sitting in a Room* loops the sound of Lucier's voice so many times that the reinforced frequencies of the room eventually render his words unintelligible; listeners must hear these transformations over time if they are to have their greatest effect. The piece is most impressive when heard live within the very room where the speaker's voice is slowly being fossilized and rendered unintelligible. In short, *I Am Sitting in a Room* treats space but also the embodiment of listening, the fact that we listen not only as minds or ears but as entire bodies. The concept of space risks reifying electronic works as objects separate from their surroundings, whereas any practical treatment of space in music always hinges on the listener's relationship to sound.

Many other electronic works also address the theme of space, although they, too, end up reflecting back on listening as much as, if not more than, on space. Instead of structuring this discussion around space, we would do well to expand our focus to *site*, which entails not only the environments in which sound propagates but also those that listeners physically and metaphorically occupy. The terms at play in discussions of music and site are *space, place,* and *location. Space,* according to Lefebvre (2000), refers to large-scale sites that could be physical, mental, or cultural in nature and either imaginary or real. *Space* often appears in treatments of acoustics, since it is through the manipulation of sound reverberations that music communicates, truthfully or otherwise, information about the spaces in which it is heard. *Place,* according to Castells (2000), refers to sites that are local and governed by interpersonal, ecological, or political relationships. *Place* entails reflection on the conditions, whether man-made or natural, that produce sound. By *location,* I mean the sheer physical placement of listeners and sound objects. Location can be actual or perceived but is often the latter, since recordings excel at suggesting acoustical situations that do not or cannot exist in real life. When talking about these terms together, I employ the word *site,* which can refer to acoustics, source origins, or cultural associations of sound. In short, the aim of this chapter is to delve into works that regard sound as *situated,* as inextricably bound to a particular spot or trajectory, whether real or imagined, physical or metaphysical. But we should also keep in mind that any musical work, and especially any electronic-music work, is by definition concerned with site. The technologies that enable the capture of temporally and physically distant sounds automatically address the theme of situation, creating schizophonic (when sound is transported from its original cultural context into a new one) and acousmatic (when the source of sound production is hidden from view) conditions that would never otherwise be possible.

Why are the terms *space, place, location,* and *site,* and the admittedly subtle degrees of distinction among them, so important? They all affirm the special quality of sound as a directional phenomenon. In terms of physics, sound is always traveling as vibrations through a medium, which, for our purposes, is usually air. Sound is a vector. It emits from one location and travels to many other locations, and our perception of it depends on our own location in relation to both the sound and our other surroundings. Sound contains information about its origins and trajectories. As Smalley (2007, 38) puts it, sounds are "space-bearers" that "carry their space with them" and even "produce space." But Smalley's enthusiastic reading of sound should be tempered by a more sober realization that sounds do not, *cannot,* indicate as clearly and precisely as visual objects can to those who rely predominantly on sight. The film theorist Christian Metz cautions that

> spatial anchoring of aural events is much more vague and uncertain than
> that of visual events. The two sensory orders don't have the same relation-
> ship to space, sound's relationship being much less precise, restrictive, even
> when it indicates a general direction (but it rarely indicates a really precise
> site, which on the contrary is the rule for the visible). (1980, 29)

Metz's observation chafes against much space-related discourse in electro-acoustic music, which insists on the accuracy with which listeners of acousmatic music can pinpoint sound. These assertions help justify surround-sound systems such as 5.1 or its sequel, 10.2, which have become increasingly common in electroacoustic works of the past ten years (Otondo 2008). Whatever the limits of spatialization, however, it is undeniable that sound is a tantalizing phenomenon that simultaneously discloses and hides a great deal about its origins. Sound is the perfect sign for artists but a maddeningly imprecise one for logicians; it points without confirming and suggests without asserting.

Sound can transmit information about space, place, and location. And depending on the music and the type of listening approach, the same sound can bear different messages about site. This chapter investigates some of those messages. I address the manifestations of site according to genre; thus, I approach space through ambient music, place through soundscape composition, and location through field recording. I conclude by discussing what I call graphic music, which admittedly is not a genre but is still pertinent, since graphic music anchors itself to a particular site by existing as an acoustic translation of visual code. Graphic music does not emit from a location in the same way that the sound of trickling emits from a stream but exists rather as a semiotic emission, a code linking a visual component with an acoustic component.

Throughout this chapter, I intermittently draw on works that are perhaps best described as sound art rather than music because of their direct interaction with the sites in which they are heard. I want to avoid a protracted examination of the aesthetics of sound art and how it is distinct from music but instead refer selectively to electronically produced sound artworks that, in some manner, indicate site. Taken as a whole, the genres and styles at stake in this chapter may seem to have little to do with one another, but what they do share is a propensity for using sound to refer not to abstract concepts but to specific sites and locations. This will prove to be the case even with sound artworks such as those of Francisco López and Toshiya Tsunoda that assert the nonreferentiality of their materials. Their insistence on reduced listening notwithstanding, such works use identifiable materials and evocative titles to gesture far beyond the confines of the work.

Various manifestations of site have generated intense discussion, particularly in Doyle (2005), LaBelle (2006), Licht (2007), Prendergast (2000), and Toop (1995; 2004). These treatments have done the heavy lifting of describing the techniques and specific motivations of site evocation. My purpose here is to reflect on the undercurrents connecting approaches to site that might otherwise seem utterly disconnected. The genres in this chapter all place stock in sound's ability to convey a sense of space, place, and location—to gesture beyond itself, to represent the outside world as a sign. If it seems obvious that sound should act as a sign, consider that this sentiment runs counter to many tendencies in the musical examples covered earlier in this book. Schaeffer's impact on electronic music was to conceive of an ideal (however unattainable) listening experience that brackets out interpretation of signs. Microsound aspires to a blank meaninglessness through its use of base acoustic materials. A great deal of EDM revels in its impassive sounds that defy categorization. Yet the genres considered in this chapter take for granted that sound always indicates some place beyond itself, that it can communicate concretely and clearly to its listeners. The emphasis on site distinguishes these genres from those covered in chapters 1 and 2, which also treat sound as a sign but one that refers to concepts or entities rather than sites or locations. Post-Schaefferian electroacoustic and electronica use sounds as symbols or metaphors, while the music considered here uses sounds for their ability to situate the listener.

AMBIENT MUSIC AND LISTENING SPACE

Ambient musicians in general seem a highly secure bunch, content to make music to be ignored. From Erik Satie's furniture music to Brian Eno's first excursions into contemplative, synthesized repetition, ambient music has lurked on the periphery of the listener's attention, sometimes delightful and other times delightfully boring, always hinting at, rather than imposing, an environment (Toop 1995, 1–22). So it is no small irony that ambient music today invites such close study. Possibly more than any other genre, ambient has encouraged scholars to dissect and critique the listening process, enlisting disciplines ranging from phenomenology and psychoacoustics to aesthetics. The particular quality I want to spotlight here, listening space, is not something easily discussed with technical vocabulary, and I apologize for that in advance. Listening space, especially as writers like Doyle (2005) explain it, is a composite of the perceived spatial characteristics of a work, usually in recorded form, as well as the emotions that those characteristics elicit from the listener.

The listening space that ambient music creates is markedly different from the space we experience in, say, a recording of a Beethoven symphony. One reason for this distinction is the fact that a Beethoven recording (or a recording of virtually any Western art-music work) has a very clear foreground, or area of central activity. Recording engineers mix most commercial recordings to give the impression that one is attending a concert in which the musicians are seated from five to thirty feet in front of the listener and centered according to the axis of the listener's ears. Engineers base their calculation of this acoustical sweet spot on the traditions surrounding the musical material, as well as techniques for spatialization or determining the mix of intensities between the left and right channels in the stereophonic field.

Thanks to its representations in the media, classical music still enjoys prestige in many cultures. Listeners who may not have had much exposure to symphonies might nevertheless have the impression that such works demand concentration. But the manner in which a Beethoven recording is mixed also makes clear that it is intended to occupy the listener's attention. When it is played too softly or at too great a distance to be heard, it still comes across as music to be pondered, albeit at too far a remove for ideal contemplation. Ambient music, on the other hand, uses a slew of methods to make it sound as if it lacks a foreground and thus easily melts into its surroundings. Brian Eno's *Ambient 1: Music for Airports* (1978) provides the template for many later works: repetitive, tonal harmonic language, an absence of abrasive or abrupt attacks, long decays, and nonteleological writing, as if the melody could continue on indefinitely. More recently, KLF's landmark album *Chill Out* (1990) updates this formula with its surgical control over volume and intensity.

Chill Out appeared amid the height of the acid-house craze in Britain during the mid-1990s (Toop 1995, 59–63). Artists Bill Drummond and Jimmy Cauty wanted to create an antidote for acid house's frenetic, incessant rhythms, and *Chill Out*'s static, intermittent samples and pensive drones were the result. *Chill Out* is exotic easy listening, at least for British listeners, because it features the "foreign" sounds of African-American preachers, steel-string guitars, Elvis Presley's stab at social commentary ("In the Ghetto"), freight trains, and Tibetan throat singing. These far-flung sampling choices conform to the habit in hip-hop and EDM of sampling unusual sounds as a form of sonic tourism. But the manner in which the album structures and mixes these samples is what distinguishes *Chill Out* as an ambient work. Many tracks contain the sound of the wind, interrupted occasionally by a train whistle. The centerpiece of each track is usually a guitar slide or else a few enigmatic phrases from a preacher. But each type of material is mixed very softly, so that one has to turn up the recording quite loudly to make out distinct details. *Chill Out* seems to position itself in the background of any space in which it is played, even when it is heard through headphones. A track like "Madrugada Eterna," whose title uses the Portuguese word for the wee hours of the morning, aims at a quietness that is less the result of objective volume than of the stillness often experienced at late hours, when not only sounds but motion and life itself seem muted.

Tetsu Inoue's ambient album *World Receiver* (1996) accomplishes a different goal in referring simultaneously to sounds of public spaces and to the interior of the mind. That Inoue succeeds in invoking public space is no small technical feat. The identity of such sounds, from the murmur of a crowd to the half-hearted grinding of a merry-go-round organ, establishes a sense of being outside, but as so often happens in sample-based music, these materials could have simply been left untreated so as to sound as if they really derive from a studio and only later are replayed in an outdoors location. What makes listeners identify these materials as public and not as something heard privately are reverb, delay, and other types of effects processing, which create the illusion that these sounds are traveling through large, partially enclosed areas. *World Receiver* superimposes these supposedly public sounds, such as a bit of Muzak guitar being played in an outdoor shopping mall, onto static chords or riffs with an entirely different spatial profile. The result is a collision of two different types of acoustics—a reverberant open one and a more restrained private one that suggests interiority, or the music and sounds heard only in the mind. Neither type of material occupies the foreground of the recording. The reverberant acoustic seems positioned far away from the listener, and the interior one seems to emit from within the listener. *World Receiver* ends up resembling less a work of music than the soundtrack of a film that combines diegetic materials, or those that happen inside the narrative frame of public space, with nondiegetic sounds, or those the viewer alone hears.

Normally, discussions of sample-based works such as *Chill Out* or *World Receiver* focus on the provenance of the samples themselves, an approach that, as described in chapter 2, risks overemphasizing listeners' ability to recognize sounds. But I'd prefer to think of these two albums in terms of how they construct listening spaces, which really amounts to how they emphasize listeners' embodiment. Phenomenology can help in this regard, since it has served as a reference point for many ambient and electronic musicians. Merleau-Ponty (2002) builds on Husserl's phenomenological approach, namely that we experience the world through a composite of several different impressions of any one object or phenomenon. From these various individual moments, we construct a gestalt, representative image. Merleau-Ponty's study of World War I amputees led him to conclude that perceptual experience is always inherently corporeal. It is impossible, in other words, to divorce perception from the body, because we have no other frame of reference for experiencing the world.

Merleau-Ponty's embodied phenomenology explains a great deal about the experience of modern artistic practice. Minimalists and site-specific artists drew on Merleau-Ponty to justify their reliance on large objects that filled entire exhibition spaces or even natural objects found outside. Such objects confront the viewer by exceeding the safe protections of frames and museum walls. But Merleau-Ponty's work goes only so far in describing the nature of that corporeal experience. We could react to an artwork by recoiling, by falling asleep, or by laughing. So how does phenomenology connect to the creation of particular types of space? Bachelard (1994), also a seminal source for many electroacoustic musicians, provides the missing link between phenomenology and spatialized music. Bachelard examines how poetry and art invoke memories of the houses in which we grow up, which for Bachelard are the spaces to which our minds return for the rest of our lives. Poetry, says Bachelard, succeeds in returning the reader to feelings experienced in the spaces of childhood, spaces long forgotten or abandoned. These spaces are especially comforting and reassuring against a backdrop of a storm or a loud city; they make the viewer feel protected, bundled, and warm. Bachelard identifies the tendency in numerous artworks to dictate the circumstances—literally, the situation—of their consumption. Just as large, voluminous minimalist sculpture confronts a viewer physically, ambient music excels at creating the impression of an acoustic cocoon that surrounds the listener.

Sound, in other words, can create space, but following Lefebvre (2000), such a space is not merely physical but also psychological, drawing on memory and nostalgia as much as bodily sensation. The two types of space at play in *Chill Out* and *World Receiver* might initially seem to be operating at cross-purposes: the peripheral ambience of *Chill Out* and some moments of *World Receiver* seem distant from the listener, while the interior moments of *World Receiver* seem incredibly close. But both types of space lack the acoustical foreground on which listeners are accustomed to focusing their attention, especially in classical recordings such as Beethoven's Fifth. This foreground encourages a perceptual experience in which the subject is at some remove, but not too far away, from the object, and can therefore listen dispassionately but attentively. The absence of foreground in ambient music undermines the division between the subject and the object by putting the contingencies of our own bodies—their limited ability to hear, their tendencies to intermingle thoughts with sounds—at the forefront of listening.

We turn next to works that go even further than ambient music in thematizing listening. Soundscape compositions make listening a subject in itself rather than taking it for granted as a means of addressing another topic. Some soundscape works achieve this through the creation and manipulation of acoustic spaces, particularly interior spaces, in a manner similar to ambient music. As Stankievech (2007, 56) illustrates, such manipulation achieves an intimacy and introversion that would be unthinkable in works that construct a distanced listening landscape. In soundscapes, however, the purpose of space manipulation is not simply to evoke otherworldly experiences like those in *Chill Out* or *World Receiver*. Through provoking listening experiences of an intensely personal nature, soundscapes hope to attain a higher degree of truth content than that experienced in other forms of art.

SOUNDSCAPE AND TRUTH

In writing about music, there is a robust tradition of personal accounts of listening. During the nineteenth century, music scholars regularly presented public programmatic readings of works. Such educational lectures were intended to make abstract musical language accessible to a wider public. Although modernists looked unfavorably upon these sorts of freely associative interpretations, they enjoyed a resurgence of sorts in the second half of the twentieth century. Barthes's essay "The Grain of the Voice" (1977) bases its discussion of performance on his own personal relationship to Dieter Fischer-Dieskau's voice. More recently, first-person descriptions of the listening process are gaining credibility in music scholarship. Koestenbaum's *The Queen's Throat* (2001) chronicles opera queens' obsessions with vintage recordings, while Ouzounian's work on sound installations (2006; 2009) and Smalley's writing on space in electroacoustic music (2007) number among the latest efforts to ground listening in personal experience.

The motivations behind such listening accounts are at odds with one another. On the one hand, personal accounts of listening claim to document the experience in an objective fashion by including details such as the associations triggered by a particular sound or the listener's physical reaction to a performance. On the other hand, such accounts underscore the contingency of listening on culture, history, physiology, and emotional receptivity. In short, these accounts may aspire toward scientific rigor in their method of representation, yet they also demonstrate the idiosyncrasies of listening, its dependence on a set of circumstances that may not easily be reproduced.

Listening descriptions lie at the consumption end of the spectrum of musical activity. The production-end counterpart to these descriptions is the soundscape composition, a work consisting in large part, if not exclusively, of audio footage of specific locations. Soundscape works can feature purely natural sounds or those of machines or other forms of technology; human voices can be present or absent, depending on the work. Although soundscape compositions might also contain newly composed material, the use of audio footage stakes a claim on objective representation, a quality usually perceived as lacking in material that is entirely composed or improvised. Audio footage ties a soundscape composition to the ecological, social, historical, or cultural dynamics of a specific location, which both personalizes and politicizes the act of listening.

Soundscape compositions grew out of the earliest soundscape recordings by R. Murray Schafer, who during the late 1960s railed against what he perceived as the undesirable encroachment of industrial noise on the city of Vancouver. Schafer taught at Simon Fraser University, where he assembled a group of graduate students to record local environments; this group called itself the World Soundscape Project (WSP). The WSP's first release was *The Vancouver Soundscape* (1973), and in subsequent years, it has made soundscape recordings of towns and cities across Canada as well as western Europe (World Soundscape Project Web page). The lasting contribution of Schafer and his students (among whom Barry Truax and Hildegard Westerkamp in particular have gone on to lead successful careers as composers) has been the creation of the field known as "acoustic ecology," a composite of scholarly, artistic, and political approaches for studying sound's relationship to the environment.

Thanks to its origins within the WSP, soundscape composition often reflects the values of acoustic ecology, chiefly the desire to represent natural acoustic environments free from human-made sound and noise.[1] But soundscape techniques have traveled far beyond the Vancouver clique to permeate electronic music made all over the world, and not all soundscapes are concerned with the protection of natural environments. Soundscapes have been made not only of preindustrial natural settings but also of loud urban neighborhoods, as Tony Schwartz did with his series of sound ethnographies of Puerto Rican immigrants in Manhattan during the 1940s and 1950s (Stoever 2007). The common trait linking ecologically minded soundscapes with cosmopolitan soundscapes is the use of found sounds as documentary footage. Whereas musique concrète composers abstracted found sounds in order to recontextualize them in musical works, soundscapes use footage in a reconstructive manner to convey what it feels like (or at least sounds like) in a given place.

Drever (2002) notes the affinities that soundscape compositions share with ethnography, the strategy of observing a community on its own terms. Ethnographers attempt as much as possible to let a community speak for itself through interviews and testimonials rather than imposing interpretations of a group's behavior or values. Drever points out that because soundscape is so often grouped under the banner of acousmatic music, its connections to ethnography are minimized, if not completely effaced. This is an oversight, because soundscape's reliance on audio footage puts it in line with a trend throughout recent art toward anthropological representation, the use of field materials within the artwork. Drever's touchstone is Hal Foster's essay "The Artist As Ethnographer," which describes the habit among many contemporary artists of incorporating ethnography into their work. One passage in Foster's essay bears quoting in its entirety:

> With a turn to this split discourse of anthropology, artists and critics can
> resolve these contradictory models magically: they can take up the guises of

---

[1] For another approach to music and ecology using conventional musical instruments, see the work of the composer John Luther Adams, as explored in Morris (1998).

*cultural semiologist and contextual fieldworker, they can continue and
condemn critical theory, they can relativize and recenter the subject, all at the
same time.* In our current state of artistic-theoretical ambivalences and
cultural-political impasses, anthropology is the compromise discourse of
choice. (Foster 1996, 183; emphasis in original)

Drever's final assessment of the ethnographic strain in soundscape is quite
positive. He feels that ethnography leads the composer to relinquish complete control over authorship of a work, "engaging in a collaborative process,
facilitating the local inhabitants to speak for themselves" (2002, 25). This
smacks of the inclusive multiculturalism toward which so many artists and
scholars currently gravitate, an attitude informed by poststructuralist and
postcolonial criticism that seeks to reveal and dismantle mechanisms of
power inscribed within artistic practice. Addressing the silent tools of
repression within and outside of composition is a commendable goal, but
the ethnographical impulse in soundscape feeds a belief at odds with this
goal, the idea that sound can be used to imitate reality and impart truth in
an unambiguous manner.

Compared with vision, listening is often valorized as a more inclusive,
passive, and accepting sensory modality. Berendt (1992) characterizes listening as a tool for peaceful resolution of conflict and argues that listening
allows the observed object greater control over how it is represented. This
distinguishes listening from looking, an activity that entails a "gaze" or uni-
directional perception in which the viewer can perceive and objectify without being seen. Berendt goes so far as to ascribe genders to the senses, with
vision being the aggressive masculine while hearing demurs as the nurturing
feminine.

There is some physiological basis for this privileged interpretation of listening. Vision tends to be both more elective and more selective than
listening; we can choose to focus on one object to the relative exclusion of
other things, but we have greater difficulty listening to only one particular
sound object if other sounds are occurring simultaneously. We can close our
eyes to sight altogether, but it is much more difficult to close our ears to or
otherwise disregard sound, as most city dwellers can attest. Listening, in
other words, lies only partially under the control of the listener and provides
a greater opportunity for objects of perception to exercise agency.

Yet the hope inherent in ethnographic soundscape is essentially a scientific one, that objectively true representation is attainable. Westerkamp's
most well-known soundscape, "Kits Beach Soundwalk" (1989), profiles the
sounds of water lapping in tide pools on a beach within earshot of down-
town Vancouver but also features Westerkamp herself narrating the sounds.
She states early on that while she could use studio equipment to fool listeners

into thinking that these tidal sounds are louder than they really are, she chooses instead to filter out the sounds of the city that "interfere" with the sounds of the barnacles Westerkamp wants to hear, the "tiny" voices of nature drowned out by the city. She praises these tiny voices as "healing," "intimate," "energizing," and dream-inspiring, ultimately hearing in them a truth that she finds absent in a city she calls a "monster." Westerkamp's piece idealizes a few different underdogs: women at the mercy of violent men toting guns, nature at the mercy of industrialization, and quietness at the mercy of loudness. Westerkamp clearly intends with these choices to liberate and empower voices that normally go mute. But once sounds are inscribed onto a recording, they, too, assume objectified status, becoming rigid and unchangeable. No matter how inclusive or diverse soundscapes claim to be, they reflect the same sorts of authorial choices made in any other determined work, in which some materials are retained whereas others are discarded. Westerkamp herself admits this when she states in her text for "Kits Beach Soundwalk" that she is using band-pass filters to block out noise from Vancouver. The temptation in listening to soundscape, even if it is not the composer's intention, is to receive the work as a sonic tour, as a slice of life sampling an exotic local or culture. The word *soundwalk* only confirms this—a sonic voyage taken on foot.

The premise of soundscape may be that perception is contingent on culture, history, noise pollution, and the willingness and ability to listen, but soundscape also subscribes to the idea that sound possesses truth content. By this, I mean the belief that sound is unmediated and thus communicates more truthfully than other sensed phenomena. Andra McCartney, a sound artist and composer who has studied and collaborated with Westerkamp, refers to the close connection in soundscape composition between hearing and the sense of touch, repeating the common trope that hearing accesses information more directly and intimately than other senses (2004). This faith in the universally meaningful properties of sound should be surprising, because one thing on which virtually anyone in electronic music can agree is that there is no one unmediated or natural experience of sound. Whether a sound is produced in nature as opposed to in a city does not change its fundamental physical characteristics, the fact that it is a set of vibrations through a medium such as air or water. Certainly, forest sounds are different from freeway sounds, but they are in no way truer or, to vocalize the unspoken implication in much acoustic ecology works and writings, better. Yet the ethnographic impulse in soundscape compositions suggests precisely that: sounds captured in natural environments are more beautiful and enlightening than those we normally hear. Take, for instance, the liner notes to soundscape artist Peter Cusack's album *Where Is the Green Parrot?* (1999), which states: "The pieces use bird song and calls, plus other environmental sounds, to given an aural perspective on some of the attitudes that we humans take towards other species on the planet." Soundscape compositions at their most polemical conceive of nature's sounds, and, by extension, all of nature, as existing in an adversarial relationship with humanity. This leads to the distinction between soundscape works and field recordings, which also use audio footage from a location but do so with a very different intention.

FIELD RECORDINGS AS MUTE OBJECTS

Sound artist Alan Licht complains that the term *sound art* has become a fashionable affectation for experimental musicians who want to "play the art card" (2007, 210–211). For Licht, *music* and *sound art* cannot be regarded as interchangeable terms because of two critical distinctions: music is heard in performance venues, whereas sound art is heard in exhibition spaces; and music is narrative, whereas sound art is immersive.

At first blush, this sort of insistence on the boundaries between two art forms whose own definitions are murky might seem like quibbling. There is also the risk of overgeneralization: not all music is narrative in the sense that Licht means of having materials that develop and transform through the course of a work. But Licht's desire to explain what makes sound art unique is nonetheless understandable. The prevalent definitions of *sound installations* and *sound art* (Cox and Warner 2004; Davis 2003; Licht 2007; LaBelle 2006) assert that this difference amounts to site-specificity, meaning that sounds are constructed to interact with the locations where they are heard. Through this emphasis on location, site-specific artworks expose the artificial demarcation between themselves and the venues in which they occur, venues that, according to the logic of autonomous art, are meant to be invisible and thus exempt from critical examination. This interaction with location could be acoustical, as in enlisting the particular spatial characteristics of an environment, or it could be thematic, as in incorporating aspects of a particular location's history, culture, or ecology (Kwon 2002). In both scenarios, site-specificity critiques the boundaries that have traditionally separated the artwork from the outside world. Sound art therefore encompasses not only sounds but the architectural and acoustical properties that shape and nurture them, as well as the larger societies that generate them.

While it is certainly true that many works of sound art are site-specific in the sense outlined above, not all are. Consider field recordings by two people frequently described as sound artists, Toshiya Tsunoda and Francisco López. Although Tsunoda and López have done extensive work with site-specific installations, the recordings I discuss here—Tsunoda's *Scenery of Decalcomania* (2003) and *Ridge of Undulation* (2005) and López's *La Selva* (1998),

Buildings (New York) (2001), and *Wind (Patagonia)* (2007)—are commercially available, inherently mobile, and thus detached from any particular venue or aural architecture. They can be heard whenever and wherever the listener likes, and seem best suited to the interior experience of headphone listening. In other words, they are not site-specific in the typical sense. Yet they seem equally ill served by the moniker of *music*. Sparse and long-lasting, these field recordings display little of the editing or compositional intervention that categorize much musique concrète and acousmatic music. Tsunoda's and López's works are found objects of long duration and minute detail, studied explorations of natural phenomena whose status as aesthetic objects is nonetheless patent.

How, then, can these field recordings count as site-specific sound art? One answer is to interrogate one of the primary criteria of site-specific art, that its materials foreground culture and history. I propose a more inclusive definition, namely that the boundaries that separate the work from the outside world are blurry. In other words, we can understand site-specific sound art as any art that *in some manner* (but not necessarily through the lens of culture) addresses the topics of site and location. A great deal of site-specific art launches the work into the outside world while also drawing the outside world into the artwork through explicit appeals to social issues. In Tsunoda's and López's field recordings, however, these same boundaries are semipermeable: the artwork leaves the exhibit space to inhabit the world, but the world does not impinge on the artwork's materials, which the artists treat as self-referential, autonomous, and primary. This difference distinguishes Tsunoda's and López's field recordings from soundscape compositions such as those considered above that also make use of audio footage from a particular location but do so in order to address issues pertaining to ecology or culture.

To elaborate on this position, I want to situate Tsunoda's and López's field recordings amid Pierre Schaeffer's advocacy for reduced listening, which emerges as an important tool for larger reflections of site-specificity, because it provides a vocabulary for discussing works whose relationship to a particular location is not based on the usual concerns of social relevance. In particular, reduced listening is pertinent for such field recordings because it clarifies some artists' efforts to appropriate specific locations as autonomous objects free of residual associations.

For the past two decades, Toshiya Tsunoda has made field recordings that capture the collisions and interactions of vibrations. He works mostly in and around his hometown of Yokohama, Japan, and has recorded sounds both large (ferries as they shuttle across harbors) and small (birdsongs as heard through the tailpipe of an automobile) in scale. During the 1990s, Tsunoda was affiliated with WrK, a collective of artists who focused on discovering latent materials within natural processes and cultural formalities. This tenure with WrK honed Tsunoda's talent for unearthing the aesthetic out of the mundane. His two recent releases, *Scenery of Decalcomania* (2003) and *Ridge of Undulation* (2005), contain largely anonymous sounds: the wind as it blows through a metal railing, low resonances as heard through very large pipes, waves gently breaking on beaches covered with coarse sand and stones, and so on. His choices tend toward sounds that invite treatment as raw materials: "I don't have a decisive reason for choosing a location, but rather, it's simply that places I know well have a sense of familiarity. However, it must be a location without any sort of special characteristics, such as a fishing port, warehouse, etc." (Tsunoda 2007, 86).

Locations "without any sort of special characteristics" yield sounds that are anonymous and become abstract after only a few moments. The track "Wind Whistling" from *Scenery of Decalcomania* is a seven-minute recording of the wind blowing through the rails of a metal footbridge. Changes in wind intensity produce what sounds like a wandering atonal melody with occasional dyads and triads. The duration of the track is long enough to lull any initial curiosity about the way these sounds are produced. The hermetic melody is offset at times by intrusions from the outside world—a ferry horn or a distant airplane engine. These brief incidents draw attention to the place of the microphone (and, by extension, the listener) in relation to the wind sounds; the microphone must be close to the railing, very close, as the outside world seems very far away.

Tsunoda is forthcoming about the origins of his sounds; his titles describe them in general and sometimes even specific terms ("Filmy Feedback," "Curved Pipe," "At Stern, Tokyo Bay, 11 December 1997," etc.), and his liner notes give even more information, notably the claim that he does not edit or process any of his materials (Haynes 2005), limiting his intervention to the choice and placement of microphones. It is unclear why Tsunoda makes this statement, given that his recordings do, in fact, display some signs of processing. What is clear is that Tsunoda treats these materials as integral materials, and for the most part, if editing or processing have taken place, that is not manifest. And despite the transparency with which he reveals his sources, Tsunoda regards the provenance of sounds as purely incidental: "Hearing an incident as music is a matter of cultural backgrounds. That's also interesting but I never expect . . . it" (Plop 2007).

Sound artist Francisco López assumes a similar approach in his numerous field recordings. I focus here on the trilogy of *La Selva* (1998), containing sounds of a rain forest in Costa Rica; *Buildings (New York)* (2001), containing sounds of offices, apartments, and studios in Manhattan and Brooklyn; and *Wind (Patagonia)* (2007), containing sounds of the wind blowing through open spaces in southern Argentina. Unlike many of López's works that are referred to simply as "Untitled" with a number, this trilogy lists explicit information concerning sound origins. All three works feature copious liner notes with photographs of the locations, as well as precise timings for each event within the recording. For example, *Buildings* captures the repetitive, mechanized sounds of air conditioners, computers, and boilers. The recording features ten different building environments, each of which plays for a few minutes before fading into the next. By following along with the liner notes, the listener can know at any moment where and when a particular section was recorded. Despite this wealth of detail, however, López discourages attention to the sources of sound, or causal listening. In his preface for *Buildings*, he writes:

> You might want to know about the background philosophy behind this work and about its specific spatial-temporal "reality." I didn't want to omit these referential levels, because they irremediably exist and I have indeed dealt with them. But I also wanted to emphatically give you the opportunity to skip them, to have them in your hands and decide purposefully not to access them. My recommendation is—having the knowledge of their existence—to keep them closed. This is not a game or a trick; it is a confrontation with the relational frameworks that blur our experience of the essential.

The approaches outlined by Tsunoda and López are clearly indebted to Schaeffer's reduced listening, which has been discussed extensively elsewhere (Chion 1983; Emmerson 2007; Kane 2007) and which I also treat in chapter 1, so I only touch on the most pertinent concepts here. Schaeffer describes reduced listening as the intention to listen only to the sound object (*objet sonore*), his term for sounds divorced from their source, medium, and notation. Reduced listening does not come easily; listeners are naturally inclined to hear sounds either for their informational value (i.e., where they come from, how they are produced) or for their signification (i.e., what they mean). Reduced listening thus entails a phenomenological reduction, a bracketing out of information in order to arrive at an essential sound or a sound before associations have been ascribed to it. With practice, listeners can develop the discipline necessary to free themselves from the habits of acculturated listening.

Of the works considered here, Tsunoda's encourage a modified form of reduced listening, not through hiding the origins of his sounds but through acknowledging them in an understated manner. The titles of tracks on *Scenery of Decalcomania* are indicative of this approach, because they provide less information about the specifics of the recordings than do the titles of the later album, *Ridge of Undulation*. "Unstable Contact," the opening track on *Scenery*, makes manifest that the sounds therein are of some sort of electrical signal. But with a duration of more than seventeen minutes, the listener's curiosity about how that unstable contact is produced gradually dissipates. These repetitive sounds, which do not evolve much over the course of the track, instill a sort of semantic fatigue, so that eventually, they seem cut adrift from the source origins announced in their titles.

López's proposed reduced listening poses more challenges to the listener. He goes to great pains to document his sources, yet he then asks listeners to choose not to attend to this information, recalling Schaeffer's descriptions of reduced listening as a "discipline" and an "intention of listening" that must be practiced in order to overcome our natural tendencies toward causal listening. As with Schaeffer's original formulation of reduced listening, López's ambivalent stance toward sound identification might require from the listener a certain indulgence in order to appreciate the intention behind López's directives, even though the execution of his premise actually elicits causal listening. And while López is also savvy enough to acknowledge the cultural character of the sounds he uses—

> My music is loaded with a multitude of cultural references, from the soundtrack of "Eraserhead" to some sound approaches in Buddhism. Whether or not these are apparent is more a question of perception than of explicit explanation. What is essential to it, though, is the fact that I don't attach myself to any specific system of aesthetic, conceptual or spiritual beliefs. I think its universal reach potential is dependent upon the individual—more than social or cultural—attitudes concerning listening and creation. (López 2000)

—he feels strongly that musical materials should not be reduced to their associative properties:

> There can only be a documentary or communicative reason to keep the cause-object relationship in the work with soundscapes, never an artistic/musical one. Actually, I am convinced that the more this relationship is kept, the less musical the work will be (which is rooted in my belief that the idea of absolute music and that of *objet sonore* are among the most relevant and revolutionary in the history of music). . . . A musical composition (no matter whether based on soundscapes or not) must be a free action in the sense of not having to refuse any extraction of elements from reality and also in the sense of having the full right to be self-referential, not being subjected to a pragmatic goal such as a supposed, unjustified re-integration of the listener with the environment. (López 1997)

The universal qualities to which López refers are those qualities that remain *after* sounds' cultural references have been bracketed out, resembling what in Schaeffer's reduced listening is the repression of the information-gathering and meaning-gathering listening modes, *écouter* and *comprendre* (Kane 2007, 18).

The stumbling blocks interfering with the reception of these field recordings have to do with their allegiance to reduced listening as well as their mobility and detachment from any particular site of listening. First, as detailed in chapter 1, reduced listening is problematic on two fronts. It is difficult to do at a practical level, because humans are conditioned to attend to the source origins of a sound. More fundamentally, reduced listening assumes an a priori listening experience that precedes history and culture, a stance that sharply diverges from the general consensus that sound perception is necessarily a socially inscribed experience. Second, anticipating Licht's insistence on the site-specificity of sound art, Hegarty writes that sound art

> either has to be an installation where the sound occupies a certain space (or exceeds it) or a performance. Transportable works can be sound art (particularly if we take self-description as a useful marker), if they are headphone pieces that "guide" you around a town aurally (Hildegard Westerkamp, Janet Cardiff) or maybe set up an environment, through site-specific sound recordings, other than the one you are in (Richard Long, Chris Watson), even if only listening on headphones in the gallery. A CD of sound art that gets played at home seems less fully part of sound art—despite the growth of field recordings, ambiences, and recordings of installations. (Hegarty 2007, 171)

One might quip that under Hegarty's criteria, all that is necessary for a work to be counted as sound art is a stereo set up in an exhibition space; playing a recording in a gallery of Beethoven's Fifth Symphony, something otherwise universally agreed to be music, could therefore be considered sound art. This is a flippant joke, but Hegarty, in fact, discusses a very similar installation by Janet Cardiff, her "Forty-Part Motet" in which sixteenth-century composer Thomas Tallis's "*Spem in alium nunquam habui*" is played back with forty speakers, each transmitting the voice of an individual singer. As observers walk through the installation, their perception of the piece changes according to which speaker they hear most closely. The resulting effect is of both the totality of the Tallis work and the ways in which a single singer contributes to the whole listening experience.

Cardiff is one of the most prominent sound-installation artists active today, and there is (to my knowledge) no debate about whether "Forty-Part

Motet" counts as sound art.[2] This is fine, and I agree with Licht and Hegarty that the category of sound art is more meaningful if it is distinct from the category of music. But if works such as "Forty-Part Motet" are accepted as sound art solely on the basis of their anchoring in a physical location (since the material of this work is unoriginal and firmly established as music), would it not be fair to take into account works that exist conversely as being sound art entirely on account of material, in the absence of such anchoring? Is site-specificity determined only by physical placement, or can it also be invoked through materials?

To answer these questions, it's helpful to consult minimalist visual art, which inspired so many subsequent site-specific artworks. In Michael Fried's 1967 critique of minimalism, "Art and Objecthood" (an essay discussed in detail in chapter 3), he seizes upon one undesirable trait of minimalist sculpture in particular: its cultivation of *presence* at the expense of *presentness*. Presence coincides with theatricality, which Fried says

> confronts the beholder, and thereby isolates him, with the endlessness not just of objecthood but of *time*; or as though the sense which, at bottom, theatre addresses is a sense of temporality, of time both passing and to come, *simultaneously approaching and receding*, as if apprehended in an infinite perspective. (Fried 1998, 167)

That is, minimalist art asserts itself physically so that the observer is forced to contend with it as a corporeal presence rather than as simply an artwork removed from the sphere of the observer (Davis 2003, 208–210). In other words, the boundaries between the artwork and the outside world are breached. Fried contrasts minimalism's presence with modernism's present-ness, which for him is inherently better, because "*at every moment the work itself is wholly manifest*" (Fried 1998, 167). A work that exhibits presentness is instantaneously manifest, while a work that lacks presentness requires that the observer absorb it from different perspectives over time. Presentness takes the beholder out of the work, while presence necessitates the physical presence of the beholder.

Admittedly, both presentness and presence would be elusive for any recorded work, the former because recordings unfold over time and thus cannot be apprehended in a single moment, the latter because the listener is aware that he or she can never truly be in the presence of the event because it has already happened in the past. Nonetheless, Tsunoda's and López's

---

[2]Cardiff refers to her work as sound "installations" rather than sound art, a designation that under-scores her interest in the relationship of the perceiver's body to the work. This specification notwith-standing, Cardiff's output is routinely mentioned in inventories of sound art.

explanations of their field recordings resonate with this idea of presence and thus suggest an alternative mode of site-specificity. Tsunoda distinguishes between the ideal of universal perception (an ideal because perception can never be the same for everyone) and the lived experience of perception, which entails an awareness of the listener's body in relation to sounds. Because Tsunoda's recordings capture sounds that are often so unusual and require unusual microphone placement, they draw heightened attention to the placement of the listener's body in relation to the sounds. "Curved Pipe" (from *Scenery of Decalcomania*), for instance, contains drones captured near the opening of a pipe. The track encourages the listener to imagine hearing these same sounds directly, even if this would require the impossible situation of fitting into a pipe. López's appeals for reduced listening also downplay the importance of objective knowledge about sounds in favor of an undetermined, individual engagement with sounds as standalone objects. The textures of his sounds in *La Selva*, for instance, are so rich and multileveled, from close-by frogs to distant birds, that the listener has a strong sense of the breadth of the sonic environment. So even when the listener can successfully disregard the origins of sounds, their placement within the stereophonic field conveys the sense of a large, voluminous space. Thus, while these recordings are in reality mobile and untethered, they intimate that the listener is in a specific location in close proximity to the sounds.

Tsunoda's and López's field recordings ultimately demand a high price from their listeners in asking for a type of listening that simultaneously attends to and disregards site. But even this type of listening benefits from the close relationship between the sounds and the things they are supposed to represent. "Curved Pipe" does, at some level, seem like something that could be heard from inside a pipe. The works discussed in the next section take the idea of site to its most abstract extreme in translating sound not from other sounds but from visual image.

GRAPHIC MUSIC

Kittler (1999) observes that the three technologies of the gramophone, film, and the typewriter operate as media, mechanisms by which one type of information is transferred through another type of messenger. The gramophone, for instance, translates acoustic vibrations into physical etchings on a record that are then transmitted as electrical signals into an amplifier, where they are subsequently reanimated as acoustic vibrations. Kittler also notes that contemporary technologies are eroding the very boundaries that used to justify separating different sorts of data. In the coming years, Kittler anticipates the rise of pure data, of flows and streams of information that could be experienced as music, film, statistics, or other phenomena. (Perhaps coincidentally, Miller Puckett, the developer of the digital signal-processing application Max/MSP, has also developed a programming language called Pure Data for use in interactive computer music and multimedia works.)

In keeping with Kittler's work, many media theorists have speculated about the slippage between sound and vision throughout the twentieth century, leading to numerous attempts to create a music that could somehow translate visual information. Rilke's famous 1919 essay "Primal Sound," which Kittler reproduces in its entirety, sets the scene: the poet remembers his science teacher's construction of a rudimentary phonograph and, upon studying anatomy several years later, is inspired to "read" the sutures of a human skull with a gramophone needle, leading to what Rilke expects would be a primal ur-sound. Kittler writes of Rilke's fantasy:

> What the coronal suture yields upon replay is a primal sound without a name, a music without notation, a sound even more strange than any incantation for the dead for which the skull could have been used.
> Deprived of its shellac, the duped needle produces sounds that "are not the result of a graphic transposition of a note" but are an absolute transfer, that is, a metaphor. (Kittler 1999, 44–45)

In the wake of Rilke's essay, the urge to translate visual images into sound and vice versa has become nothing short of an obsession. Kittler relates Moholy-Nagy's 1923 envisioning of a music that would inscribe marks directly onto a record, marks that lacked "any previous acoustic existence" (Kittler 1999, 46). Other examples beyond Kittler's make clear the fascination that visualized music commands. Although Adorno initially distrusted phonographs for their poor audio quality and what he perceived as their tendency to stultify listeners' attention, he later praised recordings precisely for their capacity to isolate and render repeatable musical moments that would simply pass fleetingly in live performance. He also called for the rise of a music that would be performed directly from the grooves of a record, a music in which those grooves would be the primary material rather than a weak method of secondary capture (Levin 1990). And in 1953, Iannis Xenakis began composing *Metastasis*, a work for strings deriving from a visual design whose smooth, continuous lines recall architectural blueprints. (Those lines would go on to inspire Le Corbusier's design for the Philips Pavilion, which was the installation site for Edgard Varèse's *Poème électronique* in 1958.) Xenakis assigned specific pitches, durations, and instruments to points along these lines, arguably culminating in the first music composition to make good on the promise of sonicizing visual image.

Xenakis also conceived of a mechanical device that would convert visual images directly into musical notation. By 1977, Xenakis made this device a reality: the UPIC, or Unité Polyagogique Informatique du CEMAMu (Centre d'Etudes de Mathématiques et Automatiques Musicales). Xenakis used the UPIC to draw the contours that became musical materials in his composition *La Légende d'Eer*.

Ryoji Ikeda's album *Test Pattern* (2008) still adheres to musical forms even though it

> is based around a cross-platform conversion system that takes any format of data (whether auditory, textual or pictorial) as a source to be transformed into barcode patterns. This product is then re-constituted as audio data, ready to be sculpted into composed structures by Ikeda. Consequently, the sound artist is able to standardize all media and all types of information, reconfiguring everything within the parameters of that familiar language of his: high frequency tones and digital noise. (Boomkat 2008b)

This review somewhat overstates the novelty of Ikeda's work. *Test Pattern* certainly sounds like music; its regular, rhythmic grooves make that apparent. I wonder if Ikeda might, in fact, have worked backward from rhythmic patterns to bar codes, or at least whether he might have generated data streams on the basis of their ability to translate into regular rhythmic patterns. Regardless, *Test Pattern* continues the early-twentieth-century project for hearing the music in visual images.

Veteran noise musician and Fluxus artist Yasunao Tone offers the most radical answer to Rilke's challenge. His *Musica Iconologos* (1994) is a computerized, acoustic realization of two images, "Jiao Liao Fruits" and "Solar Eclipse in October," whose titles come from the names of Chinese characters. Rather than using the characters themselves as the source image, Tone assembled for each image a composite of multiple photographs, which he then digitized into pixels that could subsequently be translated into acoustic code. *Musica Iconologos* sets up an arbitrary relationship of the signifier (pixels in the two images) to signified (sounds), an arrangement that demands absolute "faith"—the term Robert Ashley uses in his introductory essay in the liner notes—that "the sound is an encoded description of the picture in utmost detail. In the mythical future (or today) somebody can translate the sounds of this compact disc back into pictures." Given these variables, one might expect *Musica Iconologos* to sound chaotic and unmusical, but for a listener sympathetic to post-1945 experimental music, this work sounds no less musical than any serialist or aleatoric work. And *Musica Iconologos* complicates the tension between highly determined serialism and supposedly author-free indeterminacy. The piece displays authorial control to the extent that Tone and his collaborators, principally sound editor Craig Kendall, decided how to translate image into sound through converting a pixelized version of each image into binary ones and zeros that are then translated into different types of sound. But the choice of which binary codes lead to which sounds is arbitrary; a given combination of pixels could just as easily have resulted in the sound of a plucked string or a pitchless drum attack as the digitalized chirps in Tone's realization. In other words, there is no one preferred correlation between the images and their sonic analogs. But the description of *Musica Iconologos* makes it impossible to hear the piece as a Cageian exercise in compositional self-effacement. Once the composer claims that this piece is an acoustic translation of a graphic image, he opens a Pandora's box in the listener's mind, inciting us to speculate about how a given musical figure could relate to a given aspect of the image.

Graphic music implies a source that lies halfway between idea and reality. The "sites" on which *Test Pattern* and *Musica Iconologos* dwell are abstract, digital codes, yet they are also visible, physical objects that we can view while listening to the works. However impossible it might be to discern in those visual objects some correlation to the sounds we hear, such sites present themselves as texts or scores that generate music. Graphic musical works are signs whose signifiers are not concepts but locatable objects. In this sense, they depart substantially from most musical works, which take as their basis either ideas or, in the case of music that imitates sounds of the outside world, sounds. Even in the case of the latter, the source from which the work derives lies within the realm of sound. Graphic music, by contrast, derives from outside itself and from specific locations. For this reason, graphic music is an anomaly, an anchoring of a phenomenon that is by definition always in flux and never tied to one location.

In the next and final chapter of this book, I approach the theme of situation not in terms of specific musical or acoustic materials but rather in terms of how electronic-music participants perceive themselves in relation to one another. Aesthetic theory can easily focus on the intrinsic qualities of artworks while ignoring *why* those qualities exist. Chapter 6 examines how notions of genre and experimentalism situate electronic-music practice, as well as why it is so important for practitioners to feel that they are breaking new ground.

6

Genre, Experimentalism, and the Musical Frame

The questions inherent in genre—what it does for listeners, why so many genres exist—dog any discussion of music aesthetics, but especially so for electronic music, since so many genres and subgenres seem to qualify as some form of electronic music. In the first five chapters of this book, I have refrained from addressing the topic of aesthetics head-on and likewise have taken as self-evident the existence of certain distinct genres of electronic music. But we cannot take definitions of either aesthetics or genre for granted, nor can we assume that the two exist independently of each other. This chapter addresses the relationships between aesthetics and genre: How do aesthetics determine our understanding of electronic-music genres, and, conversely, how do genres affect our understanding of electronic-music aesthetics? I argue here that what motivates the effort to categorize and demarcate different genres is a growing confusion about the experience of listening to electronic music. The word *music* might no longer adequately describe the strange sounds, structures, and situations of this new acoustic landscape. Insistence on the small-scale distinctions among genres delays larger reflections on how *all* of electronic music differs from everything that has preceded it. Yet we often disregard patent similarities between otherwise disparate forms of electronic music simply because we have grown accustomed to the idea that different spheres of electronic-music production are unrelated.

Much of the difficulty in talking about electronic-music aesthetics lies in identifying what electronic music is and deciding whether it is too big to discuss as one entity. Most practitioners would probably agree that electronic music as a whole is too heterogeneous to be considered as a single genre. But if so, at what level of specification do the genre demarcations appear? Is it enough to distinguish between high and popular forms of electronic music, or should those entities constitute metagenres instead of genres? What do *high* and *popular* now mean, anyway? And if we hone down the level of specification to what an online music store might consider style, whether ambient, electroacoustic, or techno, does the specificity we can gain from such labels outweigh the confusion that an ever-proliferating number of styles creates for listeners and practitioners alike? In short, we can ask one succinct question: What do we expect genre to do for our understanding of electronic music?

I want to answer these questions with the help of three texts having to do with genre: John Frow's book *Genre*, Kembrew McLeod's article on genres and subgenres in EDM, and Charles Kronengold's article on genre slippage in disco, album-oriented rock, and New Wave. Frow explains genre as a method of communicating knowledge: "Genre, we might say, is a set of conventional and highly organized constraints on the production and interpretation of meaning" (Frow 2005, 10). With even a passing awareness of the genre to which a work belongs, audiences can make predictions about what the work will and will not do. This, of course, does not commit the work to follow the dictates of a genre to the letter but instead informs audiences that may react with surprise, disappointment, curiosity, or approval when a work breaks its genre's rules.

Genre is, of course, not an abstract quality but a quotient of social relations and consumer decisions. McLeod (2001) makes this clear in his discussion of the multitude of dance-oriented electronica genres, which often amount to a series of provocative labels for types of music that a nonexpert might hear as indistinguishable from one another. Genre labels are effective marketing tools in formats such as electronica where insider information and subcultural capital are prized possessions and where media pit authentic music undergrounds against a repressive music mainstream (Thornton 1995, 116–137). So while genre can, according to Frow, illuminate something about a work, it can also place great expectations on a listener's knowledge. Genre is, in other words, a way of cultivating an us-and-them attitude that divides the public into those who know something about a given music and those who do not.

Kronengold's examination (2008) of late-1970s genres such as disco and New Wave reminds us that just as songs fit into genres, songs also contain genres. Many disco songs casually invoke the conventions of other genres such as Top 40 pop without abandoning their own disco-dance format. A good disco producer would have thus manipulated genre as easily and with as much latitude as song structure or instrumentation. But unlike other malleable musical parameters like structure or interpretation, genre communicates knowledge about the context of a musical work. It situates works in a manner analogous to the way a particular sound in a field recording or a soundscape composition situates a work within a geographical locale or cultural background.

To bring this discussion back to electronic music, consider the term *minimalism*. I already mentioned the disagreement about its definition in chapters 3 and 4. Some listeners think that minimalism refers to the works of American composers such as John Adams, Philip Glass, Steve Reich, and La Monte Young, from which they deduce that minimalist music features repetitive rhythms with consonant harmonies. But there's the rub: there are many examples of music with these characteristics that might otherwise seem unrelated to one another. Fink (2005) gives an analysis of one such piece, Donna Summer's "Love to Love You Baby" (1975), which he compares with Reich's *Music for 18 Musicians* (1976). Most people would agree that these two works fall into different genres. "Love to Love You Baby" counts as disco, while *Music for 18 Musicians* counts as Western art chamber music. So if we consider both as minimalist, is minimalism therefore a metagenre, a style, or a subgenre? And is there any point to quibbling over such fine points of nomenclature?

Fink's solution to this Gordian knot is to sidestep definitions of genre altogether and instead to divest minimalism of its pretensions toward abstraction and meaninglessness. By demonstrating the structural affinities between Summer's and Reich's work, he affirms minimalism's connection to American culture, particularly to the use of repetition in advertising. Many genres are minimalist for Fink, in other words. Fink's book scores two blows in rooting minimalism in history and culture, as well as arguing for the aesthetic legitimacy of disco. But Fink also gives the impression that minimalism's pretensions at abstraction and autonomy are mere snobbery. I'd like to question this assumption, for while we might personally disagree with the claims of an artist or of a work toward aesthetic superiority, we nonetheless have to be aware of the existence of such claims. Opinions about aesthetic distinction and excellence are important, because they create a feedback loop among artists and audiences, reinforcing certain musical traits while stifling others. Aesthetic theory, in other words, can and should recognize opinions about artistic value, because genre is, after all, a mechanism for practitioners to maintain the value or quality of an art form. Genre tells us that artworks will behave a certain way, and when they don't, either they have a good reason for doing so, or else they have failed to heed their genre's rules. The existence of so many genres and subgenres in electronic music begins to make sense if we understand genre as an outgrowth of aesthetic theory.

AESTHETICS AND EXPERIMENTALISM

Many humanists and artists look warily on aesthetics as being commensurate with assertions of artistic worth, and with some reason. For many years, aesthetic theory boiled down to arguments about the superiority of one artwork at the expense of another. In the present academic climate of multiculturalism and canon deconstruction, aesthetic theory might seem dangerously reactionary. Yet aesthetic theory can offer more than proclamations about artistic quality. In the case of electronic music, returning to the basic questions of aesthetic theory can, in fact, help clarify some of the messy issues that the proliferation of genre has stirred up. This book's introduction presented some of these questions, such as what exactly are aesthetics, anyway? Are they synonymous with preferences for taste or style, or do they entail something else in addition to taste and style? Can we derive one common aesthetic from a disparate collection of electronic genres? And if so, does the effort to find this common aesthetic contradict the project in cultural studies and sociology of demonstrating the contingency of art on culture? More to the point, is it necessary to separate aesthetics from cultural studies? The answers to these queries are, of course, far from self-evident: the field of aesthetics is widely contested, and there are many arguments for and against its usefulness.

One preliminary response to these questions is that aesthetics are the shared values concerning what is good, entertaining, and compelling art. But if aesthetics were only this, then this book would and should be nothing more than a case study of opinions, an ethnography of the views about the field of electronic music—in short, something resembling more a work of journalism or scientific investigation rather than philosophy. I have felt it necessary to intervene, however, and to introduce observations that do not necessarily square with predominant views in electronic-music communities. In other words, I am not an invisible or transparent observer in this field but bring to this discussion my own ideologies and values.

My reasons for what to discuss and what to exclude in the aesthetics of experimental electronic music are obviously not exempt from scrutiny. My perspective reflects my social, cultural, and economic situation. I have written about the music to which I have access, and a great deal of that access hinges on my having heard or read about an artist (something that is frequently a result of coincidence or good fortune), as well as on the availability of the artist's recordings. My status as a privileged academic who has attended universities with generously endowed music departments that support electronic music also informs my perspective. This set of circumstances naturally gives me a view of electronic music that might strike some as myopic but to others might seem overly generalist at the expense of exhaustive knowledge of one particular genre.

Yet taking the generalist approach is, in fact, the point of this book. The first five chapters describe elements related to the preoccupation with sound as either meaningful or mute. Each genre I consider has its own values and methods for approaching sound and for deciphering any meaning it might possess, but all strategies share one trait: a subscription to the ideal of experimentalism. The first task of this chapter is thus to reexamine what I regard as an unquestioned quality shared among all forms of experimental electronic music: the persistent subscription to what Bourdieu (1987) explains as a rhetoric of distinction, when listeners tout a genre's or subgenre's high-culture status, independence from commercialism, and resistance to mass culture. The distinctions among electronic-music genres and metagenres reflect beliefs about how experimental music should behave in relation to some vaguely defined mainstream. Fundamental, then, to this aesthetics of recent experimental electronic music is a consideration of what experimentalism entails and how the concept of experimentalism simultaneously unites and divides both listeners and genres.

Experimentalist discourse rides on two assumptions: that experimental music is distinct from and superior to a mainstream-culture industry and that culture and history determine aesthetic experience. It is strange that experimentalists embrace both of these positions, since the two originate from opposite sides of a debate between Kantian aesthetic theorists and Marxist critical theorists. Wolff (1993) has fruitfully mapped out the terrain of this debate as it applies to art criticism in general, and I rely here on her summary as well as a few key texts pertaining to music. Kant (2000, 55–56) himself wrote that aesthetic experience entails the appreciation of beauty, which all humans universally can recognize and appreciate. Beautiful art is something that is *autonomous* and possesses *purposive purposelessness*—autonomous because its pleasing qualities reside within the artwork itself and do not reflect the conditions that led to its creation and purposively purposeless because the artwork does not need to "do" any work in order to legitimize its existence. Kant maintains that while questions of taste are subjective, beauty is objective and self-evident—anyone can recognize it. Many philosophers and critics have upheld Kant's position since the late eighteenth century. One of his more notable advocates was Hanslick (1986), who argued that music needs to be detached from programmatic narrative and even text. Scruton (1997) has provided a comprehensive aesthetics of Western art music that seeks meaning within the musical text itself, in terms of its structure, syntax, and performance. Scruton dismisses attempts to "read" music as either a language or a reflection of cultural or sociological concerns outside itself. What Hanslick and Scruton both take from Kant is the position that good music is universally recognizable because it conveys eternal messages rather than those contingent on social situation, time, or place. Good music is also universally meaningful and cannot be reduced to one specific reading, whether that reading emerges from a composer's program or a scholar's analysis. In the hands of Scruton as well as Adorno (2002a; 2002b), the Kantian position has justified the superiority of Western art music over pop, jazz, and world musics.

The Marxist refutation of Kantian aesthetics contends that aesthetic experience cannot be disinterested, autonomous, or divorced from everyday experience. This position reflects the larger Marxist project of dismantling notions of ahistorical transcendence. In the Marxist worldview, power relations always mediate aesthetic experience, which means that universal standards of good art simply cannot exist. Bourdieu (1987), for instance, identifies "cultural capital," the perceived prestige we gain through aligning ourselves with specific types of art, as a motivation behind aesthetic experience. People gravitate to either high- or low-brow art depending on their level of education as well as their socioeconomic aspirations. Likewise, people judge one another on the basis of their aesthetic preferences. In the wake of Bourdieu, cultural-studies scholars such as Bennett (1990), Frow (1995), Hebdige (1979), and Thornton (1995) have shifted the focus of aesthetics to how individuals and communities define themselves in relation to the art they consume. Marxist aesthetic theory thus amounts to a sociology of cultural production—what the art we like says about our values and personalities.

There are naturally shades of gray between the Kantian and Marxist extremes. Adorno (1997) argues that artworks contain within their very material and structure the traces of their surrounding cultural situation. Modern art for Adorno must reflect its particular historical moment by rejecting the false consolations of harmony, happy endings, and natural beauty. The tension in Adorno's work results from his simultaneous acceptance of the contingence of art on culture with his disdain for popular music. Adorno bases his rejection on popular music's piecemeal construction and interchangeable materials, which for him make meaningful expression impossible. Wolff, meanwhile, acknowledges that aesthetic criticism emanates from specific historical conditions even thought it might try to efface those origins (1993, 16). But Wolff concludes that while awareness of culture naturally informs any worthwhile study of art, aesthetic experience cannot be reduced to sociology, because art is unique and separate from daily experience. Finally, within popular-music studies, Frith (1996) identifies music as a special type of aesthetic product because it simultaneously cultivates a sense of community while facilitating transcendence of community. We listen to the music we like because it reflects our social placement but also because it allows us to escape that placement.

The rhetoric of experimentalism, which Cage (1961a, 39) defined as an action "the outcome of which is not foreseen," displays a mixture of Kantian and Marxist beliefs. Experimentalism at once clings to notions of aesthetic superiority and autonomy from market forces even as it regards aesthetic experience as inseparable from culture. All of the genres that I consider in this book, and indeed nearly all electronic-music genres that exist in general, claim to be experimental in that they are creating something new rather than perfecting old practices. As Benitez (1978) and Nyman (1999) point out, experimental music in the United States during the 1950s developed in response to the highly determined European avant-garde centered around the Darmstadt School and composers such as Boulez and Stockhausen. But notions of experimentalism have since broadened to include not only works with elements of indeterminacy, such as Cage's, Christian Wolff's, or Earle Brown's, but also works that break sharply with existing generic norms, such as Ornette Coleman's *Free Jazz: A Collective Improvisation* (1961) or the Velvet Underground's subversion of pop songs. The predominant definitions of experimentalism cast it as an essentially apolitical action, the aesthetic equivalent of a scientific experiment that pursues truth dispassionately. Experimentalism occurs in any attempt to experiment, to take risks, to do the unexpected. As such, experimentalism can occur anywhere, in any economic class or social situation, and with any type of technology.

Benitez and Nyman both understand mid-twentieth-century experimentalism in music as an alternative to avant-garde music, which usually was a politically charged activity. As Poggioli (1968, 106–108) explains, avant-gardes thrive in liberal-bourgeois democracies and suffer under fascism and communism. The avant-garde by definition posits itself as alienated from mainstream society, yet it simultaneously needs that mainstream in order to sustain itself financially. If 1950s American experimental music could be, but was not necessarily, political, avant-garde music's political commitment was more definitive; it sought to critique mass culture, insisted on its own alienation from both prestigious high art and popular culture, and dispensed with the ideal of autonomous art, arguing instead for art's embeddedness within life (Bürger 1984, 49). Whatever the initial merits of distinguishing experimentalism from the avant-garde, though, the two have merged to become indistinguishable in recent electronic music. Experimentalism today is synonymous with the avant-garde because both impulses claim independence from mass culture and consumerism, just as both claim aesthetic superiority on the basis of their difficulty and institutional pedigrees.

METAGENRE

Experimentalism, then, is a repudiation, but of what? First and foremost, of mass culture, even though the definition of mass culture is far from clear. Let's return to the three metagenres of experimental electronic music that have served as structural underpinnings of this book: institutional electro-acoustic music, electronica, and sound art. Participants in each metagenre generally perceive themselves in an oppositional relationship to a main-stream made up of the other two metagenres as well as different forms of nonelectronic music. Thus, electroacoustic music pits itself against both sound art and electronica but also against Western art music and popular music.

These metagenres also define themselves on the basis of institutions, media, and criticism. Electroacoustic music has done best in research uni-versities and institutes and, during the first few decades after World War II, at radio stations subsidized by state governments. Among the most famous of such educational institutions are IRCAM (Institut de Recherche et Coor-dination Acoustique/Musique) and GRM (Groupe de Recherches Musi-cales) in Paris and, in the United States, CCRMA (Center for Computer Research in Music and Acoustics at Stanford University), CRCA (Center for Research in Computing and the Arts at the University of California, San Diego), and the Computer Music Center (at Columbia University, formerly the Columbia-Princeton Electronic Music Center). These institutes see themselves as conducting scientific research that need not result in commer-cial gain and spurn associations with mass culture or critical success (Bab-bitt 2003; Richard 1994). Nevertheless, these institutions depend on the largesse of governmental subsidies or private companies, many of which have ties to the defense industry or to commercial electronics. IRCAM, for instance, received support money from some of France's defense contractors (Born 1995), and Stanford's CCRMA functions thanks to underwriting from numerous corporations, including Apple, Hewlitt-Packard, IBM, and Yamaha.

By contrast, the various genres encompassed under the umbrella of elec-tronica display a less predictable attitude concerning capitalism and mass culture; some critique capitalism, while others quite happily embrace it. Electronica, especially EDM, emanates from recording labels possessing distinct aesthetic profiles, and electronica fans often describe their tastes according to the labels whose music they follow. Composer Taylor Deupree's label 12k is well known for releasing glitch and postminimal techno. EDM fans revere labels such as Warp, Kompakt, and Basic Channel, while labels such as Touch, Thrill Jockey, and Microcosm cater to larger cross-sections of electronic music, both dance-oriented and otherwise.

Sound art poses the most vexing challenge in terms of genre. Some prac-titioners insist that sound art simply cannot qualify as music but is rather a form of art incorporating sound, acoustics, and space or architecture. And even for those who do tolerate overlaps between sound art and music, sound art does not necessarily count as electronic music; it may just as easily be rendered through acoustic instruments or other nonelectronic means. Nevertheless, the same media channels that treat experimental electronic music, especially through academic journals and monographs, also treat sound art. Similarly, commercial music labels often release works of sound art. The subsidiary label of 12k, LINE, specializes in extremely quiet, minimal works that it advertises as sound art.

Let there be no misunderstanding—all three metagenres here constitute high art for a number of reasons. In terms of the revenue they generate and the numbers of people who listen or make the music, these metagenres represent only a small portion of the total musical activity of any culture. They also operate best in environments with one or more of the following conditions: well-funded research institutions and universities, a critical mass of listeners and practitioners with postsecondary education who are conversant with computers and the Internet, access to sound or music software and equipment, and disposable income. Yet all three metagenres are also inherently commercial despite any claims to the contrary, since all three depend on recording and ticket sales. The goal of record labels—to sell recordings—is undeniably a commercial one, but most electronic-music labels are independent from major corporations, run on tight budgets, and net only modest returns. In contrast to institutional music and sound art, electronica generally embraces its commodity character with the understanding that it is possible and indeed productive to make money from selling recordings and merchandise. The trade-off implicit in this position is that most such labels release and sell only small numbers of records, sometimes fewer than 500 copies of a particular album. Institutional electroacoustic music and sound art also circulate on commercial recording labels. But commercial release in these circumstances seems like a secondary goal to that of the initial creation of the artwork. And many other electroacoustic and sound-art recordings never receive commercial release.

The true indication of how institutional electroacoustic, electronica, and sound art regard themselves and one another lies in the criticism that the three metagenres generate. Electroacoustic music and, recently, sound art receive treatment and analysis in peer-reviewed academic journals such as *Organised Sound* and *Computer Music Journal*. *Organised Sound* serves as a case study of the difficulties inherent in maintaining strict generic divisions within electronic music. The editor of *Organised Sound*, Leigh Landy, teaches composition and electroacoustic music studies in the Music, Technology and Innovation Centre of De Montfort University in Leicester, U.K. In *Organised Sound* and elsewhere, Landy has written essays that consider the place of electroacoustic art music within contemporary culture. Most notable among these writings is his monograph *Understanding the Art of Sound Organization* (2007), which begins with the premise that electroacoustic music deserves a larger audience than the one it currently enjoys. In order to expand that listenership, Landy and his colleagues at Leicester developed the "Intention/Reception" project, which asks listeners to complete surveys about the music they hear both before and after hearing the composer's descriptions or explanations. With the data retrieved from these surveys, Landy hopes to educate composers and sound artists on the most successful methods for communicating with their audiences.

Landy's efforts make sense, considering that very few electroacoustic works attract any sort of public attention. But as pointed out in chapter 1, the project of collecting data to chart listeners' reactions runs the risk of turning music into a scientific experiment where repeatable procedures yield predictable results. Also, Landy seems less than enthusiastic when forms of sound organization other than his own garner greater commercial success:

> It should come as no surprise that, given fine art's greater public acceptance than contemporary music's in general, sound art is more publicly available as well. During the period in which this book was written, Bruce Naumann created a sound installation for the Tate Modern in London. It consisted of the simultaneous presentation of twenty-two single human voices, each one heard on an individual loudspeaker in the huge entrance to the Tate Modern. I can remember only a handful of contemporary composers' works drawing nearly as much attention as this one. Although it was in a museum, there was virtually nothing to look at. Does this make Naumann's work that much better or more important than any other major contemporary sonic art work? . . . Granted, a Jean-Michel Jarre *son et lumière* city work gets headline exposure as well, but that accompanies the huge investment and spectacle status the work receives. This was, instead, just a sound installation in a museum entrance. (Landy 2007, 162)

It would be unfair to judge Landy on the basis of this statement alone, a statement whose apparent bitterness might well be understandable coming from anyone who has spent years writing and cultivating electroacoustic music, only to be eclipsed by an artist whose aesthetic position is so different. To their credit, Landy and the editors of *Organised Sound* have made efforts to incorporate various types of sound art and electronica, especially in the Vol. 13, No. 1 issue of the journal from 2008, which centers around "work not supported by the academic economy." Articles in this issue address works by well-known artists such as Alva Noto, Björk, and Merzbow. Yet even this gesture of inclusion affirms, rather than breaks down, generic barriers. The fact that *Organised Sound* sequesters electronica from other forms of electronic music is simultaneously heartening and troubling. Electronica certainly deserves to be taken seriously on its own terms, and its inclusion in an academic journal devoted to music technology speaks well for the capacity of scholars to venture beyond their institutional ivory towers. But by corralling electronica within its own issue, *Organised Sound* might, in fact, be building yet another ivory tower, one that ensconces electronica safely away from other genres it might otherwise threaten. Surely, the variety of electronic-music genres cannot simply be reduced to a distinction between funding mechanisms, whether originating from academic economies or free-market capitalism. Tony Myatt, the guest editor of this nonacademic issue of *Organised Sound*, says that while the defining characteristic of the musics considered is the fact that they are produced outside of academe, these musics share another trait, namely that they are "not primarily influenced by Schaeffer, or spectromorphology, or constructs derived from instrumental music or structuralist approaches to the manipulation of sound and audio parameters" (Myatt 2008, 1). Myatt draws an easy connection between institutional affiliation and commitment to Schaeffer, who himself founded the GRM as well as indirectly led to the foundation of other institutions like De Montfort's electroacoustic department. Yet many independent sound artists whose work might have easily fit into Myatt's issue, such as Francisco López and Toshiya Tsunoda, espouse clearly Schaefferian positions even as they pursue careers as independent freelance artists.

The example of *Organised Sound* indicates that while institutional electroacoustic communities might bear popular culture good will (or, at least, no ill will), they may lack the necessary knowledge to catch affinities among electronic-music genres. Other sources of institutional electroacoustic scholarship affirm this conclusion. For instance, Curtis Roads's textbook *Microsound* spends many pages discussing Xenakis, Roads's own compositions, and other institutional composers. Yet Roads mentions only briefly that electronica musicians employ microsound techniques, and the only electronica artist Roads feels fit to mention is Kim Cascone (Roads 2001, 323). Similarly, Simon Emmerson's *Living Electronic Music* (2007) often talks generally about the mutual admiration among art and popular musicians yet himself discusses the work of only one recent electronic musician, Aphex Twin.

A foil to the example of *Organised Sound* is the online music store Boomkat, based in Manchester, U.K. Boomkat sells experimental music, especially electronic dance music, electronica, and noise music. Unlike the music magazine *Pitchfork*, whose staff reviews music independently and often critically, Boomkat publishes descriptions that teeter between journalist review and advertisement. An alarmingly high number of featured releases earn accolades such as "essential purchase" or "massively recommended." Yet Boomkat displays a surprisingly broad palette of musical taste, and its writers know their electronic-music history cold. For instance, the unidentified Boomkat writer who reviewed a 2008 rerelease of Michel Chion's *Requiem* (1978) on the label Sub Rosa recommended the work highly, acclaiming it as "an amazing, defining work from the second wave of musique concrète" (Boomkat 2008a). It is frankly astonishing that any popular source of journalism would describe a musique concrète work with such warm terms, let alone refer to the different historical periods of the art form. Boomkat also released its own collection, *14 Tracks of Early Electronic Music,* which contains works by institutional electroacoustic composers such as Stockhausen, Bernhard Parmegiani, and Jean-Claude Risset, as well as independents such as Terry Riley, Raymond Scott, and Edgard Varèse. Boomkat congratulates itself for this collection, calling it "life affirming" and inspirational for "contemporary music of all colors," including the successful electronica group Boards of Canada.

In 2009, *Organised Sound* devoted an entire issue to sound art and logically chose Alan Licht to write an introductory article on the ambiguities inherent in the term. Licht offers a more conciliatory definition in this article than he did in his monograph from 2007:

> As a term, "sound art" is mainly of value in crediting site or object-specific
> works that are not intended as music per se. Much like rock and roll, a
> purist view of sound art becomes very narrow, and much of what is called
> or categorised as sound art can be just as easily viewed as a hyphenated
> fusion of sound art with an experimental musical style. . . . A universal
> definition and definitive history of sound art may not be likely, for these
> reasons; but ultimately it is better to honour sound pieces created in a
> non-time-based, non-programmatic way as being sound art as opposed to
> music than to simply shoehorn any sound work into the genre of experi-
> mental music, or to practise the lazy revisionism of blanketing any
> experimental sound composition, performance or recording under the
> rubric of sound art. (Licht 2009, 9)

Here, Licht sounds rather generous in his provisional acceptance of many types of work as sound art, but earlier in the article, he speculates that museums embrace sound art and popular music indiscriminately to increase admissions sales (2009, 7). Licht's essay sets the tone for many subsequent articles in this *Organised Sound* issue, which examine individual works and discussion issues germane to sound art, such as site-specificity and types of listening. Yet these authors describe works that are often unavailable as recordings. Sticklers to Licht's notion of sound art would probably approve, since they would feel that the mobility of a recording would destroy the site-specificity that sets sound art apart from music. But such critical treatments of sound art run the risk of excluding readers and listeners through focusing on works that, on a practical level, are inaccessible.

ALIENATION AND COMMON GROUND

Clearly, musicians are independent human beings who think freely. An *Organised Sound* reader might compose highly inaccessible works even while building extensive collections of techno recordings and might disagree with Landy's frustration concerning the success of sound art. But the examples above are still useful in indicating trends about how scholars, journalists, and critics conceive of the three electronic-music metagenres. Two assumptions appear consistently: (1) each metagenre exists in alienation from the other two metagenres and from a mainstream culture that barely supports its existence, and (2) alienation from mainstream culture is a sign of aesthetic integrity. In short, all three metagenres conceive of themselves as subcultures struggling against the culture industry for meager resources. And as Hebdige (1979), Fonarow (2006), and Thornton (1995) detail, subcultural rhetoric frequently presumes that financial success (however modest that success may be in reality) is a sign of lower artistic quality.

We can easily identify this sort of subcultural cliquishness in academic and institutional circles. Stockhausen (Stockhausen et al. 2007), responding to the music of Aphex Twin, Scanner, and other recent electronica artists, criticizes their use of repetitive rhythms and loops as simplistic and (alarmingly) "post-African." As Neill (2002) explains, this bias against dance-oriented rhythms is nothing new but is rather the one distinction to which art musicians can cling in a landscape where art and popular culture are permeating each other. Yet cliquishness exists among sound and electronica artists as well. Licht (2007) reproaches experimental musicians who claim to create sound art as if it were simply a classier synonym for music. For Licht, music is narrative, while sound art is cyclical and site-specific. Licht's position is vulnerable to attack on many fronts—the drone works of Phill Niblock or Éliane Radigue, for instance, arguably lack developmental or narrative qualities and are frequently performed in exhibit spaces. And as Licht himself acknowledges, the definition of site-specificity is itself no longer clear, given the proliferation of surround-sound technologies and recorded versions of sound art, which untether works from their original venues. Licht's aversion to the popularity of the term *sound art* suggests a certain discomfort, as if outsiders were sullying sound art's cultural cachet.

Even within the supposedly homogeneous confines of popular music, there are cracks within the façade of solidarity. The famous divisions between 1970s progressive rock and punk stand as witness to this: claims for intellectual cultivation and sophistication help rival genres compete in tight economic markets (Gendron 2002). The electronica subgenre called intelligent dance music (IDM) begs the question: what would stupid dance music sound like? Record labels touted IDM in the 1990s as the thinking person's answer to what many perceived as mindless dance music (Reynolds 1999,

181–183). The term unfortunately recalls some disagreeable tenets of aesthetic theory originating as far back as Plato: music that encourages bodily movement is less desirable than music that engages the mind.

Still, there is no sinister cabal at work. Distinction and aesthetic value are inherent in any musical genre, and especially in experimental electronic-music genres where financial and critical success ride on the listener's ability to distinguish among any number of works or artists. But if the electro-acoustic, electronica, and sound art camps regard themselves as irreconcilable with one another, how can we talk about the aesthetics of electronic music, as if something approaching an aesthetic consensus existed?

One subject for which common ground undoubtedly exists is history. The journalistic and academic histories of electronic music and sound art all read as if from the same script. This narrative inevitably begins with the early days of phonography and the related attempts to encode sound into visual data. The fetch of texts such as Friedrich Kittler's *Gramophone, Film, Typewriter* has been enormous, especially in English-speaking countries. Chanan (1995), Katz (2004), Levin (1990), and Sterne (2003) all view the phonograph as a turning point not only for music but for the very experience of sound and hail Rilke's desire to "play" the coronal sutures of the human skull with a phonographic needle as a prescient anticipation of later purely phonographic musics like scratch hip-hop and Marclay's turntable pieces. The list of founding fathers (and a few mothers) of electronic music repeats the same few names: Babbitt, Messiaen, Oliveros, Schaeffer, Stockhausen, and Theremin. Even Licht (2009) cites many of these same influences for the creation of sound art.

But then that history splinters off into different branches. *Modulations*, an edited volume of interviews and essays, places academic and institutional electronic music on equal footing with trip-hop, dub, and techno, noting that many DJs revere musique concrète pioneers such as Schaeffer and Pierre Henry (Shapiro 2000, 8–23). *The Ambient Century* (Prendergast 2000) offers an exhaustive listing of art-music and popular composers who contributed to the general project of ambience, and *Ocean of Sound* and *Haunted Weather* (Toop 1995; 2004) juggle Western art music with sound art and electronica in rapid succession, long past the point where genre boundaries begin to lose significance. Yet the revised edition of *Electronic and Computer Music* (Manning 2004) devotes only thirteen pages to "rock and pop electronic music." Similarly, the second edition of *Electronic and Experimental Music* (Holmes 2002) contains short descriptions of commercial synthesizers and turntablism but does not spend any time on popular genres. There are clear reasons for the relative absence of popular music in academic textbooks, which profile academic music almost exclusively and which only in later editions have acknowledged the existence of nonacademic and popular music. Many people still believe that high culture is more prestigious than popular culture. Popular music often compares itself with art music in order to access some of that prestige, just as art music frequently avoids comparisons with popular music lest it seem trivial or commercial.

Still, the manner in which the three metagenres represent their primal histories reveals a common belief that electronic music is fundamentally different from anything that came before it. And to return to my opening statement in chapter 1, this difference boils down to a simple phenomenological fact: electronic music sounds different from conventional music. At the heart, then, of electronic-music aesthetics is a continued interrogation of whether electronically produced sound can or should convey meaning. But, as illustrated in the first five chapters of this book, there is no consensus on this issue. For some post-Schaefferians, soundscape artists, and field recordists, sound should represent the outside world mimetically. For some microsound and electronica artists, sound should aspire to abstraction and meaninglessness. For many musicians in all three metagenres, sound should fall into predictable musical patterns of rhythm, pitch, or harmony. But for many others, sound should avoid the trappings of music as much as possible.

No matter the aesthetic platform of the artist, though, one issue is clear: contemporary electronic music erases the frame that has encased music for centuries. I have touched on what I call the musical frame: a collection of expectations for how music should behave and what distinguishes it from nonmusical sound. In nonelectronic Western art music, the frame consisted of instrumental timbres that make musical instruments quickly identifiable; it also included the customs governing behavior, such as the prohibition of talking during a concert or applauding between movements of a work. The frame excluded certain types of nonmusical sounds such as noise (however defined) in musical works. Electronic music is certainly not solely responsible for the destruction of the musical frame; Schoenberg, Cage, the circulation of non-Western music, and the advent of commercial recordings have all taken their toll as well. But electronic music concentrates several antiframing techniques: its performance in nonconcert venues, its use of objectlike audio footage, its blurring of the divisions between "live" and "recorded" performance. In the next section, we can reflect on methods of deconstructing the musical frame and what this deconstruction means for the future of music.

THE MUSICAL FRAME

It's instructive to return to nonelectronic Western art music as a point of comparison. Although the diversity of various forms of Western art music is obvious, until musicians began to use electronics to produce and capture music, certain elements contributed to the musical frame irrespective of the type of music it encased. The most basic of these elements has been instrumental timbre. Listeners who may know nothing else about a musical practice tend to be able to recognize the sounds of musical instruments native to their culture. This explains why people who admit to being tone-deaf can at least tell the difference between a radio broadcast of music and radio static. Other elements that many listeners can identify include predictable rhythms, melodies, harmonies, and forms. As Scruton points out, these elements encourage musical listening because they make "use of a particular kind of sound: an acousmatic event, which is heard 'apart from' the everyday world, and recognized as the instance of a type" (1997, 19). Scruton's use of the term *acousmatic* is less stringent than Schaeffer's. He does not mean that listeners completely disregard the source of musical sounds; if they did, listeners would be indifferent to the fact that the solo instrument in Gershwin's *Rhapsody in Blue* is a piano and not a violin. Scruton does, however, correctly state that listeners hear conventional music as a *special* event that is distinct from the sounds heard in the outside world, sounds that we tend to identify primarily on the basis of their source causes.

Again, I realize that nonelectronic music includes an enormously heterogeneous collection of listening experiences, but an analogy can help justify this generalization. We can liken nonelectronic Western art-music traditions, such as Renaissance polyphony or Classical string quartets, to spoken languages. Just as many languages employ recurring structural elements such as subjects and predicates, certain structural elements in music occur regularly and assume a functional role. In Renaissance polyphony, for instance, one such element could be the alternation between fleeting dissonances and cadential consonances, while in string quartets, it could be the sense of conversation that occurs when a motive travels from instrument to instrument. Even if one does not "speak" the language of Renaissance counterpoint or chamber music, one can usually recognize that these languages are musical in nature and not, for instance, representations of forest birds or babbling brooks. In many instances, electronic music lacks these linguistic elements that help alert listeners to the fact that they are hearing music. This absence leads many listeners to hear electronic music not as a language but as something else (I'll address what that something else is below).

The confusion about whether sound in electronic music can convey meaning results from the fact that so many electronically produced sounds imitate the world outside the musical work. As the post-Schaefferian listening theories profiled in chapter 1 affirm, it is very difficult to hear such sounds in a reduced manner, to disregard their source causes. We usually hear mimetic sounds, especially those in electroacoustic, soundscape, and field recordings, not as music but as signs. And even when electronic music contains nonmimetic sounds, it can also destroy musical frame if such sounds are not organized according to predictable musical parameters of rhythm. In microsound, for instance, tiny sounds can create a sense of voluminous space, but in their more abstract manifestations, these sounds rarely combine to form rudimentary musical patterns such as melodies or recurring rhythms.

So far, I have mentioned only the most idiosyncratic examples of electronic music—instances when electronic music does not behave musically. Yet electronic music does often behave like music, most clearly in EDM, with its preponderance of a four-on-the-floor beat. It is absolutely true that EDM is electronic dance *music*, but the musical experience that EDM affords is nonetheless quite different from that in Western art music. To understand this point, it's revealing to consider EDM alongside its antithesis, drone music. In both, the fact that duration is completely arbitrary dismantles the musical frame. Both a techno track and a drone work could last five minutes, fifteen minutes, or three hours, and all three scenarios would be equally consistent with the confines of their respective genres. Yet in Western art music, the conventions of form and length dictated the range of a work's duration; five-hour or five-second symphonies do not exist, because the former case exceeds and the latter case undershoots the time necessary for adequate harmonic and melodic development according to the symphonic style of the Classical and Romantic eras. Musical genres in which development is no longer expected or required assail the musical frame by making it purely incidental when the piece starts and ends.

The absence of a musical frame is a crucial change in the history of music, but I by no means intend with this statement that musicians will no longer create music or that listeners will no longer listen to it. Listeners will no doubt continue to use the word *music* to refer to these frameless works, even though the experience of listening will be markedly different from what art-music listening meant a century ago. Experimental electronic music encourages a type of listening that would be highly uncharacteristic for non-electronic music in which discrete beginnings and endings and development are standard and where predictable forms, instrumental timbres, and structures are the norm. We can think of this new manner of listening as "aesthetic" rather than musical, although I do not mean some judgment of the value of the listening experience. Aesthetic listening heeds intermittent moments of a work without searching for a trajectory that unites such moments; Adorno (2002c) dubbed this practice "regressive listening," because it attends to the transient delights of a pop song, whether a catchy chorus or a syncopated rhythm. Despite his official advocacy of modern music, Adorno's position grew out of the German Romantic tradition of works that adhered to a particular set of formal codes governing the relationship and growth of themes and harmonic areas. Aesthetic listening would be ill suited to this repertoire, because it would ignore many of the features composers intended as markers of craft such as thematic growth, interconnection of harmony with melody, and relationships among different movements of a piece. Works that do not follow such schema but instead repeat smaller units over long stretches afford momentary attention that does not necessarily demand hearing larger-scale patterns or growth. It is certainly possible to hear such works with large-scale growth in mind, just not expected.

The comparison with Adorno's regressive listening is apt, because aesthetic listening is more similar to the sort of listening many already practice with Adorno's dreaded popular music and jazz as well as numerous forms of non-Western music. Whereas in art music listeners are expected to pay full attention to the music and ignore almost everything else around them, listening to electronic music, dance music, and popular forms is a composite of sensory experiences. In dance clubs where EDM plays, attendees listen to and feel the pulse of the music in their ears and guts and move their hips and limbs to accompany what they hear. But dancers also pay attention to other dancers, notice clothing, flirt, drink, talk, and laugh. They might listen assiduously to a particular aspect of a track such as a sample or rhythmic pattern in one moment and start a conversation in the next. The medium that inspires and incites such activity might be music in the sense that it is organized sound, but it permits and encourages attention to many simultaneous occurrences. That popular music should call on different ways of listening from art music is certainly no surprise. What is astonishing is that the same sort of diffused, aesthetic listening that previously was unique to Western popular forms has become routine in experimental electronic music, which on the basis of its funding and support, listenership, and criticism, aligns itself more with high art than with mass culture.

Aesthetic listening lies somewhere between nonelectronic musical listening and the type of listening we experience when we listen for information. Schaeffer's *Railroad Study* highlights this new experience. Before its composition, it is unlikely that anyone had ever thought to hear train noises as musical objects. The sounds of a train whistle notified the listener of an approaching source of transportation or, perhaps, danger. The ability to hear sound not for its informational value but for its aesthetic qualities is not precisely the same thing as the acousmatic or reduced listening experiences that Schaeffer described, where listeners try their best to ignore source causes altogether. But this ability does involve a type of aesthetic reduction, akin to when we listen to an unintelligible foreign language for its sounds and cadence since we cannot make out its meaning. Aesthetic listening thus also includes the experience of appreciating the characteristics of nonmusical sound as aesthetic objects. This does not preclude hearing the source causes or external associations of a sound, which Schaeffer advocated as reduced listening. It instead means that listeners can contemplate a sound from the outside world for its own aesthetic merits.

One of Cage's goals was to enable listeners to hear all sounds as if they were music, and it would be impossible to talk about any of the music featured in this book without also acknowledging Cage's influence. But experimental electronic music demonstrates not merely that music has expanded or should expand its boundaries but also that musical listening constitutes only one very limited type of aesthetic listening experience. And while insiders might still insist on the distinctions among various metagenres and genres, outsiders might well perceive in electronic music as a whole not only a new musical experience but a new *medium* in which sound is aesthetic but not especially musical. This book's conclusion begins with this premise, that electronic music forecasts the end of music as we have known it in the West for several centuries. I don't make this claim lightly or for dramatic effect. Music, as any form of organized sound, will continue to exist, and listeners and musicians will continue to argue and obsess over its meanings and significance. But the rituals and expectations surrounding this experience have changed and promise to continue to do so.

Conclusion

In 1986, at the age of seventy-six, Pierre Schaeffer gave an interview with Tim Hodgkinson, former member of the avant-garde rock group Henry Cow. The interview is perplexing and disheartening, showing the twilight years of a man who should have been enjoying the esteem of his colleagues and students. By 1986, Schaeffer had apparently revised his opinions about the hierarchy of music and sound. Now the move from purely representational sound to abstract sound *rightfully* culminates in music. This differs from his statements in the *Traité* that musicians and composers had *wrongfully* chosen to make music abstract, to remove it from its concrete origins in raw sound:

> We have to not call music things which are simply sound-structures. . . .
> There's thus a gradation between the domain of raw sound, which starts by
> being imitative, like the representational plastic arts, and the domain of
> language. Between, there's a zone of gradation which is the area of
> "abstract" in the plastic arts, and which is neither language nor model, but
> a play of forms and material. There are many people working with sound.
> It's often boring, but not necessarily ugly. It contains dynamic and kinaes-
> thetic impressions. But it's not music. (Hodgkinson 1986)

The in-between zone between sound and music for Schaeffer is where musique concrète resided, and musique concrète evidently failed to measure up to music. Indeed, Schaeffer dismisses practically all subsequent electronic music as a failure and instead advocates what he quizzically calls "baroque music." He answers the question "So a new music is impossible?" as follows:

Yes, a music which is new because it comes from new instruments, new theories, new languages. So what's left? Baroque music. . . . It will be when our contemporary researchers abandon their ludicrous technologies and systems and "new" musical languages and realize that there's no way out of traditional music, that we can get down to a baroque music for the 21st century. Such a music has been prefigured in popular music—not that I rate it very highly. Jazz, rock, etc., the music of "mass" culture, and I'm not talking about good jazz, the marvelous negro spirituals which are completely traditional, but the kind of utility-music which is widely used for dancing, making love, etc.; this is a baroque music, a mixture of electricity and DoReMi. (Hodgkinson 1986)

Here, Schaeffer acknowledges a phenomenon I have called "aesthetic listening" or what Adorno would call "regressive listening," a type of activity-centered listening that courts intermittent rather than absorbed listening. And, like Adorno, Schaeffer seems to mourn an earlier era when music took up the listener's complete attention.

Schaeffer also offers this dismal assessment of his life's work:

I was always deeply unhappy at what I was doing. . . . Each time I was to experience the disappointment of not arriving at music. I couldn't get to music—what I call music. . . . Seeing that no one knew what to do anymore with DoReMi, maybe we had to look outside that. . . . Unfortunately it took me forty years to conclude that nothing is possible outside DoReMi. . . . In other words, I wasted my life. (Hodgkinson 1986)

How can the inventor of musique concrète and a beloved figurehead of electronic music, electronica, and sound art dismiss his accomplishments as a waste? Why the sudden longing for the abstraction of music, after a career of insisting on the virtues of concrete sound? Did Schaeffer hear something that legions of his students and devoted fans around the world did not?

We can partially explain Schaeffer's regret as a function of his insecurity about not being a musician proper. Schaeffer mentions his father chiding him as a boy to grow up, stop tinkering, and make real music. And in describing his collaborations with Pierre Henry, Schaeffer apologetically identified himself as an engineer rather than a musician (Schaeffer 1967). These personal details notwithstanding, Schaeffer seems to regret not only his own inadequacies but also the passing of an era when music making came naturally. Good music, for Schaeffer, had long since died, having been replaced with either acoustic abstraction or functional light music.

Schaeffer's dysphoria mirrors a crisis felt throughout the arts but articulated particularly well in visual-arts discourse. Many people over the last century have proclaimed the "end of art." We all have anecdotal evidence of this, such as the countless reproaches from professional and armchair critics that some new artwork is so simple or so bad that a child could have done better, usually followed by a comparison with an earlier point in history when painters knew how to paint. Academia has frequently anticipated the end of art, though not always as a catastrophe. Hans Belting's book, *The End of the History of Art* (1987), demonstrates how "art" arose when the function of painting shifted from devotional aid to object of disinterested contemplation. For Belting, the end of art history simply means the end of this era of disinterestedness, not an end of artistic quality or activity. Donald Kuspit, on the other hand, foresees the worst in his jeremiad *The End of Art* (2004), a reactionary dismissal of Marcel Duchamp and Barnett Newman and the artists they inspired. Most important, however, is Arthur Danto's book *After the End of Art* (1997), which agrees with Belting that such an end hardly means that art will no longer exist. Rather, Danto argues, the central concern in this new postart landscape is not whether art has meaning but how it differs from nonart—that is, reality.

There is clearly no consensus about what the end of art means or how we should react to it. Kuspit published *The End of Art* seven years after Danto's *After the End of Art* and does not mention Danto at all, meaning that either Kuspit did not know about Danto's work, or, more amazingly, he chose to ignore it. I want not to make this same mistake and so will center some concluding thoughts about experimental electronic music amid some canny observations that Danto makes about this interstitial moment in the history of aesthetics. These ideas might, in turn, explain why Schaeffer disavowed his career and why he longed for a return of music.

Danto writes that art aesthetics (and by this he means mostly painting) concerned itself from 1300 to 1900 with mimesis and representation. The success or failure of an artwork hinged on how well it imitated something in real life. When photography was invented, painters seemingly overnight lost their reason for existence. Why struggle for better perspective when photographs could trump anything produced with paint and a brush? Not surprisingly, Impressionism and Modernism emerged soon after the first photographs and gradually shifted attention away from representation and toward those materials intrinsic to painting and painting alone—paint, canvas, and brushstrokes. Modernism, in turn, gave way to the paradigm of the ready-made, the pop-art object, and the Brillo box. Marcel Duchamp and Andy Warhol introduced patently unaestheticized objects into the museum and exhibition space, not in order to celebrate their beautiful or aesthetic qualities but to render strange the concept of art in the era of mechanical reproduction and consumerism. Danto returns again and again to Warhol's *Brillo Box* as an epicenter for this new era when aesthetics and beauty cease to matter and when manifestos about the superiority of one type of art over another have long since become irrelevant. For Danto, the end of art history means an era where *any* type of art is possible and legitimate, whether perspectival painting, Fluxus installations, cartoons, or candy bars. The only question Danto says we must answer is what is the essential ingredient that makes art art, if it is not quality, narrative, or meaning?

With some minor adjustments, we can adapt Danto's thesis about the progression of visual-arts aesthetics to Western art music. From approximately 1400 through 1900, a period roughly overlapping with Danto's period of mimesis, Western art music's chief concerns were with beauty and compositional craft. Divisions between musical sound and sound from the outside world were clear thanks to instrumental and vocal timbre, musical forms and structures, and rituals surrounding music performance and listening. Just as photography instigated a philosophical crisis in visual arts, so did the introduction of electricity into music making at the turn of the twentieth century change musical aesthetics forever. Inventors and composers quickly realized that electronic instruments were good for more than merely imitating acoustic ones. Tonality endured multiple assaults, first at the hands of serialized harmony, then with the microtonal gradations that electronic instruments suddenly made possible. Phonographs resurrected sounds of the past into the present, freeing music for the first time from its imprisonment within the present. Noise and silence quickly evolved from their second-class status as forbidden objects to novel coloristic tools and then to legitimate musical materials. As in the visual-arts world, musicians and music listeners find themselves asking questions quite similar to Danto's. If silence and noise are now musical, if a live music performance can consist of prerecorded sound, and if music can consist exclusively of sounds of the outside world, then what is it that makes electronic music music and not simply sound?

The three preoccupations this book has identified—sound as sign, object, and situation—indicate how much electronic music has departed from traditional music aesthetics. To refer again to Danto, they point to the end of the history of music, not an era in which music is no longer being made but one in which all types of sound in art have become equally legitimate. Post-Schaefferians (and others) hear sound as a sign and debate the extent to which it should function mimetically, as well as how much composers can impose meanings on listeners. Microsound composers (and others) hear sound as an object, a phenomenon stripped of any meaning it might once have carried. Field recordists, soundscape artists, and ambient composers hear sound as embedded within a location, whether physical, cultural, or psychological. And just as the new philosophical question in visual arts asks how the artwork differs from reality, the new question in musical aesthetics should be how nonmusical, electronic sound differs from traditionally musical sound. Does it carry meaning? Must we hear it differently from the way we would hear it in the real world, simply because it still occurs within an artwork?

I divided this book into its three parts for the sake of clarity, as a means of isolating examples of signs, objects, and situations from one another. But as common sense would suggest, some electronic works can display the traits of more than one element, or even three simultaneously. I now turn to two examples of such works in order to illustrate the difficulty in pinpointing the boundaries between sound inside and outside the artwork.

Kim Cascone's *Music for Dagger and Guitar* (2008) departs sharply from the composer's recent output. It is made up mostly of field recordings but occasionally features electronically produced pitches or noise. Cascone packages the recording in a box that looks like a DVD case and uses a font often seen in movie posters on the liner notes. This reference to cinema resonates with two of the inspirations for the work: Béla Tarr's *Sátántangó* (1994) and Michael Haneke's *The Seventh Continent* (1989). The influence of Haneke on the work is unmistakable. *The Seventh Continent* propels its various storylines through brutally unaestheticized cuts between scenes, interspersed with a few seconds of a black screen. In *Music for Dagger and Guitar,* Cascone uses brief sections of evocative material that abruptly cut to a few seconds of silence before starting with new material. The affinities with *Sátántangó* are less literal, amounting to the slow pacing of the work, which allows the listener time to form conclusions without heavy-handed narration (Cascone, personal communication, July 6, 2009). But these parallels are more red herrings than keys to the work. Cascone deliberately refrained from charting a series of correspondences between sound materials and meanings, counting instead on the listener's own ability to do so. And yet the work relies on easily recognizable sounds of the outside world—lawn sprinklers, airport intercom announcements—that carry residual meaning. *Music for Dagger and Guitar* thus skews any easy classification of either its intentions or its genre.

Conveyance (2009) is a "sound art documentary" by Inouk Demers. Lasting about an hour, *Conveyance* combines voiceover commentary with field recordings. Purely in terms of the types of materials it uses, *Conveyance* recalls Hildegard Westerkamp soundscapes such as "Kits Beach Soundwalk" (1989), although *Conveyance* operates according to very different principles. The theme here is the history of water policy in Los Angeles. Occasional voiceover statements refer to William Mulholland's construction of the Los Angeles Aqueduct leading from the Sierra Nevadas, quote job descriptions for a position with a local water authority, and point to the dire need for better water management in Southern California. Unlike "Kits Beach

Soundwalk," however, the voiceover in *Conveyance* occurs only intermittently and tends toward indirectness rather than clarity. There is no clear agenda here, whether political or narrative; some statements seem cryptic and even unmotivated, such as allusions to water lilies in ancient Egypt or the exchange of water among different organizations. Documentaries putatively aim for some sense of objectivity, and although total objectivity is, of course, impossible, the supposition in a documentary is that the authorial voice is educating the audience. *Conveyance* does its best *not* to aspire toward clarity, even though the voiceover assumes the position of educated informant.

What qualifies *Conveyance* as a work of electronic music, though, is not its voiceover but rather its field recordings, footage taken from water-treatment facilities, the docks of the Port of Los Angeles, the bus terminal at Union Station, and storm drains near Elysian Park. Unlike a López field recording, *Conveyance* does not identify any of its audio footage in its liner notes, and the sounds themselves are usually so abstract and unidentifiable that they don't seem obviously connected to the specific voiceover commentaries that accompany them. Most of the time, in fact, there are no obvious connections between the subject matter of the narration and the recordings. Frequently, the recorded materials lock into a repetitive stasis of drones or machine-powered gear shifting. Since the voiceovers achieve some amount of clarity by dint of using words and sentences, the field recordings in comparison sound increasingly abstract and even faintly musical in the sense that one fixates on their regularity and predictability to the exclusion of their source causes. At its conclusion, *Conveyance* doesn't seem to be *about* water usage so much as it uses the theme of water as a point of departure for another altogether unrelated theme. It is difficult to listen to *Conveyance* without feeling that one has missed something, that one didn't concentrate enough to grasp a detail that would make all of the recordings and statements gel into a coherent whole. The obscurity of the text, a material that normally would guide the listener, scrambles the experience. *Conveyance* behaves like neither a documentary nor a field recording such as López's or Tsunoda's. It is certainly not a soundscape that immerses the listener in the sounds of a particular environment; the cuts between different field recordings are often abrupt and dispel any illusion that one has traveled to a new, discrete location. Everything about *Conveyance*, in other words, is strange and unsettling because it is generically untethered.

I by no means suggest here that most electronic works of the future will resemble *Music for Dagger and Guitar* or *Conveyance*. In many respects, the future after the end of music will seem much like the present. EDM will continue to pound away, electroacoustic works will continue to explore the acousmatic condition, drones will continue to approach a state of acoustic nirvana. But the appearance of generically confusing works such as Cascone's or Demers's bring to Danto's questions a particular urgency. Why would we consider *Music for Dagger and Guitar* as music? Even less than in Cascone's abstract microsound work *Cathode Flower*, it has very little to do with music, and as its packaging and listed inspirations suggest, it might, in fact, make more sense as the soundtrack for a film. *Conveyance* refuses to assume the traditionally commanding presence of an authorial speaker, and this refusal jolts and invigorates the listening process. Should we take as fact the statements in this work? Should we hear the field recordings as more or less factual, illustrative, informing than the elusive voiceovers?

The uncertainties in these two works return us yet again to the issue of genre in electronic music. If the distinctions between real-world sound and sound in the artwork are blurry, the differences between genres and even media are even more so. If all sounds are possible in electronic music, what distinguishes it from nonmusic? From sound art? If we collapse music and sound art into one overarching category of Art, what is the difference between sound in art and sound as a sheer sensory phenomenon? I want to refrain from answering these questions, partially because I myself am unsure of the answers but also because it is the questions themselves that make recent electronic music so relevant. If we could easily classify such works into neat genres and smugly decode their meanings and intentions, we would return to the sort of philological detective work that Adorno decried (1997, 128)—the type of aesthetic interpretation that treats the artwork as a secret treasure map where a particular gesture yields a particular meaning.

Nevertheless, let me offer some manner of response to my questions above. I have argued in this book that electronic music has dismantled the musical frame. But it has imposed another type of frame, one much more invisible and inaudible. If electronic music affords aesthetic listening, it does so because it encases its materials in an aesthetic frame. What I mean by this is that electronic music, or sound art, or sound that we simply happen to listen to with aesthetic interest in mind (what Scruton [2007] would call the "aesthetic gaze"), is somehow cordoned off as being interesting not for its meaning or communicative properties but simply because of its sound. This is a neo-Kantian notion, but it does not mean that we need to insist on the disinterestedness of sound. Sound can continue to have residual signification; we need not aspire toward reduced listening. We can hear both meaning and syntax simultaneously. And the experience of hearing in both ways at the same time lends electronic music a quivering sort of energy, because we will never be able to pin down its meanings decisively. This is the danger in electronic music but also its strength. We can never fully relegate it to the world of the concert hall, exhibition space, or museum, because it is already too enmeshed in the real world. Yet we know that we will never run into a work like *Music for Dagger and Guitar* or *Conveyance* in the real world, while walking in a shopping mall or waiting in line at the grocery store. Such works are still special, aesthetic objects.

Adorno (1997, 81) identifies one of the few preelectronic phenomena that displayed this same ambiguity. Fireworks are a strange sort of art, for while they undoubtedly have aesthetic qualities meant to please the viewer, they serve a functional role in punctuating a celebration or festivity. Adorno refutes what would be a Kantian assumption that fireworks cannot be art because they possess use value. For him, it is precisely the fact that fireworks are real, phenomenal, and empirical that makes them artworks. And, like fireworks, the sounds in electronic music are similarly alienating. These sounds are strange in the real world, but they also succeed in making the real world strange.

GLOSSARY

This glossary includes only terms discussed in the main text. For comprehensive definitions of terms pertaining to all aspects of electronic music and acoustics, see Augoyard 2006 and Truax 1999.

absolute music   Western art music that supposedly transcends language and forsakes explicit associations with the outside world. Absolute music is instrumental music that lacks a program or other extramusical narrative or explanation. For advocates such as critic Eduard Hanslick, absolute music reached its pinnacle in the compositions of Beethoven, although even Beethoven's Sixth Symphony had a program. Absolute music's traces can be felt in twentieth-century modernist works that claim to be completely self-contained and formally coherent, such as the works of Babbitt or Boulez or some works by Stockhausen.

acid house   A subgenre of Chicago-based EDM that became popular in Britain during the late 1980s, featuring fast tempi and exotic samples of birds, women speaking foreign languages, and drum machines. Most acid-house tracks were released on "white-label records" by virtually anonymous artists and enjoyed only momentary popularity in a highly competitive climate where novelty was more important than longevity. However, a few acts gained some degree of success and recognition, the most famous of which is 808 State, whose "Pacific State" (1989) is a representative example of the genre.

acousmatic   The condition of listening without being able to see the source of sound production. The word derives from *akousmatikoi,* disciples of

Pythagoras who supposedly listened to their teacher from behind a curtain so as not to be distracted by his appearance or gestures. Pierre Schaeffer resurrected the word in his discussions of musique concrète, applying it to situations in which radios or phonographs replayed sound removed from its origins. Acousmatic music refers to post-Schaefferian electroacoustic music played over loudspeakers or headphones.

aesthetic listening   Electronic music and sound art afford aesthetic listening rather than the musical listening typical for Western art music, because they usually place no demands on the listener to focus attention exclusively on music and to listen for development or cohesion. Instead, aesthetic listening allows for intermittent attention to sound as well as other sensory stimuli and acknowledges the aesthetic characteristics of sounds typically heard as non-musical. Aesthetic listening corresponds somewhat with what Adorno (2002c) critically labeled "regressive listening," or listening for momentarily pleasing fragments of popular songs. But aesthetic listening enjoys legitimacy among many electronic artists who claim high-culture, rather than popular, status.

aesthetics   The branch of philosophy concerned with the values by which we perceive and judge sensory stimuli. Aesthetics used to address beauty specifically but in recent decades has broadened to include the perception of elements once perceived as unbeautiful or even ugly. In electronic music, aesthetics can address the use of previously taboo phenomena such as noise or silence. Aesthetics can study both sensory stimuli triggered in the outside world and those specific to art; the latter is a subject also discussed in the philosophy of art, the branch of philosophy that interrogates what art does and how it is different from nonartistic activities. In recent decades, aesthetics and the philosophy of art suffered criticism for insisting on the universality of aesthetic experience, as well as for claiming to be objective measures of aesthetic value.

ambient music   Unobtrusive or atmospheric music; music not meant to occupy the center of the listener's attention. The concept arguably began with Erik Satie's "furniture music" or live music performed in social spaces as a sort of wallpaper or subliminal decoration. Brian Eno famously coined the phrase *ambient music* to describe his instrumental compositions from the late 1970s onward that featured unobtrusive tonal melodies and repetition. Ambient music was the first type of Western art music to dissent from the expectations of rigorously attentive listening.

Belleville Three   Juan Atkins, Derrick May, and Kevin Saunderson, three high school friends from the Detroit suburb of Belleville who invented techno in the 1980s.

break beat The break is the section in a funk or R&B song when melody drops out, leaving only the percussion. Break beats are the rhythmic patterns that occur during break sections. Two of the most famous break beats ever recorded are those in the Winstons' "Amen, My Brother" (1969) and James Brown's "Funky Drummer" (1970). The drum solos in these two songs contain syncopated patterns that have been heavily sampled or reperformed in numerous hip-hop and EDM tracks. Break beats distinguish rhythmically complex EDM subgenres such as jungle and hip-hop from disco-derived forms of EDM such as house and techno.

CCRMA Center for Computer Research in Music and Acoustics, in the music department at Stanford University. One of the foremost centers for the composition of electroacoustic music, CCRMA also supports research in psychoacoustics, signal processing, and multimedia art. PhD students enrolled in the departments of music, electrical engineering, or computer science can take classes and pursue independent study through the center. CCRMA has received support from numerous technology-related corporations, including Apple Computer, Hewlitt-Packard, IBM, and Yamaha.

CRCA Center for Research in Computing and the Arts, at the University of California, San Diego. CRCA is an organized research unit whose participants draw from the departments of computer science and engineering, music, psychology, theater, and visual arts. Like CCRMA, CRCA specializes in research on multimedia, psychoacoustics, and signal processing.

disco A genre of dance music originating in the early 1970s, combining elements of R&B, salsa, soul, jazz, and synth-pop. What eventually became known as disco started as continuous dance music played at private parties in New York City, particularly at David Mancuso's famous venue, the Loft. Disco clubs catering to black and latino gay men became prevalent by the mid-1970s in several cities around the world. Disco went mainstream later in the decade thanks to radio-friendly acts such as the Bee Gees and the film *Saturday Night Fever* (1977), whose heterosexual main character reassured viewers that disco dancing was masculine. The commercial craze surrounding disco led to a backlash after the 1979 Disco Demolition event in Chicago, where a local radio DJ sponsored a massive burning and explosion of disco records at a baseball game. The success of Disco Demolition indicated widespread homophobia but also general distaste for the decadence and frequent monotony of much disco. Instead of dying, however, disco retreated to underground dance clubs in New York, Chicago, and Detroit, eventually re-forming into EDM genres such as house and techno. The hallmarks of disco include a steady four-on-the-floor bass-drum beat, orchestral accompaniment, and a female lead singer singing in a soul or gospel style.

DJ In general usage, a DJ, or disc jockey, is anyone who plays recordings on the radio or at a club, party, or concert. In live settings, the DJ plays record players, compact-disc players, or laptops and, in the case of the first two, often turns the disc backward and forward to change the speed of playback or to add scratching noises. In disco and EDM, DJs typically play twelve-inch disks in their entirety, using a fader and mixer to create a seamless transition from one song to the next. In hip-hop, DJs often work with two turntables simultaneously, extracting a fragment of a song to play repeatedly. In many genres of electronic music, the DJ enjoys the status of an auteur and constructs elaborate collages of sound.

drone Any sustained or unchanging pitch or group of pitches. Drones are very common in musics throughout the world. In Western experimentalist music, drones came to prominence thanks to minimalist composers Phill Niblock, Charlemagne Palestine, and La Monte Young, who created drone works lasting long periods of time, often several hours. Drones are especially common in recent electronic music and have also entered experimental popular music by way of the Velvet Underground, whose violist, John Cale, was collaborating with Young roughly simultaneously with the Velvet Underground's first recordings.

dub A variant of Jamaican reggae that subjects instrumental tracks to heavy echo and reverberation effects and often removes vocals and emphasizes bass lines. Dub reggae developed thanks to the practice among Jamaican producers of releasing instrumental versions of popular songs. Many versions added unusual psychedelic effects not present in their original forms. Among the two most influential dub musicians are King Tubby and Lee Scratch Perry, both of whom became popular among British ska, punk, and postpunk musicians.

dub techno A subgenre of EDM that combines the minimalism of techno's mechanistic beats with echo and reverb effects. Dub techno came into being in the mid-1990s thanks largely to Basic Channel, the Berlin-based duo of Moritz von Oswald and Mark Ernestus. Techno until then consistently featured dry, precise attacks, but Basic Channel introduced modulating synth pads and impossibly reverberant acoustics. Oswald collaborated with Belleville Three pioneer Juan Atkins on some of his Model 500 tracks, including "M69 Starlight" (1995), and is responsible for the ambient turn that many techno artists have taken in the intervening decade and a half.

electroacoustic music   General term for electronic music that might also involve acoustic instruments. Electroacoustic music also unites two activities once considered polar opposites: musique concrète, which uses found audio footage, and exclusively synthesized music (what the Germans called *elektronische Musik*).

electronic dance music (EDM)   A catchall term for several genres of post-disco dance music, including house and techno as well as their various subgenres. In the years after disco's demise, EDM essentially repeated the disco formula but with synthesizers and sequencers. Techno constituted the first substantive departure from disco with its near complete absence of vocals and spare, mechanical beats and fast tempi. During the 1980s, EDM was mostly intended for dance clubs, but following the acid-house craze in the late 1980s in Britain, a new variant of intelligent dance music (IDM) appeared that claimed to be intellectual enough for living-room listening.

electronic music   Term referring to a large, disparate collection of genres and metagenres of musics involving one or more of the following: electronic instruments, signal processing, and phonographic technology. Electronic music appeared in the early twentieth century with instruments such as the Telharmonium, the theremin, and the Ondes Martenot. During the 1950s and 1960s, it flourished on state-supported radio stations in France and Germany and at universities in the United States. Meanwhile, electronic music gradually made its way into Hollywood film, especially science-fiction movies. Thanks to a precipitous drop in the price of synthesizers in the early 1980s, synthesizers and sequencers made their way into hip-hop and mainstream pop. An analogous drop in the price of audio software during the 1990s made it possible for amateur musicians to produce high-quality recordings at home, further contributing to the democratization of the medium. Today, electronic music can be understood as including three metagenres: institutional electroacoustic music, which aspires toward high modernist autonomy and rigor; electronica, an umbrella for a number of ambient and dance-related genres; and some electronic forms of sound art, or organized sound that in some way relates to the space in which it is heard.

electronica   Electronic music that flourishes primarily outside of academia but also claims some independence from the mainstream music industry. Electronica is split between dance genres such as house or techno and non-dance-oriented music such as drone, ambient, or glitch. No specific formal or stylistic parameters govern what counts as electronica; the one common factor seems to be a sense among artists and listeners that electronica is ideologically distinct from both mainstream culture and institutional electronic music. The term began to appear in the 1990s as a music-industry tool to brand what had become an explosion of niche EDM subgenres such as acid house and jungle. Along with electroacoustic music and electronic sound art, electronica is one of the three metagenres of recent electronic music.

elektronische Musik German for "electronic music," this term describes the music that emerged during the 1950s from the studios of WDR, specifically that of Karlheinz Stockhausen. *Elektronische Musik* was diametrically opposed in its ideology and means of execution to musique concrète, which was being cultivated in Paris at the ORTF studios under Pierre Schaeffer. *Elektronische Musik* involved the creation of entirely new sounds using synthesis and rejected the use of prerecorded sounds in musique concrète for destroying the artwork's ability to signify independently.

experimental music A branch of modernist Western art music emerging in the United States during the 1940s and 1950s that emphasized process over material, relied on aleatoric and chance-related techniques, and often gave performers unprecedented say in how to interpret scores. Experimental musicians often perceived themselves in opposition to the institutional avant-garde that prevailed in postwar Europe, spurning academic or governmental support and avoiding political associations. In the intervening decades, experimentalists have permeated universities and have assumed many of the trappings of the older avant-garde, including commitment to leftist politics and a belief in its own aesthetic distinction. John Cage described experimentalism as an action "the outcome of which is not foreseen" (1961a).

field recording Audio footage taken on location. Field recordings are used in disciplines like anthropology and zoology to document sounds in their natural contexts, such as languages or animal sounds. They have also become a popular form of sound art. Unlike musique concrète and recent electroacoustic music, which edits audio footage and often uses small portions of material, field recordings often focus on the sounds of one location for several minutes. Although any act of recording necessarily involves some editorial decisions on the part of the recordist, many field recordings also aspire toward an unmediated representation of reality. Notable field recordists include Peter Cusack, Francisco López, and Toshiya Tsunoda.

genre A collection of works sharing a common set of conventions. Works establish genre when they repeat formal attributes to the point of establishing listening expectations that those attributes will continue to exist. The most striking moments, however, occur when genre rules are broken or when a work seems to belong to more than one genre. Genres are prevalent through-out popular music, where they serve as effective marketing tools encouraging connoisseurship among fans and consumers. Electronica features a particularly high concentration of genres and subgenres, especially among variants of EDM.

glitch   Literally, the sound of a digital "mistake" that occurs through the mistranslation or deterioration of digital data. It also refers to the electronica genre alternatively known as "clicks and cuts." Glitch (i.e., "glitch microsound") contains what sounds like compact-disc-player skips and low loudspeaker buzz. Well-known glitch musicians include Alva Noto and Oval.

GRM   Groupe des Recherches Musicales, a large research institution in Paris dedicated to the composition and research of computer music. Pierre Schaeffer founded the GRM in 1958; since then, major participants have included François Bayle, Michel Chion, Luc Ferrari, and Bernard Parmegiani. The institution is committed to acousmatic music, while its counterpart and rival institution IRCAM tends to support real-time synthesis of electronics with acoustic instruments.

hip-hop   A hybrid art form developed in the Bronx during the 1970s. Hip-hop includes music as well as graffiti, breakdancing, and fashion. It is an art of (often illicit) appropriation: hip-hop music samples or borrows from pre-existing recordings, graffiti marks public transportation, breakdancing incorporates robotic and mechanistic movements, and hip-hop fashion lit-erally rips off car emblems and fashion labels to make new collages. Hip-hop music won commercial and critical success by the mid-1980s and became a mouthpiece for disenfranchised African-American youth. By the mid-1990s, however, most hip-hop listeners were white, middle-class, suburban teenagers. During the 1980s, hip-hop music sampled from a wide palette of music, often illegally. By the early 1990s, several high-profile lawsuits pre-cipitated a chilling effect in which record labels refused to release material with unlicensed samples.

house   One of the most important postdisco genres of EDM, house emerged in underground dance clubs in Chicago and New York during the early 1980s. House in many respects retains the most effective elements of disco: a steady mid-tempo beat with R&B or funk grooves. But house updates disco by using sampled rather than performed vocals in the upper register of the track and replaces some of disco's acoustic instruments with synthesizers. A seminal early house track is Frankie Knuckles's "Your Love" (1987). As house began to attract listeners outside Chicago, it evolved into acid house, a faster, more frenetic variant of house featuring more far-flung samples.

installation   An artwork that occupies a specific space that is not necessarily an exhibit space or museum. Installations often require spectators to interact physically with the work through actions such as walking, touching, sitting, speaking, and smelling. Installation art arose in tandem with other attempts (minimalist, site-specific, environmental, and conceptual art) to dispose of the frame and the museum as preferred vehicles for separating the artwork from the spectator and the outside world. Sound and/or music often play a role in installation art, usually underscoring the contingency of perception on bodily placement.

institutional electroacoustic music   Electronic music produced in academic or research institutions that features electronics, often paired with acoustic instruments. Institutional electroacoustic music generates a good deal of scholarship and criticism in peer-reviewed journals and monographs. This discourse is heavily theoretical and emphasizes the interaction between compositional intention and listener reception. Along with electronica and electronic sound art, institutional electroacoustic music is one of the three metagenres of recent electronic music.

intelligent dance music (IDM)   A subgenre of electronica that originated in Britain during the early 1990s as a reaction to the frenetic excess and commercial saturation of acid house. Most artists despise the term, although record labels have found it a useful tool for appealing to consumers' elitism. IDM includes chill-out music, literally the ambient, beatless music that ravers would relish after long nights of clubbing. It also includes forms of techno and jungle that seem just as amenable to headphone listening as to dancing. Many consider Aphex Twin, Autechre, Boards of Canada, and KLF as definitive examples of IDM.

IRCAM   Institut de Recherche et Coordination Acoustique/Musique, a center for the composition and research of electronic music and new media. IRCAM opened in Paris in 1977 under the leadership of Pierre Boulez. The institute was created at the behest of French president Georges Pompidou and has received unrivaled support from the French government, as well as from sectors of the French defense industry. For the past three decades, IRCAM has offered highly selective fellowships and residencies for composers studying signal processing and electronics. Many have noted the ongoing rivalry between IRCAM and its Parisian counterpart GRM.

metagenre An organizational grouping this book employs to illustrate affinities among the many genres of recent electronic music. The three metagenres identified here are institutional electroacoustic music, electronica, and sound art. A metagenre contains multiple genres; thus, electronica includes techno and house plus their various progeny such as ambient house, dub techno, and so on. Participants in these three metagenres define their music in relation to other metagenres as well as to a vaguely defined musical mainstream. Inherent in the discourse of metagenre is the irreconcilability of aesthetic quality with commercial success.

metaphor In semiotic theory, a sign in which the relationship between signifier and signified is generally abstract and not based on literal imitation. Electronica often propagates metaphors linking different types of sounds with larger concepts. For instance, the sounds of synthesizers, especially vintage instruments of the 1960s and 1970s, frequently evoke science fiction and futurism. Phonographic noise such as the pops and scratches of a record player's needle can serve as a metaphor for the age of the underlying music, even if those noises were artificially constructed rather than innate to the material.

microsound Literally, sound of extremely short duration, typically lasting only a fraction of a second. Microsound as a genre includes music based on the smallest particles of sound, called grains. One of the most common means of generating microsound is granular synthesis, where small grains function as elementary particles for constructing new sounds and textures. Microsound techniques are popular among institutional composers and also among many electronica artists, especially those dealing in glitch, a genre that uses the sounds of digital decay as aesthetic materials.

mimesis Imitation. Mimetic materials in electronic music emulate something outside the musical work. Before the advent of electronic music, musical imitations were necessarily constrained by the limitations of musical instruments, whose timbres did not necessarily approximate nonmusical sounds with any precision. Thanks to sampling and synthesis, however, electronic music can produce mimetic representations that are virtually indistinguishable from their real-world counterparts. A point of contention in post-Schaefferian electroacoustic music is whether materials can be mimetic or should adhere to the modernist ideal of abstraction.

musical frame   The conventions that maintain the separation between the musical work on the one hand and the listener and the outside world on the other hand. In preelectronic Western art music, elements of the frame have included performer attire, the stage, rituals governing listener behavior at concerts, and the use of musical parameters (instrumental timbre, rhythm, harmony, form) that quickly identify a musical work as music and not as noise or random sound. Electronic music has assaulted the musical frame on many fronts, by confusing the distinction between live and prerecorded sound, incorporating nonmusical sound, and relying on nontraditional venues and spaces that thrust listeners into the performance space.

musique concrète   A genre of electronic music whose materials consist of prerecorded materials. Pierre Schaeffer invented musique concrète in his search for a musical language that would begin with concrete, basic material from which he extrapolated abstract structures. Schaeffer explained his efforts as a refutation of German *elektronische Musik,* which he faulted for beginning with abstract principles instead of sound. Schaeffer's earliest concrete works used recognizable sounds, although Schaeffer advocated "reduced listening" as a way of bypassing external associations to focus on a sound's inherent qualities. Schaeffer taught numerous composers, who incorporated elements of musique concrète into their own works, although many broke with Schaeffer in recognizing the value of synthesis as well. Karlheinz Stockhausen famously bridged the *elektronische Musik*/musique concrète divide with his *Gesang der Jünglinge* (1956), which used both synthesized and taped sounds.

noise   In general usage, any undesirable sound. For acousticians, pure or "white" noise is any random auditory signal in which the intensity of all frequencies is uniform. Musicology and sound studies note the communicative aspects of noise. It can function as a tool of resistance to dominant notions of beauty or order. In electronic music, noise has been recuperated as an aesthetic entity, particularly in genres such as glitch and hip-hop, where phonographic noise is common.

noise music   A variant of recent electronica featuring distortion and loud volumes. Precedents include Italian Futurist music, which utilized the *intonarumori* (literally, "noise intoners"), and American experimentalists such as Henry Cowell and John Cage, who used alternative techniques to produce sounds from conventional instruments such as the piano. Noise music as such emerged with industrial groups such as Cabaret Voltaire and Throbbing Gristle in the early 1980s, bands that used harrowing electronic sounds along with imagery of dread, violence, and fear.

Several Japanese musicians, most famously Merzbow, use noise at deafening levels.

objecthood   Art critic Michael Fried's concept for describing what distinguished 1960s minimalist sculpture from Abstract Expressionist painting (and, by implication, all previous art). Fried criticized artists such as Donald Judd for creating works whose sheer size and physicality intruded into the space of the viewer. Objecthood's reliance on objects rather than aestheticized and mediated material destroyed art and replaced it with theater. Glitch microsound and other forms of recent electronic music attain a similar state of objecthood but do so intentionally as a way of avoiding musical signification.

organized sound   Edgard Varèse's term for what he predicted as the future of music, when electronic instruments would be liberated from the dictates of conventional music to produce any type of sound. The term also serves as the title for one of the leading academic journals specializing in electronic and electroacoustic music.

programmatic music   During the eighteenth and nineteenth centuries, Western art music that relied on extramusical narrative or explanation. Frequently, these explanations were known as "programs" and were printed in leaflets distributed at concerts. Programmatic works such as Berlioz's *Symphonie fantastique* (1830) espoused the view that music should demonstrate an idea or illustrate an image. Advocates of absolute music attacked programmatic works for relegating music to a secondary mode of expression. Echoes of programmatic music can be heard in institutional electroacoustic works that use sounds to convey an extramusical story, image, or idea.

reduced listening   Pierre Schaeffer's term for listening that ignores the source and origins of sound. Schaeffer advocated reduced listening for his musique concrète, a genre that often relied on recognizable footage of everyday sounds such as trains. Several composers, including many of Schaeffer's own students, have criticized or rejected reduced listening for placing unrealistic expectations on listeners. A few composers (Francisco López, Denis Smalley) advocate reduced listening as one facet of a larger listening practice.

sampling   In signal processing, the process by which a continuous signal is converted to a discrete signal. In music, sampling refers to the act of replaying preexisting recordings in new works. The term applies to digital sampling as well as (but with less precision) to turntablist and splicing techniques that interject old recorded material into a new context. Hip-hop in the 1980s and 1990s relied heavily on sampling of unlicensed material. A number of high-profile lawsuits created today's environment in which it is highly risky to sample without permission.

semiotics The study of signs. Writings on the subject date back to antiquity, but the field has been especially busy during the past hundred years thanks to the rise of structuralism. Ferdinand de Saussure, who originated one of the predominant modern approaches toward semiotics, wrote that every sign is composed of a signifier and a signified; this theory influenced musique concrète inventor Pierre Schaeffer. Competing theories have been put forward by Umberto Eco and Charles Peirce, among others. Several notable works on semiotics in music have appeared in the last thirty years, most notably Kofi Agawu's *Playing with Signs* (1991) and Jean-Jacques Nattiez's *Music and Discourse* (1990).

sequencer A device or software that makes a musical instrument, usually a synthesizer, perform a preprogrammed series of actions. Sequencers have been popular in synth-pop, hip-hop, and EDM since the 1980s.

sign Something that refers to something else. According to Saussure's structuralist theory of semiotics, a theory that influenced musique concrète and other forms of electronic music, a sign is composed of a signifier, that which indicates, and a signified, the underlying idea of the sign.

signal processing In music, the control and manipulation of audio signals. Signal processing is one of the chief distinctions of electronic music, because it allows for the alteration of sound after it has been emitted, something that was impossible before the era of electronics.

signified In Saussure's structuralist theory of semiotics, the underlying idea to which the sensory signifier refers. In music, the signified is the concept external to the sound phenomenon, that which sound or music communicates.

signifier In Saussure's structuralist theory of semiotics, the sensory aspect of a sign that refers to an underlying idea of the sign. In music, the signified is the sound phenomenon that in some way communicates an idea external to itself.

sound art A medium that uses sound either by itself or in combination with visual or other stimuli. Most definitions insist that sound art must be site-specific, meaning that it must in some way interact with the space in which it is heard. Site-specificity typically occurs in installation works that deal explicitly with the acoustic properties of a space or that highlight how a particular space affects listening. However, strict notions of sound art are losing ground, given that many works have become available as portable recordings. Many experimental electronic musicians call their work sound art, a gesture that some have interpreted as an attempt to cash in on the prestige of visual art.

sound object   According to Pierre Schaeffer, the sound object (*objet sonore*) is sound isolated from its means of production or notation as well as the state of mind of the listener. Schaeffer's conception of the sound object is a reduction, a bracketing out of external information in order to arrive at a pure phenomenological experience. The concept of the sound object has held wide sway among post-Schaefferian electroacoustic musicians.

soundscape composition   A form of electronic music or sound art containing audio footage foregrounding the properties of a specific location. The term was coined during the early 1970s by the group surrounding R. Murray Schafer, a composer in Vancouver who campaigned against noise pollution. This group eventually founded the World Soundscape Project (WSP), which released several soundscape recordings of locations in Canada and Europe. Soundscape compositions maintain specific ties to ecological activism and often document the incursion of industrial noise into previously pristine acoustic environments. Notable soundscape composers include Hildegard Westerkamp and Barry Truax.

spectromorphology   Denis Smalley's theoretical concept for describing sound spectra and how they change over time. Smalley states that spectromorphology "is not a compositional theory or method, but a descriptive tool based on aural perception" (1997, 107). The strategy displays affinities with phenomenology in its focus on perception itself to the exclusion of the origins of sound. But it also acknowledges external associations triggered by sound, something the purely phenomenological method of Pierre Schaeffer would reject.

subgenre   A collection of works belonging to one genre yet also displaying characteristic traits not necessarily shared by all other members of the same genre. A subgenre generally contains fewer constituent works than would a genre. Subgenres are extremely widespread in electronica, especially in EDM, where they generate interest and sales because of their appeal to a listener's sense of subcultural prestige or capital. For example, techno constitutes a genre that includes subgenres such as ambient techno and dub techno.

synthesis   In electronic music, the generation of new sounds through the combination of basic sounds. Additive synthesis entails layering different wave forms in order to create a composite signal. Subtractive synthesis subjects a signal to filtering in order to distill specific frequencies. German *elektronische Musik* as practiced at the studios of WDR during the early 1950s utilized synthesis to the exclusion of other sound-production methods. Karlheinz Stockhausen's early works, such as *Studie I* (1953) and *Studie II* (1954), exemplify this approach. Stockhausen broke from this purism with *Gesang der Jünglinge* (1956), which combines synthesized materials with a recording of a boy soprano. Analog synthesizers, instruments performing synthesis on demand, grew increasingly popular during the 1960s and 1970s. By the early 1980s, less expensive digital synthesizers made electronic music more accessible to the general public.

techno   Along with house, one of the most important postdisco EDM genres. Techno's name refers to its technological aspect, its nearly exclusive reliance on synthesizers and drum machines. Unlike house, techno tends not to use samples of well-known songs, sticking instead with newly composed materials or unrecognizable samples. Techno arose during the 1980s in Detroit, the result of collaborations between the Belleville Three of Juan Atkins, Derrick May, and Kevin Saunderson. May famously described techno as what would happen if George Clinton and Kraftwerk got stuck in an elevator together; this statement points to techno's combination of psychedelic funk with robotic precision. Techno grew to prominence in Detroit dance clubs even as it gained popularity in other cities. Two representative examples of techno are Derrick May's "Strings of Life" (1987) and "Clear" (1990), a track by Juan Atkins's group Cybotron.

turntablism   The practice of playing record turntables as musical instruments. Hip-hop music provides the most famous case study. By the mid-1970s, young Bronx DJs such as Kool Herc were using turntables not merely to replay records but also to improvise collages of sections of several different songs using two tables and a fader. The most skilled DJs created percussion effects by spinning tables in reverse so that the needle produced scratch noises. These scratches functioned as the rhythmic pattern for new songs. Roughly at the same time, Swiss-American conceptual artist Christian Marclay was using turntables to play broken or damaged records and welcomed the pops and scratches of phonographic noise into his works.

Western art music   European or European-American music dating from between 1600 and the present that has received support from religious institutions, governments, or private donors and has enjoyed prestige and power.

For much of this time, Western art music operated under strict rules governing musical parameters such as melody and harmony, as well as societal controls over the interpretation of, ownership of, and access to music. Until the nineteenth century, Western art music was arguably popular in that its listeners drew from all classes; by the early twentieth century, it had lost much of that audience to become inextricably linked with the upper class. As it is practiced today, Western art music is often associated with sophistication, intelligence, wealth, and elitism, and most of its practitioners are more committed to preserving past repertoires than to supporting the composition of new works. The term *Western art music* is often used interchangeably with *classical music.*

BIBLIOGRAPHY

Abbate, Carolyn. 2004. Music—Drastic or gnostic? *Critical Inquiry* 30: 505–536.

Adorno, Theodor W. 1997. *Aesthetic Theory,* trans. Robert Hullot-Kentor. Minneapolis: University of Minnesota Press.

———. 2002a. On jazz. In *Essays on Music*, trans. Jamie Owen Daniel, 470–495. Berkeley: University of California Press.

———. 2002b. On popular music. In *Essays on Music*, trans. Jamie Owen Daniel, 437–469. Berkeley: University of California Press.

———. 2002c. On the fetish-character in music and the regression of listening. In *Essays on Music*, trans. Richard Leppert, 288–317. Berkeley: University of California Press.

Agawu, V. Kofi. 1991. *Playing with Signs: A Semiotic Interpretation of Classic Music.* Princeton, N.J.: Princeton University Press.

Anderton, Craig. 2004. *Keyboard* reports: Korg Legacy Collection. *Keyboard* 30/8: 58–64.

Atkinson, Simon. 2007. Interpretation and musical signification in acousmatic listening. *Organised Sound* 12/2: 113–122.

Attali, Jacques. 1985. *Noise: The Political Economy of Music,* trans. Brian Massumi. Minneapolis: University of Minnesota Press.

Augoyard, Jean-François, and Henry Torgue, eds. 2006. *Sonic Experience: A Guide to Everyday Sounds,* trans. Andrea McCartney and David Paquette. Montréal: McGill-Queen's University Press.

Auslander, Philip. 1999. *Liveness: Performance in a Mediatized Culture.* New York: Routledge.

Babbitt, Milton. 2003. The composer as specialist. In *The Collected Essays of Milton Babbitt,* ed. Stephen Peles, 48–54. Princeton, N.J.: Princeton University Press.

Bachelard, Gaston. 1994. *The Poetics of Space: The Classic Look at How We Experience Intimate Places,* trans. Maria Jolas. Boston: Beacon Press.

Barthes, Roland. 1977. *Image Music Text,* trans. Stephen Heath. New York: Hill and Wang.

Bataille, Georges. 1987. *The Story of the Eye,* trans. Joachim Neugroschel. San Francisco: City Lights Books.

———. 1989. *The Accursed Share,* Vol. 1, trans. Robert Hurley. New York: Zone Books.

———. 2002. Materialism. In *Art in Theory, 1900–2000: An Anthology of Changing Ideas,* eds. and trans. Charles Harrison and Paul Wood, 483–484. Malden, Mass.: Blackwell. First published in 1968 in *Documents* (Paris).

Battcock, Gregory, ed. 1968. Questions to Stella and Judd: Interview by Bruce Glaser. In *Minimal Art: A Critical Anthology,* 148–164. New York: Dutton. First published in 1966 in *Art News.*

Battier, Marc. 2007. What the GRM brought to music: From musique concrète to acousmatic music. *Organised Sound* 12/3: 189–202.

Bayle, François. 1993. *Musique acousmatique: Propositions . . . positions.* Paris: Buchet/ Chastel.

Beaudoin, Richard. 2007. Counterpoint and quotation in Ussachevsky's *Wireless Fantasy.* *Organised Sound* 12/2: 143–151.

Beal, Amy. 2006. *New Music, New Allies: American Experimental Music in West Germany from the Zero Hour to Reunification.* Berkeley: University of California Press.

Belting, Hans. 1987. *The End of the History of Art,* trans. Christopher S. Wood. Chicago: University of Chicago Press.

Benitez, Joaquim M. 1978. Avant-garde or experimental? Classifying contemporary music. *International Review of Aesthetics and Sociology in Music* 9/1: 53–77.

Benjamin, Walter. 1969. The work of art in the age of mechanical reproduction. In *Illuminations,* ed. Hannah Arendt, trans. Harry Zohn, 217–251. New York: Schocken.

Bennett, Tony. 1990. *Outside Literature.* London: Routledge.

Berendt, Joachim-Ernst. 1992. *The Third Ear: On Listening to the World,* trans. Tim Nevill. New York: Henry Holt.

Berger, Karol. 2005. Musicology according to Don Giovanni, or: Should we get drastic? *Journal of Musicology* 22/3: 490–501.

Bernard, Jonathan W. 1993. The minimalist aesthetic in the plastic arts and in music. *Perspectives of New Music* 31/1: 86–132.

Bicknell, Jeannette. 2001. The problem of reference in musical quotation: A phenomenological approach. *Journal of Aesthetics and Art Criticism* 59/2: 185–191.

Boards of Canada biography. Available at http://www.matadorrecords.com/boards_of_canada/ (accessed June 10, 2009).

Boomkat. 2008a. Review of Michel Chion's *Requiem.* Available at http://www.boomkat.com/item.cfm?id=83304 (accessed March 29, 2009).

———. 2008b. Review of Ryoji Ikeda's *Test Pattern.* Available at http://www.boomkat.com/item.cfm?id=93954 (accessed June 21, 2009).

Boon, Marcus. 2002. 12k/Line: Zen and the art of the drum machine. *Wire* 218.

Born, Georgina. 1995. *Rationalizing Culture: IRCAM, Boulez, and the Institutionalization of the Musical Avant-Garde.* Berkeley: University of California Press.

Boulez, Pierre. 1991. Concrète (Musique). In *Stocktakings from an Apprenticeship*, trans. Stephen Walsh, 226–7. Oxford: Clarendon Press.

Bourdieu, Pierre. 1987. *Distinction: A Social Critique of the Judgment of Taste*, trans. Richard Nice. Cambridge, Mass.: Harvard University Press.

Bürger, Peter. 1984. *Theory of the Avant-Garde*, trans. Michael Shaw. Minneapolis: University of Minnesota Press.

Burkholder, J. Peter. 2007. Borrowing. *Grove Music Online*. Available at http://grovemusic. com (accessed August 13 2007).

Butler, Mark J. 2006. *Unlocking the Groove: Rhythm, Meter, and Musical Design in Electronic Dance Music.* Bloomington: Indiana University Press.

Cage, John. 1961a. Composition as process. In *Silence: Lectures and Writings by John Cage.* 35–57. Middletown, Conn.: Wesleyan University Press.

———. 1961b. The future of music: Credo. In *Silence: Lectures and Writings by John Cage*, 3–7. Middletown, Conn.: Wesleyan University Press.

Cascone, Kim. 2000. The aesthetics of failure: "Post-digital" tendencies in contemporary computer music. *Computer Music Journal* 24/4: 12–18.

Castells, Manuel. 2000. *The Rise of the Network Society*, 2nd ed. Oxford, U.K.: Blackwell.

Cateforis, Theo. 2000. Are we not New Wave? Nostalgia, technology and exoticism in popular music at the turn of the 1980s. PhD diss., State University of New York, Stony Brook.

Chadabe, Joel. 1997. *Electric Sound: The Past and Promise of Electronic Music.* Upper Saddle River, N.J.: Prentice-Hall.

Chanan, Michael. 1995. *Repeated Takes: A Short History of Recording and Its Effects on Music.* London and New York: Verso.

Chion, Michel. 1983. *Guide des objets sonores: Pierre Schaeffer et la recherche musicale.* Paris: Editions Buchet/Chastel.

———. 1990. *Audio-Vision: Sound on Screen*, trans. Claudia Gorbman. New York: Columbia University Press.

Clarke, Eric F. 2005. *Ways of Listening: An Ecological Approach to the Perception of Musical Meaning.* New York: Oxford University Press.

Collis, Adam. 2008. Sound of the system: The emancipation of noise in the music of Carsten Nicolai. *Organised Sound* 13/1: 31–39.

Cox, Christoph and Daniel Warner, eds. 2007. *Audio Culture: Readings in Modern Music*, New York: Continuum.

Croft, John. 2007. Theses on liveness. *Organised Sound* 12/1: 59–66.

Dack, John. 2002. Abstract and concrete. *Journal of Electroacoustic Music* 14: 2–7.

Danto, Arthur. 1997. *After the End of Art: Contemporary Art and the Pale of History.* Princeton, N.J.: Princeton University Press.

Davies, Hugh. 1996. A history of sampling. *Organised Sound* 1/1: 3–11.

Davies, Stephen. 2005. *Themes in the Philosophy of Music*. New York: Oxford University Press.

Davis, Randal. 2003. . . . And what they do as they're going. . . : Sounding space in the work of Alvin Lucier. *Organised Sound* 8/2: 205–212.

Demers, Joanna. 2002. Sampling as lineage in hip-hop. PhD diss., Princeton University, Princeton, N.J.

———. 2003. Sampling the 1970s in hip-hop. *Popular Music* 22/1: 41–56.

———. 2006. *Steal This Music: How Intellectual Property Law Affects Musical Creativity*. Athens: University of Georgia Press.

Doyle, Peter. 2005. *Echo and Reverb: Fabricating Space in Popular Music Recording, 1900–1960*. Hanover, N.H.: Wesleyan University Press.

Drever, John. 2002. Soundscape composition: The convergence of ethnography and acousmatic music. *Organised Sound* 7/1: 21–27.

Elflein, Dietmar. 1998. From Krauts with attitudes to Turks with attitudes: Some aspects of hip-hop history in Germany. *Popular Music* 17/3: 255–265.

Emmerson, Simon. 1986. The relation of language to materials. In *The Language of Electroacoustic Music*, ed. Simon Emmerson, 17–39. London: Macmillan.

———. 2000. Introduction. In *Music, Electronic Media, and Culture*, ed. Simon Emmerson, 1–4. Aldershot, U.K.: Ashgate.

———. 2007. *Living Electronic Music*. Aldershot, U.K.: Ashgate.

Ferguson, Russell. 2003. The variety of din. In *Christian Marclay*, ed. Russell Ferguson, 19–51. Los Angeles: UCLA Hammer Museum.

Field, Ambrose. 2000. Simulation and reality: The new sonic objects. In *Music, Electronic Media and Culture*, ed. Simon Emmerson, 36–55. Aldershot, U.K.: Ashgate.

Fink, Robert. 2005. *Repeating Ourselves: American Minimal Music As Cultural Practice*. Berkeley: University of California Press.

Fonarow, Wendy. 2006. *Empire of Dirt: The Aesthetics and Rituals of British Indie Music*. Hanover, N.H.: Wesleyan University Press.

Foster, Hal. 1996. *The Return of the Real: The Avant-Garde at the End of the Century*. Cambridge, Mass.: MIT Press.

Foster, Hal, et al. 2004. *Art since 1900: Modernism, Antimodernism, Postmodernism*. London: Thames & Hudson.

Fried, Michael. 1998. Art and objecthood. In *Art and Objecthood: Essays and Reviews*, ed. Michael Fried, 148–172. Chicago: University of Chicago Press.

Frith, Simon. 1996. *Performing Rites*. Oxford, U.K.: Oxford University Press.

Frow, John. 1995. *Cultural Studies and Cultural Value*. Oxford, U.K.: Clarendon Press.

———. 2005. *Genre*. London and New York: Routledge.

Gaillot, Michel. 1999. *Multiple Meaning—Techno: An Artistic and Political Laboratory of the Present*. Trans. Warren Niesuchowski. Paris: Éditions Dis Voir.

Gann, Kyle. 1996. The outer edge of consonance: Snapshots from the evolution of La Monte Young's tuning installations. *Bucknell Review* 40/1: 152–190.

Gard, Stephen. 2004. Nasty noises: "Error" as a compositional element in contemporary electroacoustic music. MM thesis, University of Sydney.

Gaver, William W. 1993. What in the World Do We Hear? An Ecological Approach to Auditory Event Perception. *Ecological Psychology* 5/1: 1–29.

Gayou, Évelyne. 2007. *Le GRM, Groupe de Recherches Musicales: Cinquante ans d'histoire*. Paris: Fayard.

Gendron, Bernard. 2002. *Between Montmartre and the Mudd Club: Popular Music and the Avant-Garde*. Chicago: University of Chicago Press.

George, Nelson. 1998. *Hip Hop America*. New York: Penguin.

Goehr, Lydia. 2007. *The Imaginary Museum of Musical Works: An Essay in the Philosophy of Music*, rev. ed. New York: Oxford University Press.

Gradenwitz, Peter. 1953. Experiments in sound: Ten-day demonstration in Paris offers the latest in "musique concrète." *New York Times*, August 9, X5.

Greenberg, Clement. 1982. Modernist painting. In *Modern Art and Modernism: A Critical Anthology*, eds. Francis Frascina and Charles Harrison, 5–10. London: Open University Press.

Hamilton, Andy. 2007. *Aesthetics and Music*. London: Continuum.

Hanslick, Eduard. 1986. *On the Musically Beautiful: A Contribution towards the Revision of the Aesthetics of Music*, trans. Geoffrey Payzant. Indianapolis: Hackett.

Haynes, Jim. 2005. Cross platform: Toshiya Tsunoda. *Wire* 252.

Hebdige, Dick. 1979. *Subculture: The Meaning of Style*. London and New York: Routledge.

Hegarty, Paul. 2007. *Noise/Music: A History*. New York: Continuum.

———. 2008. Just what is it that makes today's noise music so different, so appealing? *Organised Sound* 13/1: 13–20.

Helm, Everett. 1961. As dead as C major: So say electronic men of 12-tone music. *New York Times*, May 14, X9.

Hesmondhalgh, David. 2007. Aesthetics and audiences: Talking about good and bad music. *European Journal of Cultural Studies* 10/4: 507–527.

Hodgkinson, Tim. 1986. Pierre Schaeffer: An interview with the pioneer of musique concrète. Available at http://www.ele-mental.org/ele_ment/said&did/schaeffer_interview.html (accessed June 5, 2009).

Hoeckner, Berthold. 2002. *Programming the Absolute: Nineteenth-Century German Music and the Hermeneutics of the Moment*. Princeton, N.J.: Princeton University Press.

Holmes, Thom. 2002. *Electronic and Experimental Music: Pioneers in Technology and Composition*, 2nd ed. New York: Routledge.

Ihde, Don. 1976. *Listening and Voice: A Phenomenology of Sound*. Athens: Ohio University Press.

Irwin, William. 2004. Against intertextuality. *Philosophy and Literature* 28/2: 227–242.

Johnson, Timothy A. 1994. Minimalism: Aesthetic, style, or technique? *Musical Quarterly* 78/4: 742–773.

Judd, Donald. 2003. Specific objects. In *Art in Theory, 1900–2000: An Anthology of Changing Ideas*, ed. Charles Harrison and Paul Wood, 824–828. Malden, U.K.: Blackwell.

Kaeppler, Adrienne. 1994. Music, metaphor, and misunderstanding. *Ethnomusicology* 38/3: 457–473.

Kahn, Douglas. 1999. *Noise, Water, Meat: A History of Sound in the Arts*. Cambridge, Mass.: MIT Press, 1999.

———. 2003. Christian Marclay's early years: An interview. *Leonardo Music Journal* 13: 17–21.

Kane, Brian. 2007. *L'objet sonore maintenant*: Pierre Schaeffer, sound objects and the phenomenological reduction. *Organised Sound* 12/1: 15–24.

Kant, Immanuel. 2000. *The Critique of Judgment*, trans. J. H. Bernard. New York: Prometheus.

Katz, Mark. 2004. *Capturing Sound: How Technology Has Changed Music*. Berkeley: University of California Press.

Kittler, Friedrich A. 1999. *Gramophone, Film, Typewriter*, trans. Geoffrey Winthrop-Young and Michael Wutz. Stanford, Calif.: Stanford University Press.

Kivy, Peter. 2002. *Introduction to a Philosophy of Music*. New York: Oxford University Press.

Koestenbaum, Wayne. 2001. *The Queen's Throat: Opera, Homosexuality, and the Mystery of Desire*. New York: Da Capo Press.

Kramer, Jonathan. 1981. New temporalities in music. *Critical Inquiry* 7/3: 539–556.

Kraut, Robert. 2007. *Artworld Metaphysics*. Oxford, U.K.: Oxford University Press.

Kristeva, Julia. 1980. *Desire in Language: A Semiotic Approach to Literature and Art*, ed. Leon S. Roudiez, trans. Thomas Gora, Alice Jardine, and Leon S. Roudiez. New York: Columbia University Press.

Kronengold, Charles. 2005. Accidents, hooks and theory. *Popular Music* 24/3: 381–397.

———. 2008. Exchange theories in disco, new wave, and album-oriented rock. *Criticism* 50/1: 43–82.

Kuspit, Donald. 2004. *The End of Art*. Cambridge, U.K.: Cambridge University Press.

Kwon, Miwon. 2002. *One Place after Another: Site-Specific Art and Locational Identity*. Cambridge, Mass.: MIT Press.

LaBelle, Brandon. 2006. *Background Noise: Perspectives on Sound Art*. New York, Continuum.

Landy, Leigh. 2007. *Understanding the Art of Sound Organization*. Cambridge, Mass.: MIT Press, 2007.

Lefebvre, Henri. 2000. *La production de l'espace*, 4th ed. Paris: Éditions Anthropos.

Lévi-Strauss, Claude. 1969. *The Raw and the Cooked*, trans. John Weightman and Doreen Weightman. New York: Harper and Row.

Levin, Thomas Y. 1990. For the record: Adorno on music in the age of its technological reproducibility. *October* 55: 23–47.

Levinson, Jerrold. 2006. *Contemplating Art*. New York: Oxford University Press.

———. 2008. *Music in the Moment*, 2nd ed. Ithaca: Cornell University Press.

Licht, Alan. 2007. *Sound Art: Beyond Music, Between Categories.* New York: Rizzoli.

———. 2009. Sound art: Origins, development and ambiguities. *Organised Sound* 14/1: 3–10.

Link, Stan. 2001. The work of reproduction in the mechanical aging of art: Listening to noise. *Computer Music Journal* 25/1: 34–47.

López, Francisco. 1997. Schizophonia vs. *l'objet sonore*: Soundscapes and artistic freedom. Available at http://www.franciscolopez.net/pdf/schizo.pdf (accessed December 10, 2007).

———. 2000. Interview with Fear Drop. Available at http://www.franciscolopez.net/int_fear.html (accessed June 1, 2008).

Manning, Peter. 2004. *Electronic and Computer Music*, rev. ed. New York: Oxford University Press.

Marclay, Christian. 1997. Liner notes to *Records '81–'89*. Atavistic ALP62CD.

Manning, Peter. 2004. *Electronic and Computer Music*, rev. ed. New York: Oxford University Press.

Marley, Brian. 2005. John Wall: The rocky road to *Cphon*. In *Blocks of Consciousness and the Unbroken Continuum*, ed. Brian Marley and Mark Wastell, 190–211. London: Sound 323.

Marx, Leo. 2000. *The Machine in the Garden: Technology and the Pastoral Ideal in America.* New York: Oxford University Press.

McCartney, Andra. 2004. Soundscape works, listening, and the touch of sound. In *Aural Cultures*, ed. J. Drobnick, 179–188. Toronto: YYZ Books.

McClary, Susan. 1991. *Feminine Endings*. Minneapolis: University of Minnesota Press.

McGonigal, Mike. 2007. *My Bloody Valentine's Loveless (33 1/3)*. New York: Continuum.

McLeod, Kembrew. 2001. Genres, subgenres, sub-subgenres and more: Musical and social differentiation within electronic/dance music communities. *Journal of Popular Music Studies* 13/1: 59–75.

Merleau-Ponty, Maurice. 2002. *Phenomenology of Perception*, trans. Colin Smith. London and New York: Routledge.

Metz, Christian. 1980. Aural objects. *Yale French Studies* 60: 24–32.

Metzer, David. 2003. *Quotation and Cultural Meaning in Twentieth-Century Music.* Cambridge, U.K.: Cambridge University Press.

Microsound list archives. Available at http://or8.net/pipermail/microsound (accessed June 14, 2009).

Moog, Robert. 1967. Electronic music: Its composition and performance. *Electronics World* 77/2: 42–46, 84–85.

Morris, Mitchell. 1998. Ectopian sounds, or, the music of Luther Adams and strong environmentalism. In *Crosscurrents and Counterpoints: Offerings in Honor of Bengt Hambræus at 70*, ed. Per F. Broman, Nora A. Engebretsen, and Bo Alphonce, 129–141. Göteborg, Sweden: Göteborg University.

Myatt, Tony. 2008. New aesthetics and practice in experimental electronic music. *Organised Sound* 13/1: 1–3.

Nancy, Jean-Luc. 2007. *Listening,* trans. Charlotte Mandell. New York: Fordham University Press.

Nattiez, Jean-Jacques. 1990. *Music and Discourse: Toward a Semiology of Music,* trans. Carolyn Abbate. Princeton, N.J.: Princeton University Press.

Neill, Ben. 2002. Pleasure beats: Rhythm and the aesthetics of current electronic music. *Leonardo Music Journal* 12: 3–6.

Nyman, Michael. 1999. *Experimental Music: Cage and Beyond,* 2nd ed. Cambridge, U.K.: Cambridge University Press.

Oberheim, Tom. 2000. 1977 Interview. *Keyboard* 26: 1.

Otondo, Felipe. 2008. Contemporary trends in the use of space in electroacoustic music. *Organised Sound* 13/1: 77–81.

Ouzounian, Gascia. 2006. Embodied sound: Aural architectures and the body. *Contemporary Music Review* 25: 69–79.

———. 2009. Impure thinking practices and clinical acts: The sonorous becomings of Heidi Fast. *Organised Sound* 14/1: 75–81.

Phillips, Thomas. 2006. Composed silence: Microsound and the quiet shock of listening. *Perspectives of New Music* 44/2: 232–248.

Piekut, Benjamin. 2008. Testing, testing . . . : New York experimentalism 1964. PhD diss., Columbia University, New York.

Plop. 2007. Interview with Toshiya Tsunoda. Available at http://www.inpartmaint.com/plop/pdis_e/plop_e_feature/toshiya_tsunoda.html (accessed June 1, 2008).

Plourde, Lorraine. 2008. Disciplined listening in Tokyo: Onkyō and non-intentional sounds. *Ethnomusicology* 52/2: 270–295.

Poggioli, Renato. 1968. *The Theory of the Avant-Garde,* trans. Gerald Fitzgerald. Cambridge, Mass.: Harvard University Press.

Potter, Keith. 2000. *Four Musical Minimalists: La Monte Young, Terry Riley, Steve Reich, Philip Glass.* Cambridge, U.K.: Cambridge University Press.

Prendergast, Mark. 2000. *The Ambient Century: From Mahler to Trance—The Evolution of Sound in the Electronic Age.* New York: Bloomsbury.

Preve, Francis. 2003. The art of extreme noise. *Keyboard* 29/9: 26–34.

Puri, Michael James. 2006. Review of *Programming the Absolute: Nineteenth-Century German Music and the Hermeneutics of the Moment,* by Berthold Hoeckner. *Journal of the American Musicological Society* 59/2: 488–501.

Rahn, John. 1993. Repetition. *Contemporary Music Review* 7: 49–57.

Recherche musicale au GRM sous la direction de Michel Chion et François Delalande. 1986. Paris: Éditions Richard-Masse.

Reynolds, Simon. 1999. *Generation Ecstasy: Into the World of Techno and Rave Culture.* New York: Routledge.

———. 2005. *Rip It Up and Start Again: Postpunk 1978–1984.* New York: Penguin.

Richard, Dominique. 1994. Computer music and the post-modern: A case of schizophrenia. *Computer Music Journal* 18/4: 26–34.

Rimbaud, Robin. 2008. Simulacra, synthesis, and sonic systems: Patching into the mesh of metaphoric malfunctions, 1–2. Foreword to Benge, *Twenty Systems*. Expanding Records ECDB1:08.

Roads, Curtis. 1996. *The Computer Music Tutorial*. Cambridge, Mass.: MIT Press.

———. 2001. *Microsound*. Cambridge, Mass.: MIT Press.

Rockwell, John. 1975. The pop life: From "Flying Saucer" to "Mr. Jaws." *New York Times,* October 10, 24.

Rodgers, Tara. 2003. On the process and aesthetics of sampling in electronic music production. *Organised Sound* 8/3: 313–320.

Rowell, Lewis. 1987. Stasis in music. *Semiotica* 66: 181–195.

Schaeffer, Pierre. 1966. *Traité des objets musicaux: Essai interdisciplines*. Paris: Éditions du Seuil.

———. 1967. *La musique concrète*. Paris: Presses Universitaires de France.

Schafer, R. Murray. 1994. *The Soundscape: Our Sonic Environment and the Tuning of the World*. Rochester, Vt.: Destiny Books.

Schonberg, Harold C. 1961. Concert without performers: Age of tape reflected by electronics. *New York Times,* May 10, 53.

Scruton, Roger. 1997. *The Aesthetics of Music*. Oxford, U.K.: Oxford University Press.

———. 2007. *Modern Culture*. New York: Continuum.

Shapiro, Peter, ed. 2000. *Modulations: A History of Electronic Music: Throbbing Words on Sound*. New York: Caipirinha Productions.

Sherburne, Philip. 2002. 12k: Between two points. *Organised Sound* 7/1: 171–176.

Smalley, Denis. 1996. The listening imagination: Listening in the electroacoustic era. *Contemporary Music Review* 13/2: 77–107.

———. 1997. Spectromorphology: Explaining sound shapes. *Organised Sound* 2/2: 107–126.

———. 2007. Space-form and the acousmatic image. *Organised Sound* 12/1: 35–58.

Smith, Marquard. 2001. Angels. In *Benjamin's Blind Spot: Walter Benjamin and the Premature Death of Aura,* ed. Lise Patt, 16–24. Topanga, Calif.: Institute of Cultural Inquiry.

Stankievech, Charles. 2007. From stethoscopes to headphones: An acoustic spatialization of subjectivity. *Leonardo Music Journal* 17: 55–59.

Sterne, Jonathan. 2003. *The Audible Past: Cultural Origins of Sound Reproduction*. Durham, N.C.: Duke University Press.

Stockhausen, Karlheinz, et al. 2007. Stockhausen vs. the "technocrats." In *Audio Culture: Readings in Modern Music,* ed. Christoph Cox and Daniel Warner, 381–385. New York: Continuum.

Stoever, Jennifer. 2007. The contours of the sonic color line: Slavery, segregation, and the cultural politics of listening. PhD diss., University of Southern California, Los Angeles.

Stuart, Caleb. 2003. Damaged sound: Glitching and skipping compact discs in the audio of Yasunao Tone, Nicolas Collins and Oval. *Leonardo Music Journal* 13: 47–52.

Szepanski, Achim. 2002. A Mille Plateaux manifesto. *Organised Sound* 7/1: 225–228.

Takasugi, Steven Kazuo. 2004. Morphology and extensibility: Resilience of musical spaces as dynamic containers. In *Musical Morphology*, ed. Claus-Steffen Mahnkopf, Frank Cox, and Wolfram Schurig, 207–222. Hofheim, Germany: Wolke Verlag.

———. 2005. *Strange Autumn*: An attempt at an interpretation. Available at http://princemyshkins.com/strangeautumn.pdf (accessed July 30, 2007).

Taubman, Howard. 1952. U.S. music of today played at concert. *New York Times,* October 29, 35.

Taylor, Timothy. 2001. *Strange Sounds: Music, Technology, and Culture*. New York: Routledge.

Théberge, Paul. 1997. *Any Sound You Can Imagine: Making Music/Consuming Technology*. Hanover, N.H.: Wesleyan University Press.

Thomson, Phil. 2004. Atoms and errors: Towards a history and aesthetics of microsound. *Organised Sound* 9/2: 207–218.

Thornton, Sarah. 1995. *Club Cultures: Music, Media, and Subcultural Capital*. Hanover, N.H.: Wesleyan University Press.

Tobias V. 2001. Matmos: Surgical beats. Available at http://www.techno.ca/targetcircuitry/mutek/matmos.htm (accessed July 29, 2007).

Toop, David. 1995. *Ocean of Sound: Aether Talk, Ambient Sound and Imaginary Worlds*. London: Serpent's Tail.

———. 2004. *Haunted Weather: Music, Silence, and Memory*. London: Serpent's Tail.

Truax, Barry. 1999. *The Handbook for Acoustic Ecology*, 2nd ed. Vancouver, B.C.: Cambridge Street Publishing.

Tsunoda, Toshiya. 2007. Toshiya Tsunoda. In *Extract: Portraits of Sound Artists*, eds. Raphael Moser and Heinrich Friedl, 84–87. Vienna: Nonvisualobjects.

Vail, Mark. 1993. Keyboard *Presents Vintage Synthesizers: Groundbreaking Instruments and Pioneering Designers of Electronic Music Synthesizers*. San Francisco: GPI Books.

Villars, Chris, ed. 2006. *Morton Feldman Says: Selected Interviews and Lectures 1964–1987*. London: Hyphen Press.

Virilio, Paul. 2003. *Art and Fear,* trans. Julie Rose. London and New York: Continuum.

Walker, Rob. 2008. Consumed: Mash-up model. *New York Times Magazine,* July 20. Available at http://www.nytimes.com/2008/07/20/magazine (accessed November 13, 2008).

Warburton, Dan. 1988. A working terminology for minimal music. *Intégral* 2: 135–159.

Whitelaw, Mitchell. 2003. Sound particles and microsonic materialism. *Contemporary Music Review* 22/4: 93–101.

Windsor, W. Luke. 1994. Using auditory information for events in electroacoustic music. *Contemporary Music Review* 10/2: 85–93.

———. 1996. Autonomy, mimesis and mechanical reproduction in contemporary music. *Contemporary Music Review* 15/1: 139–150.

————. 2000. Through and around the acousmatic: The interpretation of electroacoustic sounds. In *Music, Electronic Media and Culture*, ed. Simon Emmerson, 7–35. Aldershot, U.K.: Ashgate.

Wishart, Trevor. 1986. Sound symbols and landscapes. In *The Language of Electroacoustic Music*, ed. Simon Emmerson, 41–60. Houndmills, U.K.: Macmillan.

Wlodarski, Amy Lynn. 2007. A map of (mis)hearing: Steve Reich's *Different Trains*. Paper delivered at American Musicological Meeting, Québec.

Wolff, Janet. 1993. *Aesthetics and the Sociology of Art,* 2nd ed. Ann Arbor: University of Michigan Press.

Wong, Mandy. 2008. Action, composition—Morton Feldman and physicality. Unpublished.

World Soundscape Project. www.sfu.ca/~truax/wsp.html (accessed April 20, 2009).

Yang, Mina. 2000. *Für Elise,* circa 2000: Postmodern readings of Beethoven in popular context. *Popular Music and Society* 29/1: 1–15.

Young, John. 1996. Imagining the source: The interplay of realism and abstraction in electroacoustic music. *Contemporary Music Review* 15/1: 73–93.

Yui, Miki. 2000.Liner notes to *Lupe Luep Peul Epul.* LINE 003.

DISCOGRAPHY

Entries mention tracks and albums discussed in the text. Dates listed after artists' names refer to publication date of recording. If the original recording is out of print or difficult to obtain, the reissue date appears in parentheses at the end of the entry.

Air. 1998. *Moon Safari*. Astral Works CAR 6644-2.

Alva Noto. 2007. *Xerrox No. 1*. Raster-Noton R-N 78.

Aphex Twin. 2001. "Mt. Saint Michel's Mix + St. Michael's Mount." *Drukqs*. Warp Records 31174-2.

Barron, Louis, and Bebe Barron. 1995. *Forbidden Planet: Original MGM Soundtrack*. GNP Crescendo.

Basic Channel. 1995. "Quadrant Dub I." *BCD*. Indigo 2371-2.

Basinski, William. 2003. *The Disintegration Loops*. Musex 20620201.

Beltram, Joey. 1996. "Energy Flash." *Classics*. R&S Records 95100 CD.

Benge. 2008. *Twenty Systems*. Expanding Records ECDB1:08.

Boards of Canada. 1998. "Bocuma" and "Roygbiv." *Music Has the Right to Children*. Warp Records Skald 1/Warp CD 55.

Cale, John. 2000. *Sun Blindness Music*. Table of the Elements TOE-CD-75.

Carlos, Wendy. 1998. *A Clockwork Orange: Wendy Carlos' Complete Original Score*. East Side Digital.

Cascone, Kim. 1999. *Cathode Flower*. Mille Plateaux RIT 06.

———. 2008. *Music for Dagger and Guitar*. Anechoic TRRN 0203.

Chartier, Richard. 2000. *Series*. LINE_001.

———. 2001. *Decisive Forms*. Trente Oiseaux TOCO13.

Chion, Michel. 1978. *Requiem*. Empreintes Digitales IMED-9312-CD (1993).

Clicks + Cuts. 2000. Mille Plateaux mp79.

Cusack, Peter. 1999. *Where Is the Green Parrot?* ReR PC1.

Cybotron. 1990. "Clear." *Clear.* Fantasy 0216 (1995).

Demers, Inouk. 2009. *Conveyance.* http://mysite.verizon.net/inoukdemers.

Dr. Dre. 1992. "Let Me Ride." *The Chronic.* Interscope Records P2 57128.

Drumm, Kevin. 2002. *Sheer Hellish Miasma.* Editions Mego 053 (2007).

——. 2008. "We All Get It in the End." *Imperial Distortion.* Hospital Productions HOS-134.

Eno, Brian. 1978. *Ambient 1: Music for Airports.* Editions EG EEGCD 17.

Fennesz. 1999. *Plus Forty Seven Degrees 56'37" Minus Sixteen Degrees 51'08".* Touch TO:40 (2008).

——. 2001. "Caecilia." *Endless Summer.* Mego 035.

——. 2008a. "The Colour of Three." *Black Sea.* Touch TO:76.

Gas. 2008. Track two of "Gas". *Nah und Fern.* Kompakt CD66.

Girl Talk. 2008. "Hands in the Air." *Feed the Animals.* Illegal Art.

Goodman, Dickie. 2002. "The Flying Saucer." *25 All Time Novelty Hits.* Varese Sarabande.

Göttsching, Manuel. 1984. *E2-E4.* Spalax Music 14 241 (1992).

Ikeda, Ryoji. 2006. *+/-.* Touch TO:30.

——. 2008. *Test Pattern.* Raster-Noton R-N 093.

Inoue, Tetsu. 1996. *World Receiver.* Intraction INFX 015 (2006).

Jarre, Jean Michel. 1976. *Oxygène.* Disques Motors FDM 36140-2.

King Tubby. 1976. *King Tubby Meets Rockers Uptown.* Shanachie 43001 (2004).

KLF. 1990. "Madrugada Eterna." *Chill Out.* Wax Trax 7155.

López, Francisco. 1998. *La Selva.* V2_Archief V228.

——. 2001. *Buildings (New York).* V2_Archief V232.

——. 2007. *Wind (Patagonia).* and/OAR and/27.

Lucier, Alvin. 1969. *I Am Sitting in a Room.* Lovely Music LCD 1013 (1990).

——. 2005. *Anthony Burr/Charles Curtis.* Antiopic ANSI 002.

Marclay, Christian. 1997. "Dust Breeding" and "Smoker." *Records '81–'89.* Atavistic ALP62CD.

Matmos. 2001. "Lipostudio . . . and So On." *A Chance to Cut Is a Chance to Cure.* Matador OLE 489.

Merzbow. 2005. *Merzbuddha.* Important Records imprec052.

Microscopic Sound. 1999. Caipirinha CAI2021-2.

Model 500. 1995. "M29 Orbit" and "M69 Starlight." *Deep Space.* R&S Records RS 95066 CD.

My Bloody Valentine. 1991. *Loveless.* Sire/Warner 9 26759-2.

Niblock, Phill. 2006. "Harm" and "Valence." *Touch Three.* Touch TO:69.

The Orb. 1994. "Earth (Gaia)." *The Orb's Adventures beyond the Ultraworld.* Fontana Island 535005.

O'Rourke, Jim. 2008. *Long Night.* Streamline 1023.

Oval. 1996. "Textuell." *Systemisch*. Thrill Jockey thrillo32.

Palestine, Charlemagne. 1999. *Schlingen-Blängen*. New World Records 80578.

Parmegiani, Bernard. 2001. *De natura sonorum*. INA-GRM INA C 3001.

Radigue, Éliane. 1998. *Trilogie de la mort*. Experimental Intermedia XI 119.

Sawako. 2007. "August Neige." *Madoromi*. Anticipate 003.Schaeffer, Pierre. 1990. "*Étude aux chemins de fer*." *L'œuvre musicale*. INA-GRM INA C 1006.

Smalley, Denis. 2000. "Tides: Pools and Currents." *Sources/Scenes*. Empreintes Digitales IMED-0054.

Stockhausen, Karlheinz. 1991. "*Gesang der Jünglinge*." *Elektronische Musik 1952–1960*. Stockhausen-Verlag CD3.

Takasugi, Steven Kazuo. 1999. *Iridescent Uncertainty*. stakasugi.hotmail.com.

Tangerine Dream. 1974. *Phaedra*. Virgin 0777 7 86064 2 0.

Tone, Yasunao. 1994. *Musica Iconologos*. Lovely Music LCD 3041.

Tsunoda, Toshiya. 2003. "Wind Whistling." *Scenery of Decalcomania*. Naturestrip NS 3003.

———. 2005. "Unstable Contact." *Ridge of Undulation*. Häpna H.24.

Ussachevsky, Vladimir. 2007. "Wireless Fantasy." *Electronic and Acoustic Works*. DRAM CR 813.

Vangelis. 1994. *Blade Runner*. Atlantic 82623-2.

The Velvet Underground. 1967. "Heroin." *The Velvet Underground & Nico*. Verve 823 290-2.

———. 1969. "Candy Says." *The Velvet Underground*. Polydor 31453 1252 2 (1996).

Wall, John. 1999. *Constructions I-IV*. Utterpsalm CD4.

Westerkamp, Hildegard. 1989. "Kits Beach Soundwalk." *Transformations*. Empreintes Digitales IMED 9631 (1996).

Wishart, Trevor. 2000. *Red Bird*. EMF CD 022.

Xenakis, Iannis . 1997. "Concret PH." *Electronic Music*. EMF CD003.

———. 2008. "Analogique B." *Music for Strings*. DRAM MO152.

Yoshihide, Otomo, and Sachiko M. 1998. *Filament 1*. Extreme XCD 45.

Young, La Monte, John Cale, Tony Conrad, Angus Maclise, and Marian Zazeela. 1965. *Inside the Dream Syndicate Volume 1: Day of Niagra*. Table of the Elements TOE-CD-74 (2000).

Yui, Miki. 2000. "Torli." *Lupe Luep Peul Epul*. LINE 003.

INDEX

CPSIA information can be obtained at www.ICGtesting.com
Printed in the USA
BVOW08s1730260814

364255BV00003B/11/P